Uniform Feelings

Uniform Feelings

Scenes from the Psychic Life of Policing

JESSI LEE JACKSON

University of Michigan Press
Ann Arbor

For questions or permissions, please contact um.press.perms@umich.edu

Published in the United States of America by
the University of Michigan Press
Manufactured in the United States of America
Printed on acid-free paper

First published May 2022

A CIP catalog record for this book is available from the British Library.

ISBN 978-0-472-07525-6 (hardcover : alk. paper)
ISBN 978-0-472-05525-8 (paper : alk. paper)
ISBN 978-0-472-12999-7 (ebook)

An earlier version of Chapter 4 was published as "The Non-performativity of Implicit Bias Training" in *Radical Teacher* 112 (2018). Reprinted with permission.

The cover features Card IV of the Rorschach test, a projective test developed by Swiss psychologist Hermann Rorschach. In scoring the test, responses to Card IV have been interpreted to express possible attitudes about men and authority. It is sometimes referred to as "the father card." The Rorschach test is controversial due to concerns about reliability, validity, and online availability of test information. Despite these concerns, the test continues to be used for psychological evaluation. One application has been the pre-employment psychological screening of police officers.

CONTENTS

Acknowledgments   vii

Introduction: Compass   1

1. Gun: Relationships and Revolvers   27

2. Statistic: Frameworks of Precarity in Policing   49

3. Guidebooks: Police Psychology at the Scenes of State Violence   69

4. Manual: The Nonperformativity of Implicit-Bias Training   89

5. Museum: Heroic Fantasies at the American Police Hall of Fame   104

6. Memorial: Blue Mourning at the National Law Enforcement Officers Memorial   126

Conclusion: Abolitionist Psychologies   145

Notes   153

Bibliography   183

Index   201

Digital materials related to this title can be found on the Fulcrum platform via the following citable URL: https://doi.org/10.3998/mpub.11893694

ACKNOWLEDGMENTS

I grew up moving around with my family, living on Anishinaabe land in the Upper Peninsula of Michigan. Once a month, my parents would take the whole family in to the biggest library in the region, the Peter White Public Library in Marquette. I remember filling a plastic laundry basket with our books for the month, and feeling rich with adventures, language, poetry, and ideas. To my knowledge, I am the first person in my family to publish a book. I've been able to do it because Laurie and Charles Jackson raised me to be a reader and a writer.

Since my childhood, I have lived on Lenape, Anishinaabe, Haudenosaunee, and Coast Salish territory. I'm grateful to people who have taught me the long histories of the places where I have lived, and welcomed me into their work toward better futures. My book is built on foundations created by the intellectual labor of BIPOC scholars and organizers, especially those in the abolitionist movement and intersectional queer/feminist communities. When I was in my early twenties, trying to figure out who I was going to become, a community of Chicago abolitionists, activists, and organizers helped me figure it out. They include Wenona E. Thompson, Joanne Archibald, Salome Chasnoff, Cheryl Graves, Erica Meiners, Laurie Schaffner, Gail Smith, Ana Mercado, Mariame Kaba, the workers of the Congress Hotel Strike, the community at the Sister Jean Hughes Adult High School, and the members of Critical Resistance–Chicago. Thank you to the community of volunteers at Girl Talk Chicago and to all those who carry on the legacy of Wenona's crucial work to support girls in Chicago.

Thank you to Sara Cohen, Anna Pohlod, and the entire team at University of Michigan Press. Tyler Wall's generous critical feedback on earlier drafts was incredibly helpful. I'm also indebted to my anonymous reader for detailed and incisive engagements with this project.

Thank you to my graduate advisor Cynthia Wu, who remains my model for principled, thoughtful participation in the academic community. Thank you also to my committee members, Hershini Bhana Young and Stephanie Clare, for your careful engagements and close readings. Travers and Coleman Nye have supported me with generous and careful readings. Thanks also to Suzanna Crage for talking statistics with me. This project also benefited from the intellectual community I shared with my fellow grad students at the University at Buffalo, the members of the Graduate Group for Queer Studies, and the Lacan Reading Group. I also remain grateful to the professors who first encouraged me as an undergraduate gender-studies student at Cornell, Mary Fainsod Katzenstein and Amy Villarejo.

This project has benefited from my participation in the Institute for Critical Social Inquiry at the New School, the Stephen Mitchell Center for Relational Study, the Northwestern University Family Institute, the Toronto Institute for Contemporary Psychoanalysis, the Bavarian American Association summer institute on material culture, and the CRI-RAFTS reading group. I would also like to thank the Tuesday consult team—Lorne, Leah, Carl, Kyle, Merryn, Ryna, and Sarah—and my colleagues and friends in clinical practice. I was fortunate to experience Muriel Dimen's bracing clarity in her psychoanalytic writing, teaching, and mentorship. I continue to aspire to her level of clinical rigor and intellectual courage. I'm also grateful to Deborah Britzman for helping me figure out how to think and write.

An alternate history of this project starts in Chicago in the mid-2000s, when I was getting ready to start counseling school and Simon Elin Fisher gave me a copy of Eve Kosofsky Sedgwick's *Touching Feeling* with a note in the margin of the reparative reading chapter: "Tell Jessi." Thank you to Simon and all my other incredible friends: Caroline Boback, Coleman Nye, Carrie Gleason, Kate Rubin, Sam Worley, Mat Peltier, Tanja Ajo, Aleksandra Szaniawska, Marian Runk, Dianna Mertz, Ritchie Savage, Linsey Ly, Terra Poirier, Andrea Actis, Rachel and Mo, and of course the Black Lodge Hotdog Club. It's important to note that this book has been nourished by the strength and creativity of my queer/trans communities. Thank you for the films, poems, art projects, incredible outfits, phone calls, dance parties, mixtapes, cupcakes, roller-skate adventures, beach walks, questions about my pronouns, and seemingly endless capacity for processing. I also want to acknowledge another one of my teams: all of those who have somehow managed to think and write under the emotional weight of significant student-loan debt.

My partner Lindsey A. Freeman has supported this project across two countries, three cities, five apartments, one global pandemic, and the full range of human emotion. Thank you, Lindsey, for sharing all of the struggles and joys of this thinking, reading, and writing life with me. And thank you for finding our little dog Z., who is a fuzzy little ball of love.

Finally, I would like to thank my clients. Being a therapist is a weird job. It requires sitting with confusion, pain, frustration, self-doubt, and loss. And it's a wonderful job for a curious person. Every day that we work together, I encounter something new that transforms me: a unique way of explaining something, an unexpected joke in a moment of suffering, or another way of talking about how it is to be a thinking, feeling person navigating a difficult time. Thank you for sharing your worlds with me, and working to make those worlds better together.

Introduction

Compass

September 2012

I notice a weird look on Justin's face.

He's twelve, and I'm a mental health counselor working at his community after-school program in Brooklyn.[1] I run a parent-support group that's meeting later in this cafeteria space, and we'd been sitting at the tables, chatting at about his day when a sudden look of concern crossed his face.

"What's up?" I ask.

Justin explains, "We're doing geometry in math." He just realized that he had accidentally carried his compass—that circle-drawing tool with a sharp metal spike—out of school. He absentmindedly put it into his book bag with his notebook when the bell rang, instead of leaving it in class. He takes the object out of his backpack and places it on the table.

He is thinking ahead to the strong possibility that he will be stopped and frisked on the way home from our after-school program. He is thinking what the police might see in the compass. It is pointed. A weapon. An ordinary object suddenly becomes threatening because of its potential to be misrecognized, its function misunderstood in the backpack of a Black child. Alternately, if he throws it away, he could get in trouble at school. And what will he do in geometry?

The felt presence of police reaches into our after-school program. I tell Justin that I agree with him that the police stop-and-frisk practice is racist and wrong, and we make a plan that gets the compass to him the next day. The response feels partial and unsatisfactory. If my role as a counselor is to help shift unreasonable anxieties, I'm clearly working on the wrong side of the equation. I'm not challenging the police leaders and politicians who have made this policy, the people who support them, or the police who enforce them.

As a white woman moving through this predominantly Black neighborhood, I see a lot of police. They have never stopped me. Local residents often read me as a different kind of cop, a social worker policing through the child welfare system. I try to mark out a distinction—I'm offering a voluntary and needed mental health service in a community with less access to care, not taking kids away. But my profession has its own mandated reporting requirements and its own connections to state violence. I've been circling around my whiteness and policing in my work here, trying to figure out how to be useful in this specific Brooklyn community. The interaction with Justin punctures me. I try to leverage my tools and privileges where I can, but the fact is that I'm not doing much. I feel stuck, and I circle.

September 2014

Fast-forward two years: I have decided to return to graduate school, and I make the switch to my own private practice in counseling. At school, I am trying to bring together my interests in intersectional feminism, psychoanalysis, and prison abolition. Meanwhile, in my part-time private practice, I see clients with health insurance or the ability to pay out-of-pocket. My new clients are mostly white. Sometimes it's my explicitly queer and transpositive advertising that draws them in. At other times it's simply that I take their insurance or that my picture on the online search engine "looked friendly."

I am surprised to start getting calls from police officers and their partners, looking for a therapist. I wonder, "Is it a conflict of interest that I think of myself as an abolitionist?" But the impulse seems to be more about my own "good antiracist" anxiety than protecting my new clients or furthering any kind of solidarity with people targeted by policing. The psychoanalyst Stephen Mitchell describes this as "guiltiness," a response rooted in the desire to see myself as virtuous, rather than to repair harm.[2] I'm implicated in U.S. violence too. As I begin meeting with my new clients, I commit myself to continuing to think about race, violence, and historical context in my counseling work.

In our work, I discover that my cop clients' lives are consumed in a different way by policing. They daily embody the specter of state power. Policing has a material reality for them—it means itchy uniforms, or a rush of fear after getting poked with a sharp while searching someone's bag. As I find my own curiosity about their experiences, these counseling relationships begin to confront me with my complicity in state violence. A longtime viewer of police procedurals, I recognize that I am excited to learn insider knowledge. I review counseling manuals focused on the unique aspects of working with police and begin to learn more about my profession's involvement in supporting the ongoing power of the police. Once again, I am circling around my own relationship with police power.

Summer 2020

On May 25, 2020, a teenage girl named Darnella Frazier makes a video on her phone as George Floyd is murdered by Minneapolis police. She is a part of a small group of bystanders pleading for his life. She shares the video online, and this action sparks waves of protest, across the U.S. and internationally. Pouring into the streets, often wearing masks to prevent the spread of COVID-19, protestors insist on the value of George Floyd's life and the lives of Black people. They call out names, write them on signs, and repeat them in social media posts: Tanisha Anderson, Sandra Bland, Michael Brown, Philando Castile, Stephon Clark, Dominique Clayton, John Crawford III, Terence Crutcher, Michelle Cusseaux, Jamel Floyd, Janisha Fonville, Ezell Ford, Eric Garner, Freddie Gray, Akai Gurley, Botham Jean, Atatiana Jefferson, Dion Johnson, Bettie Jones, Quintonio LeGrier, Elijah McClain, Tony McDade, Laquan McDonald, Natasha McKenna, Gabriella Nevarez, Eric Reason, Tamir Rice, Aura Rosser, Walter Scott, Delrawn Small, Alton Sterling, Breonna Taylor, Terrill Thomas, Mary Truxillo, Christopher Whitfield.[3] For each name listed, there are thousands of other Black people killed by U.S. police whose names remain unspoken.[4] On the streets, in the media, and within the government, a mass movement makes the demand to defund the police.[5]

The protests drive broad public dialogue around policing and antiBlack racism. And yet, the presence of police remains common sense for many. In his 2020 presidential campaign, Joe Biden professed his support for police and held up the mantle of "police reform." Even the call to defund police is immediately adopted into reform. Police officer David

Hughes writes in the *New York Times*, "Yes, defund the police. But then re-fund them, better."[6] These reactions reflect widespread emotional investments in police power. They also highlight the fact that people often mean vastly different things when they talk about "the police." Some are focused on individual people or individual departments, while others draw attention to a set of institutions, systems, and materials, both inside and outside of direct government control.

Most people in the U.S. understand policing as inevitable, unchangeable, necessary, safe, or a matter of common sense. In this book, I seek to understand the intensity and persistence of this view. To do so, I examine the psychic life of police power: policing as it interacts with emotions and relationships. I start within scenes from my everyday life as a therapist, a queer white woman, and a U.S. citizen. I follow the psychic life of policing through a variety of scenes: counseling practices, professional organizations, training guides, museum displays, discussions of mortality statistics, and memorials. At each of these scenes, I work to understand how police power is functioning and to uncover the desires, assumptions, fantasies, and fears that facilitate its ongoingness.

This is not a traditional police ethnography. I did not participate in ride-alongs, embed myself within a police department, or work as a police officer.[7] Rather, *Uniform Feelings* uses a variety of methods drawn from feminist, psychoanalytic, and performance studies. The result is a qualitative inquiry into U.S. policing that incorporates clinical case studies, ethnographic research, and autotheory. Following feminist postcolonial scholar Fiona Probyn Rapsey, I use complicity as a methodological "starting point."[8] I work to avoid the role of innocent or apologist; instead I seek to understand the emotional logics that sustain policing. I want to make sense of what orients people toward state-sanctioned violence as a common-sense way of managing fear, anger, and shame, as well as a source of excitement and belonging.[9]

Through the genre of the case study, I narrate my clinical practice as a psychotherapist who has worked with people with diverse relationships to policing, including people who work in law enforcement and people who have been targeted for policing due to their race and/or gender presentation. Since the inaugural analytic treatment of Bertha Pappenheim, renamed in Josef Breuer's writing as "Anna O.," writing about the clinical encounter has raised a set of ethical questions. Some are related to accuracy and privacy, while others concern the power of the therapist.[10] The clinical vignette must be true, fair, and respectful of the client, while also carefully guarding the client's right to confidentiality. To ensure confidentiality, identifying details in all of my clinical accounts are altered. In one account (noted in the text), multiple clinical encounters are combined into a composite case study. These alterations provide opportunities for thinking about the work without compromising the confidential space that makes the work possible. It is also important to stipulate that the snapshots of my clients presented in these case studies are partial and subjective. The clients I work with have rich and complex life stories, filled with deep sorrow and despair, joyful belonging, generosity, creativity, and struggle. I only describe tiny fragments of their lives and our work together, because I believe that their life stories are not mine to tell. My focus is not on outlining extensive individual case histories. Rather, I seek to capture brief moments that helped me to understand more about how U.S. police power shapes relationships and interior lives and about how those aspects of police power might be transformed.

I explore the social alongside the psychic, inspired by the work of one of my mentors, psychoanalyst and anthropologist Muriel Dimen.[11] Examining the policing of boundary violations within the psychoanalytic community, Dimen suggests that analysts move beyond the individual response of throwing out rotten apples and "check out the barrel"—seeking to understand silence, fear, and complicity within the psychoanalytic community.[12] This is also good advice for a researcher studying policing in other settings. Dimen writes of her own experience of being harmed, and the additional harm done by her analyst's silence on the transgression as their work continued. "[I]n the context of the talking cure," Dimen writes that she was devastated by "his resounding silence, as much as his intrusive act."[13] Following Dimen, I am interested in thinking across the psychic, social, and cultural dimensions of violence and in speaking about what remains unspeakable within the frame of the "talking cure." The relationship between psychoanalysis and state-sanctioned violence is often one of those unspeakable topics. By examining clinical practice, I work to explore my own personal and professional complicities and silences.

In fact, what Freud called "auto-analysis" has been a part of psychoanalysis since the very beginning. Feminist psychoanalytic scholar Carolyn Laubender notes that the founding text of psychoanalysis, *The Interpretation of Dreams*, insists on the method. Freud found that in order to articulate a new theory of psychic functioning, he would need to analyze his own dreams; the method had to be personal and autobiographical.[14] This practice of auto-analysis aligns with the feminist method of autotheory, using embodied experiences as a point of connection to critical theory.[15] The term "autotheory" was popularized by Maggie Nelson's exploration of queer desire, family, and care in *The Argonauts*, and the practice is linked to a long history of BIPOC feminist analysis in works such as Audre Lorde's "biomythography" *Zami* and Gloria Anzaldua's *Borderlands/La Frontera*.[16]

While I begin in the psychoanalytic clinic, throughout the book I move from the consulting room into a range of other cultural sites. When I do, my approach to ethnography is grounded in my academic training in performance studies. I take on the role of participant-observer in cultural performances related to policing at museums, memorials, gun ranges, and police bias trainings. In each scene, I attend to what performance-studies scholar Diana Taylor names as the archive and the repertoire, considering embodied practices alongside written and material records of police power.[17]

The Police Power

Police power shapes life in the United States. In 2018, 6.4 million people in the United States were under some form of carceral control; this means that 2.5 percent of the total adult population was incarcerated in prison or jail or under supervision on probation or parole.[18] In the same year, there were 10.3 million arrests, with 3.1 arrests for every 100 people living in the U.S.[19] In addition to reported arrests, the police stop approximately 12 percent of drivers every year, with that number as high as 24 percent for Black, Indigenous, and people of color.[20] Many thousands more are stopped, questioned, or frisked by police in public spaces. Between 2012 and 2018, over 1,000 people were killed by police each year.[21] People who do not interact with police directly are made aware of their presence through seeing marked cars, hearing sirens, and encountering uniformed, armed officers in public spaces. We also encounter stories, news, and cultural representations of policing in television, movies, books, museums, and music.

The label "police" is expansive. It might equally be applied to the Federal Bureau of Investigation, the Tompkins County Sheriff's Office, the Illinois State Department of Corrections, a private-prison management company, or Immigration and Customs Enforcement. Policing organizations have enormous reach materially too. They have office buildings, detention facilities, training centers, archives, fleets of vehicles, and stockpiles of weapons. They have a set of ingrained practices, from written protocols to unwritten traditions, that help to organize their work. And "police" also refers to the individual workers who are paid to carry out these acts of surveilling, jailing, injuring, and killing other people.

In 2017, over 1.36 million people worked as police officers, detectives, probation officers, and jail and prison guards in the United States.[22] In the same year, 1.13 million people worked as private security guards.[23] Another 20,000 people work for Immigration and Customs Enforcement.[24] The carceral workforce shows up daily to run prisons, to patrol neighborhoods, to monitor borders, to stop and question, to direct traffic, to ensure order, and to issue tickets and fines. Around 78,000 people working in state prosecutors' offices prosecute some of the court cases created in these encounters.[25]

While they are marked by economic and geographic diversity, these workers are disproportionately white and overwhelmingly male. Though the U.S. population is only 63 percent white, the state and local police workforce is almost 75 percent white.[26] Though women are in a slight majority in the U.S. population, almost nine out of ten patrol officers are male.[27] This racial and gender disparity increases as you move up the chain of command.[28] This not-very-diverse workforce reaps the benefits of an unusually high level of union organization. While decades of attacks on unions have resulted in a U.S. workforce that is only 10.3 percent organized, police unions have been shielded from these attacks.[29] Between 75 and 80 percent of officers are represented by police unions.[30]

Police work toward a stated mission to enforce "law and order" through the use or threat of violence. Within a work environment focused on preserving the existing social order, Black, Indigenous, Latinx, and Asian American officers face even higher pressure to conform. In 2008 and 2009, two different studies by Vicky Wilkins and Brian Williams unexpectedly found increased racial profiling in units with more Black and Latinx officers.[31] Wilkins and Williams theorized that the pressure on these officers to "represent blue" led them to increased discriminatory behavior in order to fit in. A 2020 study on police killings similarly found some evidence of an increase in police killings of Black people in units with more Black officers.[32]

Adding BIPOC actors into the scene in the role of cops does not necessarily change the anti-Black scripts and repertoires of policing. In the foreword to former Philadelphia police chief John Timoney's autobiography, Tom Wolfe describes a related conversation about racial and ethnic demographics within policing:

> I remember asking Inspector Timoney if the NYPD still recruited Irish policemen. "Yeah," he said, "we recruit them, but now they all come from the suburbs . . . and to tell the truth, a lot of them are cream puffs. These days if you want a real Irish cop, you hire a Puerto Rican."[33]

Making a joke, Timoney suggests that Puerto Ricans officers are now the "real Irish cops." The "realness" here is located not in their genetic and family history, but in Timoney's perception of these officers' willingness to use state-sanctioned violence in ways that demonstrate that they are not "cream puffs."

Police institutions, police officers, and broader U.S. publics often fail to recognize how the police function, imagining police as primarily involved in "justice." This framing suggests that the primary function of police is to seek justice, stop violence, and address past wrongs. Police are imagined kicking down doors and getting "bad guys." Despite these popular fantasies, scholars agree that police in their day-to-day practices are not primarily engaged in stopping crime. Organizer Mariame Kaba argues that the behavioral repertoire of police is often misunderstood, writing, "the first thing to point out is that police officers don't do what you think they do."[34] Sociologist Robert Reiner summarizes the research: "One of the earliest findings of sociological research on policing, replicated time and time again over the last fifty years, is that—contrary to popular images—most police work does not involve crime or at any rate law enforcement."[35] Political theorist Mark Neocleous notes that "the percentage of police effort devoted to traditional criminal law matters probably does not exceed 10 percent."[36] Rather than primarily stopping crime, police work involves a variety of tasks that function primarily to maintain social order.

Policing works to maintain social order through the use of violence.[37] In the words of Micol Seigal, police are "violence workers" who the state empowers to gather information about and address threats to the current order of racialized resource distribution and life chances.[38] Sociologist Egon Bittner defines police "as a mechanism for distributing nonnegotiable coercive force in accordance with an intuitive grasp of situational threats to social order."[39] Sometimes state-sanctioned violence happens through police institutions, within the confines of their official use-of-force policies. At other times, the violence is extralegal, but either explicitly or implicitly condoned. This might include officers engaged in sexual violence toward people they encounter in their work, or deciding that there is no crime to report when asked to respond to sexual violence. In all of these situations, the state determines who can commit violence, how they can commit it, and to what ends violence can be viewed as legitimate.[40]

The history of the United States is a history of violence. The U.S. was established, expanded, and enriched through legalized violence, including the violence of settler colonialism and chattel slavery. State-sanctioned violence is now deployed to support contemporary forms of racial capitalism.[41] Policing and prisons play a key role in contemporary racial capitalism, to the point that Jackie Wang describes our economic system as "carceral capitalism." Wang argues that "the carceral techniques of the state are shaped by—and work in tandem with—the imperatives of global capitalism."[42] Within current regimes of carceral capitalism, there are unique forms of violent, racialized relationships between citizens and the state. Wang outlines techniques of "parasitic governance" that extract wealth from communities through privatization, fees, and fines.

Stories from within policing identify the role of police in "parasitic governance." Former police chief Norm Stamper reports that he was judged as a cop based on his "numbers"—arrests, tickets, and other documented interactions. The principles of equal justice, respect, and fairness were unmeasured and fell away in importance. Stamper writes, "In a bureaucracy, what gets counted counts."[43] Self-described "philosopher-cop" Jonathan Wender similarly argues that the "bureaucratic *problematization of human being*" (emphasis his) in policing results in practices that "efface human presence and translate it into an entity available for scientific analysis and methodical control."[44]

Ericson and Hagerty highlight the increasing role of police in creating knowledge through producing reports and reporting statistics.[45] Police collect a wide variety of data, write reports, engage in surveillance, and develop accounts of populations and areas and the risks they pose. In their study of rural police, Huey and Ricciardelli note that police don't often feel that this is what they signed up for, and that "of all the roles that officers adopt, the one that generates the most notable degree of frustration is . . . tied to paperwork and the need to generate statistics for internal and external use."[46]

These practices can be understood in the context of broader economic and political relationships.[47] Police stats represent resource transfers in the form of home monitoring and court fees, ticket fines, and tax investment in prisons and police. Bureaucratic reports aid the administration of insurance claims and ensure that resource distributions are insured against disruption. Whether the statistics go up or down, they can be used to argue for increased police and prison funding. More important than the numbers is the process of turning people into numbers. Wender and Stamper's critiques from within policing identify the denial of subjectivity—the effacement of human presence—as a key dynamic of policing. These are racialized practices that maintain U.S. histories of building wealth through the violent denial of subjectivity.

While scholars of policing highlight the role of police as "knowledge workers," part of police work requires not-knowing. Policing rewards the refusal to recognize alternative subjectivities; it demands contact while undermining the basis of relationship. This dynamic is rooted in white supremacy, and it is applied to people living within multiple vectors of oppression, including disability and gender diversity. Anything that might be known about people outside of their threat potential is denied. Historian Bryan Wagner notes that the long U.S. legal history of the use of "imagined threat scenarios" to define policing illustrates a persistent refusal of Black subjectivity.[48] "Seen from the standpoint of the police power, Blackness is imperceptible except for the presumed danger it poses to public welfare."[49] Historian and literary critic Saidiya Hartman writes that "Black lives are still imperiled and devalued by a racial calculus and a political arithmetic that were entrenched centuries ago"—she refers to this as the afterlife of slavery.[50] Within scenes of policing, the afterlife of slavery emerges. It is present when U.S. police are encouraged to encounter some people as undeserving of empathic connection; it shapes the misrecognition of individuals and communities as data points or threats. The afterlife of slavery is present when Black people are treated as not quite fully belonging to the category of "citizen." This refusal to recognize—to not see all people as people, to not see all violence as violence—is a key relational practice within policing. Cops sometimes struggle with its felt logics; and at times they refuse them. And many in the U.S. who do not work as police still participate in and maintain these relational practices.

Vulnerable Heroes

A number of scholars have identified and challenged the frameworks of innocence and criminality that undergird U.S. policing. Naomi Murakawa and Katherine Beckett have identified the "penology of racial innocence" that masks racial power in the study of the criminal legal system by using a limited definition of racism that cannot capture complex systems and processes.[51] Jackie Wang argues "against innocence" as an activist tactic, noting that some activist efforts "re-entrench a logic that criminalizes race and constructs docile subjects."[52] Eve Tuck and K. Wayne Yang have noted the "settler move to innocence," in which settlers disavow their investments in ongoing colonial processes, as a key dynamic in maintaining settler colonialism.[53] In the *Cult of True Victimhood*, Alyson Cole points to the appropriation of claims of victimization by figures on the Right, inverting logics of innocence and criminality to claim their own innocence.[54]

To the discussion of innocence and criminality, I bring in a third term: the vulnerable protector. Neither innocent nor criminal, this is the person who enforces social order and spouts common-sense justifications of violence. In the cultural narratives that surround policing, these representatives of the state need protection not because they are innocent, but because they are the face of a potentially vulnerable social order. As they work to preserve or expand present hierarchies, efforts for social justice or accountability are framed as violent attacks against them. These protectors embrace technical approaches to violence, and attempts to confront them with ethical or historical perspectives are seen as a threat to their emotional freedom—understood as their right to be free of shame or guilt. Efforts to transform the criminal legal system need to extend beyond critiques of racialized dichotomies between innocence and criminality. They also need to grapple with the role and the romance of the vulnerable protector.

Television shows and movies on policing present the romance of flawed-hero cops, creating extended space for contemplation of complex police subjectivities. Cop shows, as well as public discourses around policing, often work to train viewers into empathic understanding of police perspectives. Members of the public who are not targeted by policing can consume the pleasures of police perspective, while continuing to imagine themselves as innocent of police violence. The promise of becoming an idealized hero is an emotional hook that draws people into violence work. Alongside the promise of good pay is the identity of the police officer: a strong, respected public figure. Policing requires violence work, and it also requires that the public embrace the idea that some people's use of violence is necessary and good. The idealization of the hero-cop frames some violence as distinct from and opposite to the creation of harm. This is the fantasy of legitimate violence—that some forms of violence can be good for society.

Police Culture

Performances of policing function like other performances of cultural memory. In the words of performance studies scholar Diana Taylor, they "make visible (for an instant, live, now) that which is always already there: the ghosts, the tropes, the scenarios that structure our individual and collective life."[55] Policing is iterative, it is made and remade through police stops and encounters, through TV shows, through legislation that promises public safety, and through institutions that name themselves after justice. Police culture consists of all of these practices, ideas, institutions, images, documents, objects, and stories within which state violence is presented as benevolent, desirable, necessary, or inevitable. Most of U.S. culture is police culture.

A key feature of U.S. police culture is the claim that police violence is legitimate and just. The racialized specter of violent crime is invoked to make policing seem comparably benign. In contrast to crime, the police are represented as being contained within a set of boundaries and rules. Police power is presented as enforcing democratic justice—administering laws created by the people, applying them equally, and treating everyone fairly. Supposedly, police are civilian, public, and local.[56] Yet they regularly cross all of these defining boundaries, operating in coordination with the military and private corporations, organizing nationally and internationally, and defying the promise of democratic justice.

These boundaries are crossed in part because police culture consists of both archive and repertoire. The archive of policing may include commitments to antiracism, equal justice, and maintaining a nonmilitary, civilian police force. But the repertoire structures the placement of certain bodies into policing scenarios and draws on the histories of state-sanctioned violence to suggest a set of possible actions within those scenes.[57] The scene is set, and the action begins.

In the contemporary U.S., police culture is almost everywhere. People step into a police role in voluntary and impromptu ways to enforce existing social orders in schools, public parks, sidewalks, and businesses. They consume state violence in television shows, books, and movies. They justify it in everyday conversations. Police culture is every performance of identification with the existing social and economic order and the violence used to maintain it. Even among progressive activists, there can be what Alison Reed describes as a carceral psychology, "an active psychic investment" in policing that "celebrates [police] as aligned with folks most targeted for state surveillance and violence." This is reflected in shared images of cops kneeling or invited to kneel alongside protestors, or, in a case highlighted by Reed, wearing "pussy hats" at the 2016 Women's March.[58]

Micol Siegal writes that "police are the translation of state violence into human form."[59] In the U.S., much of the population is involved in these acts of translation—supporting the work of prosecutors, police, and prison guards in a variety of ways. Police culture—understood more broadly—encompasses a range of affective and relational investments in the existing social order. Even progressives and leftists who dis-identify with police act to monitor and interrogate the movement of people they deem suspicious. Teachers, social workers, store clerks, and neighbors all act as adjunct police. Police culture is present in arguments about the necessity and naturalness of police power, and in an eagerness to punish, abandon, and destroy others. Police culture shapes organizing campaigns to put violent cops behind bars. It animates fantasies of legitimate state violence.

Pointing out the contradictions of getting a permit from the police to protest the police, activist Paula X. Rojas labels these investments in state violence as "the cops in our heads and hearts."[60] She cites policing tactics within social movement spaces, assumptions about unequal resource distribution, privileging of gender-conservative organizing tactics, and investments in "professional" nonprofit status within U.S. movements as elements of police culture within social movements. Rojas highlights that challenging policing also means challenging these aspects of social-movement cultures.

Reflecting on prison as "an accurate name for our contemporary culture," the U.S. writer, scholar, and activist Alexis Pauline Gumbs states, "the moments in which prisons became a dominant feature of the U.S., our imaginations (for all, not just those of us disproportionately imprisoned) also became imprisoned. The way we imagine work, our relationships, the

future, family, everything, is locked down."[61] Police culture limits our collective imaginations of community, relationships, and safety. The first step
in moving beyond these limits is to understand how they function and how
they have shifted and persisted through time.

Rich critiques of police culture have emerged through acknowledgments of complicity. For example, the term "carceral feminism" describes
the antiviolence movement's investments in policing, prisons, and incarceration as means to achieve the goal of ending gender-based violence.[62]
Mimi Kim notes that, driven by intersectional feminist critique and organizing, mainstream antiviolence movements have now begun to question
this investment in criminalization.[63] Similarly, in the field of education,
educators have developed critiques of their institutions' participation in the
criminalization of BIPOC youth. These scholars trace the school-to-prison
pipeline and acknowledge that the school itself functions as a carceral space
in many communities.[64] Criminology educators at the college level have
also highlighted the complicity of their departments in the expansive reach
of criminalization.[65] The groundbreaking work of legal scholar Dorothy
Roberts outlines the function of the child-welfare system in racialized
policing and punishment.[66] Following Roberts's critique of the carceral
function of child welfare, Erica Meiners and Charity Tolliver highlight that
their status as "mandated reporters" situates teachers as a part of "the 'soft'
extension of [the] carceral state," alongside social service workers and many
mental health professionals.[67]

Like education, feminism, and social work, psychology has its own carceral connection. Carceral psychology links the institutions and practices
of psychology with policing, prisons, and other forms of state-sanctioned
violence. Counselors and psychologists lend their expertise and legitimacy
to police power, in exchange for promises of protection and access to
resources. In this book, I examine carceral psychology as it manifests in
counseling and research translation practices. Beyond these examples of
direct participation in policing, much of psychology and counseling practice happens within the framework of police culture. We assume policing is
natural, necessary, good, and inevitable; we do not seek to imagine the possibility of other ways of ensuring safety or responding to harm.

In suggesting an examination of police culture with the goal of developing new forms of relatedness, I am not promoting improved relationships
between police and community members. Nor am I endorsing the range of
reforms that seek to build dialogue between police and Black communities.

My focus is on understanding what draws people to the police role, on how broader publics participate in the romance of policing through celebratory and heroic narratives, and on identifying other forms of relational and emotional life that sustain U.S. policing. Policing functions at the individual, institutional, and cultural level, and each level is also a site of contestation. From my role as a psychotherapist, I identify how people in the U.S. invest and participate in policing, and how we can develop emotional and relational practices that refuse the scripts of police power. Giving up our various commitments to the hero cop means giving up the idea that interpersonal and social harm can be extinguished through the use of state violence. This is also the demand of abolitionists—that state-sanctioned violence be rejected as a legitimate response, even to acts of violence.

Abolitionists refuse the idea that people who have committed acts of violence deserve state violence. This extends to the punishment of violent police officers through the criminal legal system. In *Are Prisons Obsolete?* Angela Davis outlines the abolitionist orientation that works toward "reshaping systems of justice around strategies of reparation, rather than retribution."[68] The abolitionist organization *8 to Abolition* writes, "We believe in a world where there are zero police murders because there are zero police."[69] Drawing on Andre Gorz's concept of "non-reformist reforms," abolitionists advocate for actions that shrink the expansive reach of police power and invest instead in nonpunitive systems of care.[70]

Efforts to abolish U.S. policing need to engage with the emotional investments, identifications, and styles of relationship that maintain police power. Police culture encourages people to sink into a binary, racialized and gendered worldview that emphasizes "good guys and bad guys." In doing so, people lose skills in interpersonal problem-solving, empathy, perspective-taking, sitting with complexity, grieving, and symbolizing their own capacity to participate in harm. Movement toward abolition requires an awareness of the broad reach of police power into a variety of daily practices that make us feel safe and/or good. Shrinking police culture requires some of us to strengthen certain capacities, including the capacity to engage with marginalized subjectivities distinct from our own and the ability to hold on to mournful awareness of our own complicity in violent systems.

U.S. police cultures create structures of emotional containment that help sustain police power. But those interventions are always partial, often not quite able to contain the strong feelings associated with long histories of violence. I study the emotional culture of policing, with a psychotherapist's eye for new possibilities. In doing so, the fields of psychotherapy, psychology, and psychoanalysis are sometimes useful as a method to deepen understandings of fantasies, relationships, and emotions. Notwithstanding their usefulness, these disciplines also emerge as participants at the scene of state-sanctioned violence.

Psychoanalysis and Police Power

This project draws on queer, feminist, anticolonial, and Black engagements with psychoanalysis to think through U.S. policing. Psychoanalysis can provide tools for thinking about the complex psychic dynamics that shape policing—including identification, disavowal, and projection. And at the same time, the field emerged in its own violent social context. It is shaped by its history, structured through colonial metaphors of the "primitive" mind, disavowed racial fantasies, and heteropatriarchal stories of gender and family life.[71] As critical psychologists Derek Hook and Ross Truscott write, "we can treat psychoanalytic interpretations themselves as a form of acting out the colonial past."[72] The fields of psychology and psychoanalysis are a part of police culture. They circulate stories and maintain practices in which state-sanctioned violence is natural, unavoidable, necessary, or good. Following the strategy of Ranjanna Khanna, I encounter psychoanalysis both as a method and object of critique.[73]

Two recent cases highlight the relationship between psychoanalytic organizations and state-sanctioned violence. The first involves psychologist participation in U.S. military torture, while the second involves psychoanalytic stances toward the Israeli occupation of Palestine.

In the first decade of the U.S. "War on Terror," psychoanalysts within the American Psychological Association (APA) took a stand against their parent organization's involvement in state violence. Members of Division 39, the division that gathers psychoanalytic practitioners within the APA, led resistance to the APA's collusion with U.S. military "enhanced interrogation" torture practices.[74]

In discussing their role in opposing the practice, Division 39 members highlighted the connection between specifically psychoanalytic styles of intervention and their political work. Discussing his involvement in the protests, psychoanalyst Steven Reisner writes that when the initial stories from the APA didn't make sense to him, "I found myself listening clinically to the material. . . . I found myself listening for the hidden story—the story that was being obscured precisely as the surface narrative was being perfected." Reisner gestures toward the potential of psychoanalytic listening to political material, writing about "how a small group of psychoanalysts used psychoanalytic methods to overcome resistances and join the resistance."[75]

The successful campaign led to a scathing independent investigation and report, a 2015 ban on psychologist participation in national security interrogations, multiple resignations and early retirements from APA leadership, and an overhaul of APA ethics practices.[76] However, the 2015 interrogation ban draws a sharp line between stopping military involvement and continuing to support domestic police interrogation. The APA ban specifically does not apply to "domestic law enforcement interrogations or domestic detention settings." This exception is justified on the grounds that in these locations, "detainees are under the protection of the U.S. Constitution."[77] While the violence of military torture is opposed, the adequacy of the U.S. criminal legal system is affirmed. The surface narrative of domestic police power as offering "protection" remains intact.

In 2018, the International Association for Relational Psychoanalysis and Psychotherapy (IARPP) experienced an internal split around the organization's relationship with the Israeli occupation, following IARPP's decision to hold its 2019 annual conference in Tel Aviv.[78] The Palestinian Union of Social Workers and Psychologists opposed the conference on the grounds that it "lends legitimacy to the occupation and its innumerable violations of human rights."[79] The USA-Palestine Mental Health Network launched a "Don't Go" organizing campaign, which began with calls to move the conference location. When that initiative failed, they led a boycott of the conference.[80] One point they highlighted was the exclusion of Palestinian practitioners and people critical of Israel from the conference. The IARPP conference website acknowledged that some might have difficulty attending the conference, and offered, "We will do our very best to address and even directly handle visa approvals, including personal negotiations with the political authorities if needed."[81]

In both the APA's carving out of a police exception from the interrogation resolution and in the defense of the IARPP Tel Aviv conference, the surface narrative is one in which a democratic state is ruled by just processes of law. There is no perceived need to challenge state violence, because state processes are trusted to ensure that all violence within state borders is legitimate violence. There is activism to bring people into these states' jurisdictions, but no awareness of the states' constitutive exclusions and ongoing forms of legal violence. In other words, the actions of these psychoanalytic professional associations assume that police power is fair, necessary, and unavoidable.

The failure to hear hidden stories that might challenge the surface narrative of state power extends beyond these examples of organizational policy. Within the U.S., clinical psychoanalytic practice has often ignored the nation's foundational violence. Psychoanalyst Dorothy Evans Holmes writes of the inattention of the U.S. psychoanalytic community to the meanings of race within clinical practice:

> In particular I have found that psycho-analysis turns a blind eye to the psychodynamic meanings of being Black in America: The psychologically damaging effects of slavery and its sequels on Blacks and Whites (post-Reconstruction decimation of rights; Jim Crow and its ugly truths, including lynchings; and current-day mass incarceration of Black men) are not typically recognized by psychoanalysts as needing conceptualization and clinical attention.[82]

The traumatic impact of U.S. slavery, including its manifestations in the current carceral state, in economic inequality, and in the structuring of private lives and fantasies, is typically unrecognized in clinical contexts. Holmes writes that she has learned as a Black psychoanalyst to always inquire about childhood domestic staff in taking histories from white patients, because their early relationships with Black domestic workers often inform the treatment relationship.[83] U.S. racism matters in the clinical context. When racial context is ignored, the psychoanalytic process fails to fully encounter complex psychic processes of identity, relationship, and fantasy. When these topics are not denied or dissociated, psychoanalysis can offer rich frameworks for thinking about the interplay between the social and the psychic.

The process of identity formation is one that occurs in relation with race and gender others. Psychoanalyst Jacques Lacan describes the process of identity formation through what he terms the "mirror stage," in which individual infants look at themselves in the mirror.[84] This is a moment of recognition of the body as the self, but also a misrecognition—while the body is experienced as fragmented, it is seen in the mirror as whole and ideal, as powerful. This first recognition of self is a misrecognition: though the individual is most often physically supported by an adult caregiver in this encounter, the social and relational context is ignored as people instead understand themselves as autonomous and powerful individuals.[85]

Racialization and police power can be understood as ongoing psychic processes rather than faits accomplis. While writing *Black Skin, White Masks*, psychiatrist and social theorist Frantz Fanon was working clinically with both the colonial police and the Algerian resistance fighters who survived torture by those police.[86] His awareness of the link between police power and psychic life enriches his work. Fanon highlights that Lacan's mirror stage is a racialized description that applies to white bodies living in contexts of white power. Fanon considers the mirror stage as a doubled process for Black persons in which the mirror of the racializing gaze fragments and alienates Black persons from their own identities.[87] Fanon's famous description of this process involves a child shouting, "Look, a Negro!" In this scene, Fanon highlights the creation of blackness as an object of the white gaze rather than a subject of address. The child asks for protection from his mother, and his invisible, unnamed whiteness is reaffirmed as vulnerable, innocent, and neutral.

For the racialized individual, the encounter is a mirror that shatters, as "my body was returned to me spread-eagled, disjointed, redone, draped in mourning on this white winter's day."[88] This act also transforms the person who wields the racializing gaze, strengthening their identification with whiteness. The Black person is used as a mirror to reflect back white cohesive identity, goodness, vulnerability, autonomy, and ability to name. In the moment of "Look!," the white individual justifies violence through an experience of fear. Philosopher George Yancy writes that the white child "is learning, at that very moment, the power of racial speech, the power of racial gesturing."[89]

Racialization is, in part, enacted through a dialogue between mother and son about fear. It is significant that Fanon's scene is one in which two white people work in tandem to enact racialization *and* disavow the harms of this process. On the side of whiteness, the scene incorporates two roles that work together to construct white identity. The frightened child occupies the role of the supposed "innocent," while the protective parent serves as the "hero" who provides safety. The child says to his mother, "I'm scared!" The threat of racial violence is made through the child's calls for protection—in the face of this imagined threat, psychic dismemberment could quickly shift to bodily violence.

The white parent retains the power to determine what counts as harm, what deserves attention, and who counts as civilized. Fanon writes her words: "Ssh! You'll make him angry. Don't pay attention to him, monsieur, he doesn't realize you're just as civilized as we are."[90] The mother's comment to Fanon acts to silence him, lest he be named as uncivilized. If he should display anger in the face of this psychic violence, he may be perceived as a further threat to the child, and be a target of state-sanctioned violence. His subjectivity is absent in the parent-child encounter; it is an imagined threat scenario. Police power and heteropatriarchal protection sustain this interaction. Fanon writes of "the white man, who has no scruples about imprisoning me" as driving this process of objectification.[91] The police power supports and enables the racializing gaze and white identity formation. White parents teach white children that they are powerful, that they define civilization. Meanwhile, the parents of Black children stage a different conversation.[92]

Reading as a psychotherapist, I notice parallels between Fanon's scene and my own sessions with white clients. Entering into psychoanalytic dialogue, a white therapist and a white client can reenact this scene of racialization, as the client raises their fears and the therapist determines what counts as harm, what deserves attention, and who counts as civilized. Blackness is outside of the dialogue, an object of fantasy and knowledge, while whiteness is often unnamed, implicit, and assumed. The complicity of clients and therapists in racialized violence is seldom acknowledged or explored. Clients and therapists are implicated in the violent social order, but their involvement often remains unsymbolized, unspoken, unavailable for reflection. A question for white therapists in clinical practice with white clients is how to shift the scripts within this scene.

Psychoanalyst Lynne Jacobs argues that white shame and guilt are emotions that can serve as resources. "[I]f we cannot acknowledge our guilt, we cannot recognize our privilege. If we disavow shame we lose access to humility, compassion, and moral inspiration."[93] She notes that awareness of one's own complicity often surfaces first as bewilderment, or what she calls creeping shame, "a dawning sense of my own ignorance, and with that, a realization that I am not as innocent as my own good intentions claim."[94] Understanding shame as a resource allows one to turn toward the feelings of bewilderment, to become interested in the aspects of one's ignorance that are being highlighted, and to gain new tools to understand and act against racism.

Certainly guilt and shame can lead to a reparative impulse. But they can also work in more narcissistic ways. In his interrogation of the uses of the concept of "white privilege," psychoanalyst Neil Altman writes of an inauthentic guilt in relation to whiteness. Acts motivated by inauthentic guilt serve as "defenses against guilt, ways of putting the discomfort of guilt to rest, like a too hasty apology."[95] Altman outlines the damage of such an approach: "such lip service expressions of guilt may actually enable behaviour that violates ethical or moral principles by a show of remorse."[96]

White shame can also be recruited into the project of white supremacy. Scholars of queer shame have highlighted how shame can serve as a creative resource. Eve Kosofsky Sedgwick writes that shame "attaches to and sharpens the sense of what one is."[97] In 2016, Hillary Clinton's description of half of Trump's supporters as a racist and xenophobic "basket of deplorables" quickly shifted into a celebratory claim of shared "deplorable" identity. Trump and his supporters celebrated themselves as "deplorable," a word that literally means shameful, shifting an accusation of racism and xenophobia into a marker of community.[98] This process highlights that shame is a complex and unruly emotion. When we deploy it to try to change behaviors, it doesn't always play out as we expect.

Further, shame and guilt are not always the primary emotions associated with racism and state violence. Efforts to understand police power need to encounter other associated emotions, including pleasurable ones.[99] German-studies scholar Klaus Theweleit describes the psychic processes that facilitate emotional investments in state-sanctioned violence.[100] He turns to theories of early attachment to try to understand emotional investments in a mode of reality production that creates "life-destroying structures."[101] Rather than understanding participation in state violence as necessarily a source of shame or guilt, Theweleit explores how people become attached to a vision of a social world shaped through patriarchal and white-supremacist violence—they experience it as a positive attachment.[102]

Both Theweleit and U.S. political theorist Michael Rogin turn to British psychoanalyst Melanie Klein's work to try to understand these attachments. Rogin examines case studies in U.S. history of what he refers to as "political demonology," in which a countersubversive tradition is "dominated by splitting, by anxiety about boundary breakdown, and by invasive, devouring exterminatory enemies."[103] He notes that these themes point toward Klein's descriptions of infant life, in which rage is aimed toward either total unity or total destruction.

Police culture encourages a focus on identifying threats, as well as a binary division into good and bad citizens. This is a psychic state consistent with what Klein names as the "paranoid position."[104] Rather than treating the "paranoid position" as a specific diagnosis applied to a small number of people, Klein theorizes it as a psychic stance that occurs over the course of development, and that can be re-entered at different times. Within this stance, other people are experienced not as complex individuals, but as "part-objects." These part-objects are understood as either all-good or all-bad, depending on whether they meet the person's needs. They are assigned to poles of idealization and devaluation. The paranoid position is one from which people create and identify with strict good/bad binaries. When elements of the self are experienced as bad, the psychic defense of projection is used to maintain a sense of self as all-good. From the paranoid position, people can experience themselves as heroes, warring against evil others to promote the forces of good. This can be a pleasurable psychic position.[105]

Klein highlights that while the paranoid position seeks safety, the fantasy of total safety is inextricably linked to both terror and aggression. On patrol, at their jobs, in public spaces, police and those in the police role assess others as threats. In doing so, they assume themselves to be good—they are not the source of the threat. The encounter with others is structured as a binary sorting task—into threats and innocents. Potential violence is imagined as an unchanging characteristic of some of those encountered, manageable only through destruction. Some police refer to this through the metaphor of being sheepdogs, protecting sheep from wolves.[106]

Some might argue that the idealized hero offers a counterpoint to cynical violence, but the hero demands continued operation within a paranoid style. The good guy demands bad guys—innocence demands evil. Within this position, the threat of the hero's own violence is disavowed. Violence by "good guys" is understood as "good violence." The cynical, violent cop and the idealistic hero cop are two extremes on the same paranoid pole.

Klein describes psychic movement into another relational mode—the depressive position.[107] This shift involves learning to recognize the capacity to be simultaneously good and bad. It is marked by the ability to enter into complex relationships, including ones in which people understand their own potential for harm. Instead of supporting an identification with hero cops, one might instead accept the inevitability of failure in the stance of the hero, and to mourn this failure as a loss. This is the psychic work that might allow people to abandon an insistent defense of the goodness of policing when presented with a constant stream of conflicting evidence. In her work on Klein, queer theorist Eve Kosofsky Sedgwick terms this the "reparative position," as it is one that allows for the type of guilt that motivates relational repair. It is marked by the psychic capacity to imagine the other person's subjective experience.[108]

Challenging the current organization of our relationship with policing is not as easy as identifying "bad cops" or "bad systems" that exist outside of our hearts and minds. It may also require shifts in our own identities, relationships, and ways of feeling good. These theories resonate with calls within the field of transformative justice to interrogate our own investments in punishment. Community organizer and social worker Tanisha "Wakumi" Douglas discusses her own process toward "undoing punitive models of being" within the organization she cofounded, asking, "In what way am I undoing punitive ways of being with others?"[109]

Chapter Overview

This book considers police power as it shapes both individual emotional lives and collective social possibilities. I begin with clinical vignettes drawn from my work with police officers, to try to get inside the emotional logics of policing. I move from the individual to the institutional, examining emotional management strategies police departments employ, including efforts of police psychology to support police power at moments of crisis. I then shift from police departments to museum and memorial spaces and their efforts to shape broader public sentiments around policing through stories about history and heroism.

The first chapter explores emotional relationships with guns. I investigate the dynamics of lived relationships with firearms, with an eye toward the difficulty of shifting interpersonal relationships in the presence of dangerous weapons. I start with a client bringing a gun to my office. To think through this clinical moment, I turn to British psychoanalyst D. W. Winnicott, trying to reckon with guns in identity formation and as they enter into relationships. I then turn to contemporary best-practice "cop counseling" manuals, looking at the tools for thought provided by the emerging field of police psychology. I engage in my own fieldwork, learning to use a handgun at the American Police Hall of Fame and Museum shooting range, and I look at cultural stories about the thing-power of guns.

Some contemporary police psychologists claim that "cops and guns go together" and that any attempt to interrogate this is offensive to police and disrespectful to their culture. In doing so, they co-opt the concept of multicultural competency. In contrast, I discover moments of ambivalence and terror in the face of how firearms work to transform cops and their relationships.

The second chapter continues in the therapy office, as a jail guard quotes a statistic to me. This statistic is a familiar thing, a prediction of premature death that I've heard from other officers. Looking closely at this statistic, I consider the material bodies of police and the impact of their work on these bodies. Policing is frequently cited as an occupation that creates premature death for its workers. While the statistics about premature death for police officers are less than compelling, policing clearly manufactures misery and precarity for Black, Latinx, and Indigenous bodies. I see what happens when we look at these two accounts of premature death side by side.

To understand the emotional power of this narrative of premature police death, I argue that we need to consider the failed heroism that informs police officer's lives. They enter an occupation that promises heroic moments, while in reality it assigns them miserable bureaucratic work. The job involves encountering dead bodies, interacting with hurt and angry people, threatening and enacting violence, administering fines and tickets, staying up all night, and driving endless loops in search of something suspicious. I argue that these practices create a looming sense of deadness even in the absence of major risk.

The third chapter uses an institutional case study to further unpack the idea of trauma in policing. I zoom out from an individual to an institutional focus to critique the use of psychological power to amplify police power. In the field of police psychology, psychologists are partnering with police departments, offering support to ongoing operations. One avenue through which psychological research has entered policing is via the use of trauma-informed protocols. I examine one instance of police psychology's influence, in the International Association of Chiefs of Police's protocol for responding to officer-involved shootings. In this protocol, psychological knowledge is deployed to facilitate the ongoingness of racialized state violence. Building on Naomi Murakawa and Katherine Beckett's concept of the penology of racial innocence, I critique the psychology of racial innocence—the use of psychological intervention is assumed to be innocent of race.[110] The psychology of racial innocence makes psychological research and practice available to strengthen police organizations without questioning the ethics of facilitating ongoing state violence.

In the fourth chapter, I continue this examination of police departments' use of psychology. I look at the use of psychological research to try to stage direct confrontations with racism in policing, as research on implicit bias is brought into police trainings. Even within the context of explicit antiracist training, I find that psychological power can continue to function as a supplement to police power. I examine the transmission of knowledge about implicit bias at an implicit-bias training for police officers, noting its failure in developing police capacity to imagine other subjectivities. The training enacts what feminist scholar Sara Ahmed has termed the "non-performativity of anti-racism." This is the performance of trainings and meetings that fulfill institutional commitments to antiracism without centering the voices and experiences of those most harmed by racism. The three-ring binder of training materials functions as a shield against complaint; police trainers can use it as evidence of scientific antibias expertise, even as they continue to replicate gendered racism.

The final two chapters examine museums and memorials that engage broader public audiences and shape U.S. public feelings toward police power. Chapter 5 considers the American Police Hall of Fame and Museum (APHFM) in Titusville, Florida, a combined museum, memorial, and shooting range. One of a growing number of police museums, the APHFM creates police history and narrates violent futures. Between memorial walls honoring deceased officers, a visitor turns to see exhibits about gas chambers and nooses. The exhibits reinforce a fantasy about policing and death, describing a world fully split into heroes being killed and bad guys being destroyed. On descriptive labels about capital punishment, in plaques honoring the "officers of the year," and in the shooting range, the APHFM repeats a story about vulnerable protectors in a war against "faceless" evil opponents. I examine the museum's invitation for visitors to participate in fantasies of righteous violence.

Chapter 6 visits the National Law Enforcement Officers Memorial in Washington, D.C., to think about national narratives of police death. This site of mourning shapes both public perceptions of police legitimacy and police narratives about their work, in part by invoking ideas of familial and natural order, in practices that I term "blue mourning." I investigate how blue mourning practices at the memorial frame police as vulnerable protectors whose lives should be placed near the top of a hierarchy of national mourning, even as the nation requires their ongoing death. In their demand for grief around police death, these memorial sites and memorial practices enact multiple substitutions. At the Memorial, violent death at the hands of dangerous criminals takes the place of accidental death, and the promise of familial protection covers over the reality of heteropatriarchal violence.

Unacknowledged histories haunt every performance of policing, and sometimes these histories slip into our awareness, surfacing as shame, anger, guilt, or fear. Police culture and the emotional distress associated with policing and police culture are not problems to be resolved through best-practice intervention. Nor are they scenes of suffering to be transformed through displays of empathy.[111] Rather, these symptoms can speak, and they have something important to tell us. Each of these moments of feeling is an opportunity to challenge the common-sense perspective that sees policing as inevitable. There is an opportunity to refuse police culture and to choose instead to move toward forms of reparation and connection.

Dance scholar Andre Lepecki writes that the police power "needs not be embodied in the cop" to perform the police function of limiting imagined possibilities for movement and producing bodily conformity in the public.[112] Lepecki terms this containing and controlling of possibilities for movement as "choreopolicing." Choreopolicing restricts movement toward connection with others, the gestures of sociality that celebrate nonhierarchical and ever-shifting modes of relational life. Members of the public are encouraged to continue with this stance, refusing to sit with the complexities of contemporary and historical violence.

Just as we have the capacity for violence and harm, we have the capacity to build safety in relationships, to initiate repair, and to search for new ways to respond to one another. We can confront national narratives about state-sanctioned violence and death, and we can elevate alternate stories. We can investigate the institutions and fields in which we participate, for their own processes of supporting and naturalizing state-sanctioned violence. For me, this means challenging the involvement of my discipline, counseling psychology, in its ongoing support of police power. It also means questioning my own participation in police culture, both in and beyond my work as a counselor.

CHAPTER 1

Gun

Relationships and Revolvers

My first counseling client of the day comes into my office smiling, and we exchange a few polite remarks about the weather and parking.[1] Carl and I have been meeting for a few weeks. He talks easily throughout our sessions. In a now-familiar settling-in routine, he sets his paper cup of chai tea on the table and drapes his folded brown canvas jacket on the side of the couch next to him. This time, however, the jacket slides off onto the floor with a distinct metal thud. I am surprised at the sound, thinking, "What could be so heavy in his jacket?" Then I catch myself. Somehow I feel that I know. It's a handgun.

Until this moment I'd never thought much about the possibility that he might bring a weapon into our sessions, where we discuss his relationship with his parents and his upcoming wedding. He has spoken, in our work, about his on-the-job frustrations as a police officer. Specifically, he has traced the distance from his original excitement about being a cop to his current sense of powerlessness and frustration on the job. He feels unable to do anything to address the social problems and institutional failures that he sees daily. I genuinely like him, and I resonate with his hope to be a positive force in a deeply flawed institution.

But I'm not sure how I feel about his gun. I had not given it much thought, even as I knew that he would sometimes come directly from work, still in uniform. He must notice the surprise across my face, my attention focused on the jacket. A pause. We both avoid talking about the heavy weight in the room.

After our session ends, I wonder if I failed. I didn't know how to begin to talk about the possible presence of his gun. Even writing my notes, I found myself unsure of what was actually in the room with us that day.

Maybe it was something else? Whether it was a gun or not, I know that his potential for violence was both assumed and unspeakable in this moment. Even as I felt that a firearm could be physically present in the room, I did not name its presence. I am disappointed in my silence, and I comfort myself with the clinical aphorism that important issues tend to present again and again.

As we continue with his treatment, I notice moments when Carl's mention of the gun ends our conversation, stops our process of thinking together. One time this happens, we are discussing his difficulty sleeping. He has tried a number of solutions, relaxation training, not looking at screens before bed. I ask about medication. His response is quick and sharp. "No. I keep a gun in the house." He describes the risk that he might shoot his fiancée in a medication-induced sleepwalking daze.

In my response, I try to reflect back emotion, to create a little more space for description around this fantasy of violence. "That's a pretty intense fear to carry around."

Carl takes a breath, and then he begins a long, detailed story about something seemingly unrelated—an annoying friend. This response could be avoidance. He might be feeling fear or shame and want to avoid going deeper into such an unpleasant feeling. Or perhaps there is something that I am failing to understand, like the annoying friend. I feel myself useless.

The news reports fill once again with accounts of police shootings. Carl again expresses his fear that he could someday be the cop on the news. I nod, listen. The risk seems real, a bad day and a brief, terrible decision away. I question whether my clinical tools are up to the task of confronting the dangerous possibilities. What is an ethical way to approach, understand, and learn from these fears? And does the gun in the room change what I might do?

Winnicott and the Patient's Revolver

As I'm thinking about guns in the clinical space, another practitioner suggests I turn to the British psychoanalyst D. W. Winnicott. Winnicott has argued for the necessity of acknowledging aggression, violence, and hatred within the therapeutic relationship, as well as the crucial role of material things in psychic life. I turn to him for help in thinking about my inability to engage my cop client's fears of violence, as well as the role of this material thing—a gun—in mediating our relationship.

Winnicott first theorized the use of a "transitional object"—such as a blankie or teddy bear—as a step in developing the emotional capacity to recognize other people's subjectivity. The transitional object "gives room for the process of becoming able to accept difference and similarity."[2] The partially controlled, partially other teddy bear serves as a tool for tolerating the fact that other people have their own unique perspectives, through its unique role as an object that rides the line between self and other. He explores how investing a thing outside of oneself with a deep sense of importance and its own reactions and agency allows a child to begin to tolerate the inevitable disappointments of relationships.[3] The teddy bear has different opinions than the child and may even speak out against what the child wants to do, but the bear will not exceed the child's capacity to tolerate frustration.

Does the gun function as a transitional object? It is separate from Carl, but he controls it. It contains within it terrible fears: the fear of being attacked by others, and the terror of losing control of oneself and enacting violence. Sleeping aids are rejected, not because of his potential for violence (which might sound like, "I could hurt her"), but the potential for violence in the gun ("I keep a gun in the house"). Perhaps the gun in the consulting room enacts a question—what does one do with the capacity for violence that has been externalized and deposited in it? However, unlike the blankie, this is not a safe container. The gun not only symbolizes the potential for violence, it can also amplify it. Rather than creating a space of play in which to practice encountering different perspectives, it can silence those voices. As anthropologist Chelsey Kivland writes, "the gun's scriptive force leaves room for novel human interpretations or improvisations of the technology, but it nonetheless provides an orienting map for what to do with it."[4] It is not just a thing, it's a scriptive thing that suggests violent action. And it's in my office. Does this shift the relationship between my client and me? I turn to Winnicott again, as he thinks through the potential for aggression and violence in treatment.

Though reputed to be a gentle, caring analyst, Winnicott often spoke of the role of hatred and aggression in human relationships. He normalized moments of parental hatred toward babies and openly discussed his experiences of hatred toward patients.[5] In an essay on discussing the development of relational capacities, he describes how the patient can attack the analyst in multiple ways. He argues that the positive changes in treatment do not result from analysis of these attacks; rather, "[t]hey depend on the analyst's survival of the attacks, which involves and includes the idea of the absence of a quality change to retaliation."[6] Not only does the analyst need to survive, they need to demonstrate that they can remain cool in the face of rage and not get pulled into the temptation to punish. For Winnicott, the analyst is like a parent who calmly weathers their child's tantrums.

Winnicott notes that the attacks from the patient "may be very difficult for the analyst to stand."[7] Yet in doing so, the analyst helps the patient begin to see that they are not all-powerful. They demonstrate that cycles of reactive violence can be broken. Winnicott argues that only through recognizing aggression in relationships can this potential violence be contained. He coaches analysts to name their hatred as they refuse to act on it. Instead of being acted out, this naming makes the now-consciously symbolized idea of violence available to think about together in the psychoanalytic dialogue.[8]

As I review this argument, it seems to be a clear prompt to me to think about, and to name in session, moments in which potential violence takes center stage. I think about how to do this in a way that does not retaliate against my client, does not threaten to punish him, and that recognizes that we both have the capacity for violence. I want to figure out how to move our violence from unacknowledged, unreflective actions into reflective thought and language. I contemplate interpreting his capacity for violence. Or perhaps I could name my own hatred of ongoing police violence.

The guidance this passage by Winnicott seems to offer is muddied by a strange footnote. "When the analyst knows that the patient carries a revolver, then, it seems to me, this work cannot be done."[9] The gun enters here, as it did in my sessions with my client, as a conversation-ender. The work cannot be done in its presence.

Why does Winnicott make the argument that relational work can't be done in the presence of a patients' revolver? This is perhaps because the revolver serves as a steely reminder that it is not only the analyst's technique that determines the analyst's survival. Survival is also, always, determined by the ability of the patient's potential aggression to be contained in the space of therapy. For Winnicott, the patient's revolver shifts the balance of power. It is the opposite of a blankie, a transitional object back out of interdependent relationality. With the gun, the other must bend to your will or face the very real possibility of annihilation. It is a thing that catapults us back into a world locked in aggressive, self-centered, destructive impulses. This is a world in which the other doesn't exist outside of the patient's mind; it is a violent, lonely, and terrifying world.

In the revolver footnote, Winnicott seems to be suggesting a necessary dissociation, on the part of the analyst, of potential violence in the relationship. The revolver, for Winnicott, holds within its chambers the real possibility that an aggressive impulse will be acted on—and that serious physical injury or death might result. For Winnicott, the heightened potential for violence destroys the possibility of helpful communication; it challenges the ability of the analyst to survive their patient's aggression. In doing so, it also reinforces a dangerous sense of omnipotence in the patient. To be useful, we need to have the power to survive.

As I consider this argument, I think back on other moments of fear in the clinical situation. Through my conversations with trans, queer, and women therapists, I know that we regularly encounter moments of potential violence in our practice settings. These conversations have always begun by assuming the possibility of violence and planned from there—what to do with the patient who scares me or follows me home; how to decide if someone will be offered an evening appointment when the rest of the office is empty. In his fantasy that leaving a gun out of the room keeps potential violence away, I think Winnicott's imagination fails. He theorizes from the embodied experience of feeling physically able to defend himself against any imagined attacker, save one with a gun. Marginalized clinicians understand that the potential for violence is the situation of every therapeutic encounter. If we acknowledge present histories, violence is everywhere in the room.

And yet this stance of therapist vulnerability can also be weaponized. In *Citizen*, poet Claudia Rankine shares a vignette that involves a visit to a new therapist, a specialist in trauma counseling. The patient tries to go to the back entrance of the therapist's home as directed, but finds the gate locked. After returning to the front door and pressing the doorbell, the patient is confronted by a woman yelling "at the top of her lungs, Get away from my house! What are you doing in my yard?"[10] Rankine writes,

> And though you back up a few steps, you manage to tell her that you have an appointment. You have an appointment? she spits back. Then she pauses. Everything pauses. Oh, she says, followed by, oh, yes, that's right. I am sorry.[11]

In this example, it is anti-blackness that collapses the possibility of clinical work. At the moment of first encounter, the Black patient is attacked by the white therapist and made into the object of an imagined threat scenario—their body torn from them and handed back, narrated as though it were a weapon.

The therapist can be pulled into actions to try to quickly resolve difficult or uncomfortable feelings. These actions might include attacking ourselves, attacking others, retreating from relationship, and refusing to see connections. In our work and our social locations, both my client and I have been taught to know ourselves through our relationships with violence. My client carries a gun and its logic, which is to threaten or shoot someone if they terrify you. He is careful with this violent thing, but it is a constant companion. Guns script behavior in very simple ways; they offer themselves as solutions to violent conflict and to fear. In doing so, they may make other scripts harder to find.

I have learned a different role—that of the nonexpert and the innocent outsider, someone who has nothing to offer on questions of violence except a narrow concern for my own safety. And yet we both carry these dangerous scripts for our roles as white people in systems of anti-blackness. As a white therapist, I have my own pull toward being one of the "good guys." In my case, it's the "nice lady." I want to be seen as nice and supportive, and I avoid pressing too strongly into fearful territory. I feel the temptation to retreat, to avoid connections, to disassociate myself from the question of complicity in violence. These are all ways that I could use my privilege to avoid thinking and feeling. The pull to be one of the good white people isn't just an individual desire here—it is a crucial mechanism for the reproduction of racism. I am a white woman trying to see myself as innocent of racism.[12]

In *Good White People*, Shannon Sullivan argues that white liberals who imagine themselves as antiracist project their own racism onto working-class and poor whites. Discussions of racism serve as emotional management strategies to disavow their own racism and claim themselves as good—instrumentalizing relationships with BIPOC to reassert their own feelings of goodness.[13] Sullivan examines the relationship of demonization between good white people and historic slaveholders. She briefly carries this analysis forward into U.S. policing and incarceration, noting continuities between slavery and current criminal-legal-system racism.

Extending Sullivan, I begin to wonder about the relationship dynamic between good white people and the police. The dynamic of the good white liberal can be played out in white critiques of police racism. In critiquing police racism, good white people mark themselves as innocent of state-sanctioned violence even as they benefit from it. Good white people, living lives untouched by violence, distance themselves from the violence carried out in their names by the police. Expressing horror at scenes of police violence reassures them that they are innocent of racism. They can imagine themselves as good antiracist partners at the scene of anti-Black police violence.

I begin to wonder how my work as a counselor can acknowledge the presence of this cultural script and the unconscious aspects of our interactions. How can we begin to symbolize this encounter where race and violence are present and unacknowledged? I want to think together with Carl about this gun in the room in between the two of us, and the implicit contract between us that we will not talk about it. I want to acknowledge our differential roles as white people in ongoing anti-Black violence. And I want to build the capacity for us to relate differently. I imagine conversations in which our contributions to and investments in state violence are acknowledged, and we identify our paths to refusing ongoing complicity. And yet, the material presence of a gun can make it hard to think. These small objects condense affects and meanings. They condense the power of the state into the property of one person; they condense history into chunks of metal and polymer.

Guns in the Consulting Room

I decide to turn away from psychoanalysis, and toward the emerging field of police psychology. If I'm trying to find the overlap between my own and my cop clients' involvements in state-sanctioned violence, this seems like a good place to start. Police psychology is a field that encompasses psychological fitness for duty evaluations and counseling practices specifically targeted to the stresses of policing. I begin a review of the literature, including the recent best-practice handbook *Counseling Cops*.[14]

In *Counseling Cops*, clinicians Ellen Kirshman, Mark Kamena, and Joel Fay insist that "cops and guns go together."[15] They imagine guns as a point of cultural connection, urging counselors to form relationships with cop clients through a shared familiarity with firearms. I can see how this approach holds some promise. It rejects the idea that therapeutic dialogues can be isolated from, or exist outside of present histories of violence. While not all cops have guns, it is true that cops and guns go together in a basic way—in the U.S., the state authorizes most cops to use guns at their jobs. It seems promising that psychologists and counselors are being told that they cannot just ignore this key fact. Yet I am disappointed to learn that this acknowledgement of guns doesn't function to open their meaning up for critical reflection. Rather, clinicians are encouraged to use guns as a signal that they are on the police officers' side.

Kirshman, Kamena, and Fay frame knowledge of guns as a cultural competency and urge clinicians to signal an acceptance of police culture through their familiarity with guns. They recommend that clinicians gain proficiency with firearms and consider owning a gun. Perhaps they are concerned about the dynamics of othering that Sullivan identifies, that middle-class white counselors might treat their cop clients as scapegoats. Yet they respond to this through setting up a reactive framework, in which guns are great and further discussion of their meaning is prohibited.

In encouraging therapists to develop "cultural competency" with police gun culture, the authors appropriate the language of the field of multicultural counseling competency. This field originated as an effort to challenge the white middle-class cultural bias of the counseling profession and its tendency to relate to Black and Brown people as inferior, culturally deprived, or to view them as individuals isolated from historical and social contexts.[16] Yet in framing police as a "unique subculture," the authors work to divorce them from the historical and social context of white violence. Instead of being a weapon that helps to maintain a violent racialized social order, guns are celebrated as a marker of culture. Guns are framed as an important cultural artifact. If counselors are going to claim cultural competency working with "the unique subculture" of police, they need to understand and appreciate the particular beauty of owning and shooting guns. They approvingly cite a client who says, "If you're afraid of guns, you shouldn't be working with cops."[17]

The counseling guide does not acknowledge that the culture of gun ownership in the United States is one that is particularly racialized. Gun ownership has been a protected right for white men in the U.S., while Black people's arms have historically been confiscated. In *Dying of Whiteness*, psychiatrist and American Studies scholar Jonathan Metzl writes, "Firearms connoted tools that claimed to help white men maintain privilege or restore it when it seemed under threat."[18] He traces links between white gun culture, masculinity, and fears of Black resistance. Like gun owners, police as a whole are a group of disproportionately white and male people. They are explicitly tasked with the violent enforcement of the existing social order—one in which Black people have less wealth, less representation at all levels of government, and greater risk of premature death.

In mandating a celebration of guns as cultural objects, Kirshman, Kamena, and Fay prohibit more complex exploration of the meaning of guns. Acknowledging fear, discomfort, guilt, or shame in relation to guns is forbidden for both counselors and clients. As a clinician, this strikes me as strange. I regularly tell my clients, nothing amplifies fear or shame like avoidance. Here, fear of guns becomes unspeakable. Even more, clinicians are cautioned to avoid interpreting any meaning associated with a gun. The potential risk of the gun is downplayed, while interpretation—seeking to understand meaning—emerges as a source of terror. This is a moment of disavowal, in which the reality of violence is simultaneously known and not known. Discussing these types of disavowal, Freud notes that "they turn out to be half-measures, incomplete attempts at detachment from reality. The rejection is always supplemented by an acceptance; two contrary and independent attitudes always arise and this produces the fact of a split in the ego."[19]

The idea that "cops and guns go together" seems to suggest that this is a universal truth, one that can never change. It ignores the presence of police forces in nations that do not arm the majority of their officers, such as Britain, Ireland, Norway, Iceland, and New Zealand.[20] In constructing guns as a cultural attitude, they also fail to note how institutional policies and practices shape gun cultures. Carrying a weapon is a job requirement for most U.S. police, one that many police report feelings of ambivalence about. While many police cars are equipped with shotguns, most police also carry handguns. These guns are generally selected through department policy.[21] Some police departments issue one type of standard handgun to all officers, while others let officers choose from a list of approved guns.[22] The practice of issuing one standard firearm to all police officers in the NYPD began in 1895, under the direction of Teddy Roosevelt, with the endorsement of Colt revolvers for use as a service weapon.[23]

Changes in gun policy through time reflect changes in budgets, technology, and public feelings. In the U.S., one general trend has been that police handguns have been getting more powerful through time.[24] The first state police department to switch from revolvers to semiautomatic guns was the Illinois State Police in 1967. After decades of working with revolvers, in the mid-1980s, most departments switched from revolvers to 9-millimeter semiautomatic guns. In a 1992 article, the *New York Times* refers to one such 9-millimeter semiautomatic—the Glock 9 mm—as the "gun of choice" for police officers.[25] Seeking even more firepower, in the mid-1990s many departments switched from 9 mm to the slightly larger 40 caliber.[26] Although some departments continue to switch to 40 calibers, others are making the switch back to 9 mms. Those that switch back cite increased accuracy of and improvements in bullet technology for 9 mm bullets.[27] These constant departmental upgrades suggest the crucial role that they play in policing. Guns symbolize the legitimate use of force issued by the state to officers. Whether issued or approved by the department, police are required to demonstrate proficiency with their weapons. Failure to qualify at the shooting range is grounds for being denied the job, and most departments require periodic requalification.[28]

Kirschman, Kamena, and Fay use the language of diversity to call for the embrace of cop culture by counselors. In doing so, they suggest a universal police culture that doesn't actually exist. An uncritical embrace of something called "gun culture" is presented as a moral good. Rather than exploring the meaning of the weapon, counselors are encouraged to accept that "to separate a cop from her gun is to remove a valuable part of her identity."[29] Identity formation is not recognized as a dynamic, ongoing process that happens in the context of social, material, and historical relationships.

While Kirshman, Kamena, and Fay discuss identity, they ignore the link between gun ownership and the maintenance of white-supremacist power structures. Instead they use the language of diversity to naturalize the current distribution of firearms. And they also fail to recognize a basic feature of relationships with guns that I have already seen in my counseling sessions—that one person can have multiple and conflicting feelings in relationship to a gun. The handbook shuts down the possibility of further exploration. This refusal to explore further may stem from a fear of alienating cop clients who fear having their relationships with their guns tagged as automatically pathological—but it is ultimately a prohibition that denies them the opportunity to think deeply with another person about the social role in which they find themselves, a role that they may not have been aware that they signed up for when they decided to become cops.

Winnicott imagines the client's gun as suddenly introducing violence in a way that destroys the process. In contrast, police psychology views the client's gun as a constant and unquestionable fact of life. In doing so, it narrows the potential field of change. The mission of the therapist becomes helping the client to reconcile with their current world as is, rather than deep exploration around its possible transformations. Further, the police psychology approach seems to imagine the armed client as incredibly fragile and volatile. If I mention the gun in a way that suggests that its violence could be problematic, I might startle and scare them. And if they feel threatened, they may even meet the legal requirements to be able to justifiably discharge their firearm. Underlying the handbook's advice for counselors is a general prescription—don't challenge cops. Don't question police power.

This prohibition doesn't serve cops. The clinical refusal to engage clients' explicit and unconscious anxieties around their firearms does not help police clients figure out how to resolve these anxieties. It leaves them to face their past and potential violence without the tools of clinical reflection. My client does not need to be protected from his own process of reflection. It is a prohibition that benefits the existing social order, not my client's well-being.

Clinical reflection might explore how guns script certain responses, and how they carry different meanings across the range of relationships in that person's life. They might notice how the presence or absence of the gun shapes our dialogue; how it impacts the therapist's and client's ability to think together in relationship. They might reflect on how a gun shapes identity, including racial and gender identity. What a gun means in relation to a person may not be obvious or fixed through time. What starts as a marker of power can transform into a marker of powerlessness or of not being good enough.

If they were made available, clinical tools could provide new approaches for thinking with firearms. And yet the presence of the firearm makes the risks of being in relationship with this person clear. The role of white women in the emotional care of white men has historically been one that props up white supremacy.[30] And to step out of line is to remove myself from the class of the good white woman, deserving of protection, and to become available to policing and violence. It means trying to think together with someone who has the power to harm me.

As I move forward with this treatment, I reflect on the counselors, supervisors, friends, and teachers who have generously challenged me and helped me to see my own cruelties. Were they scared that I would retaliate? Were they scared that I would play victim and call out for protection? At times I did those things. Years later, I feel grateful to those who have helped me to see my defenses and own my aggressions.

I refuse to either ignore or celebrate the violence that exists in my consulting room, that has come into view in my relationship with this client. My goal is to figure out how to talk, and how to think, and how to begin to ask questions that can shift the implicit rules that govern both of our relationships with his gun. To be useful, I need to interrogate my own role in the violence of the state. I need to refuse the role of the innocent, vulnerable citizen in need of police protection.

Playing with Guns

A new experience can be one way to understand. I decide that I will take the police psychologists' advice to become more familiar with firearms, in the hopes that it will give me a new tool to think and feel through my own complicities. I will learn more about guns, including how to shoot a gun, noting how this process works on me. Perhaps this will give me some new ideas about how to think with and about a gun in the room. I am not sure if this is a good idea. I am nervous—I want to feel like a good person and avoid the places that make me question that "good" feeling. I tell myself that I have to understand more about my own capacity for violence if I want to shake up my role as an "innocent," a silent partner at the scene of police violence.

My first lesson in trying to get myself to the gun range is about navigating legal geographies. In New York State, it's difficult to shoot a handgun.[31] I am overwhelmed by the length and expense of the process in my home state, and instead start making plans to go to a gun range in Pennsylvania, where the laws are less restrictive. A research trip to Florida provides a similar opportunity. With Florida's lax gun laws, it's easy to schedule a trip to a shooting range with a variety of handguns and no background checks. These different legal geographies map differential rates of gun homicide and suicide. In trying to gain easier access to guns, I move myself across geographies of differential gun-related death. I stay in Orlando, the scene of the 2016 Pulse nightclub shooting. That shooting, and other lethal shootings in Florida have been facilitated by the laws that will now benefit me.

I feel nervous my first time shooting. At the range, I wait at the window, then fill out a quick one-page registration and release form. I tell the guy at the desk that it's my first time shooting, and ask if someone can give me a quick introduction. He tells me that it won't be a problem. He gives me a few different options for which handgun I can shoot. I choose a Sig Sauer 9-mm. There are even more options for targets, most of them not quite human—I notice that there are two different zombies, and a pink and neon green "Girl and a Gun" target with abstract shapes. I choose one of the zombie targets. He also hands me a pair of noise-blocking protective earmuffs.

Inside the shooting gallery, the floor is scattered with bullet casings. The people shooting around me are mostly older white men. The instructor is an older white man; he shouts so that I can hear him through my earmuffs. I hold the gun in my hand and turn to him with a question about how to load the bullets. He quickly pushes the barrel of the unloaded gun toward the gallery side with his hand, admonishing me to be careful to never point the gun at anyone, even unloaded. I feel embarrassed about my cluelessness and carelessness, and suddenly the potential lethality of this thing is present to me.

Explaining how to load the bullets into the clip, he tells me that I should treat the gun as I would treat a man. Perhaps he notices my puzzled look. "Roughly," he clarifies.

He shows me how to load the bullet into the chamber, making a crack about how it would be easier to "have a man do it for me." I'm a bit taken aback by how strongly my gender seems to be at issue here. Prior to coming, I hadn't really thought much about the fact that I was "a woman learning to shoot."

The instructor shows me how to hold my arms out and bend my knees and aim. And then, "Now squeeze the trigger." A bullethole appears in the paper target. "Good!" I take a few more shots, hit the zombie in the head and chest. "You're pretty good at this!" My instructor seems surprised. I take a pleasure in proving myself capable. In the moment, this pleasure feels feminist. *I'll show him not to underestimate me.*

After his initial demo, the instructor leaves me. I remove and reload my clip, keep firing away. As I shoot, I notice that my affect is a mix of fear and excitement. I want to be a good shot—a natural. I am a serious student, and I pay attention to the instructions. I try to be careful about where I point the gun, even when the clip is not loaded. I continue shooting, other shooters taking their places on both sides of me, the instructor off talking with a regular.

As I spend time in the range, the idea that I'd like to flee builds in my head. After twenty-five minutes, my brain feels a bit foggy and over-full, buzzing with the resonance of gunfire. It's time to go. I turn the gun in, leave quickly. Attempting to make notes in the parking lot in the rental car, I write that I feel "resistant to writing." I want to put some distance on the experience.

I drive from the gun range directly to the ocean. As I swim in the ocean, my mind wanders, opens into sadness. I reflect on the space, the zombie targets, the instructor's gendered comments. I decide that I'm not going to go shooting again. And yet, zipping back along the highway, my imagination wanders back into fantasies of violence. I think about earthquakes, wildfires, floods, fascists. If there is a catastrophic natural disaster near me, perhaps it would be good for me to have a gun. And I could protect my friends. I find myself seduced by who I could be; the fantasy of legitimate violence working in my head. I toy around with the idea of rescuing others, the idea of being a hero. I imagine that I can keep those I love safe. These fantasies always depend on the presence of some fearful other. In them, I am fantasizing about my future heroic self, my brave encounters with lethal risk.

This fantasy returns periodically in the weeks that follow. My dreams for social transformation are newly yoked to a story of apocalypse and individual heroism. I haven't dreamed this way with guns until now. I have lived at a distance from my capacity for violence, unable to fully see myself as someone who can seriously harm another person. It's a myth I didn't know I was living inside. And now, I don't like how the encounter with the gun works on me. When I point a gun, I am seeing my power to destroy. And in my fantasies, I enjoy it. For all my abolitionist critiques of the idea of innocence, I am unnerved by the complicity of my desires. I want to be a "good guy with a gun," and the fantasy of being one is a pleasure that I don't want to give up.

I'm not alone in this sense that a heroic identity and firearms are linked. Reflecting on his work as a police officer, Alec Wilkinson writes, "For a year I wore the gun on my hip, and it made me feel like someone of more substance than I was." He continues, suggesting that "a gun is the most powerful device there is to accessorize the ego."[32] Guns are often equated with power—the power to kill, to be a hero, or to protect oneself.

In his memoir, former Seattle police chief Norm Stamper describes entering the field of policing after police academy with "the rumblings of something I'd never felt before: self-confidence." He recalls, "Our instructors had drilled it into us: it was us against them, good guys versus bad guys. I knew which one I was, and set out to prove it."[33] Stamper describes the process of learning to shoot a gun as central to this transformation. Mastery of his gun was an important part of his emerging identity as a "good guy," as someone capable of heroic and decisive action. Metzl writes about white gun ownership in Missouri, recognizing that to the people he interviews, "guns function as weapons, totems, and transitional objects that promise autonomy, protection, and self-reliance."[34] He notes that "the danger [guns] pose to people who own and carry them and to their families becomes harder to acknowledge or recognize when these objects of potential self-destruction carry such weighted connotations."[35] The psychic reward of gun ownership is its promise of self-reliance and autonomy. Guns help to manage insecurities and build a sense of heroic capacity. The cost to the owner remains largely out of awareness.

Guns as Phallic Objects

The role of guns in shaping identity raises a question about masculinity and guns. Is it useful to think about a cop's gun as a phallic object? The gun promises a kind of individual autonomy that is linked to fantasies of masculinity and power. It points toward the inter-implication of sexuality and violence in creating and maintaining race and gender categories. I turn to feminist readings of the idea of the phallus, grounded in the work of French psychoanalyst Jacques Lacan.

For Lacan, the "phallus" is defined through its absence.[36] It is an imagined part that is always missing. If it were present, it would bestow its owner with power, control, and access to those things that seem to be missing from their lives. And yet it is constantly missing, and people continue to seek it out and to cover over this shameful lack. The relationship to the phallus is highly gendered, and men are socially tasked with trying to have this power, while women are tasked with trying to give others the sense of having the power. Judith Butler describes this dynamic in Lacan:

> For women to "be" the Phallus means, then, to reflect the power of the Phallus, to signify that power, to "embody" the Phallus, to supply the site to which it penetrates, and to signify the Phallus through "being" its Other, its absence, its lack, the dialectical confirmation of its identity.[37]

In psychoanalyst Patricia Gherovici's reading of Lacan, the phallus is a "symbol [that] compensates for a certain lack; it is an attribute that nobody can have, while everyone aspires to have it or embody it."[38] Guns play the role of the phallus in the psychoanalytic sense—not something that inheres to some bodies, but a feeling of power that is being chased.

Looking at the phallic representations of the police officers' gun raises questions not just about the power of the phallus represented in the gun, but about who is "having" the phallus and who is tasked with "being" the phallus. Rather than mapping cleanly onto gender lines, the cop "has" violence, manifested in the form of the gun, whereas consenting members of the public are marked by the absence of violence. Their innocence of police violence is created at the same time as the cop's violent power—they are the "dialectical confirmation of its identity."

This scene of gender and power is also racialized. As Hortense Spillers's theoretical work highlights, the force of U.S. white supremacy has historically constructed Black bodies as "ungendered" and divorced from "active desire."[39] The phallic object of the gun is about access to white patriarchal power, which is confirmed through the gendered protection of white innocence, as well as the objectification and destruction of Black bodies. In his discussion of the overdetermination of Black male sexuality, Fanon notes that Black men exist in the colonial psyche as a phallic object—"the Black man is the genital."[40] Black men are related to as threats, but not as having power. Critical legal scholar Angela P. Harris names violence between men that is intended to serve as a demonstration of manhood as a type of gender violence, arguing that violent practices within policing can express this type of racialized gender violence.[41] Building on Harris's work, legal scholar Frank Cooper describes policing as a scene of competing masculinities, one in which white men assert their power, as men, over Black men.[42] However, it is important to note that the scene of policing is not only men—rather, BIPOC women and nonbinary people are also objectified in the service of reaffirming the power of police. Andrea Ritchie outlines these forms of police violence in her book *Invisible No More*. She writes of "gender-specific *forms* of police abuse such as sexual harassment, assault, and rape by law enforcement agents," and "gender-specific *contexts* of policing such as policing of prostitution" targeted at racialized women, and the role of police in enforcing the gender binary.[43] Further, BIPOC people, white women, and white trans people are offered access to phallic power in exchange for their willingness to participate in these practices of policing.

The scene of policing is one of phallic accumulation. Police carry guns, backup guns, Tasers, and other technologies that promise power; on the job, they act to control, possess, and destroy the bodies of those marked criminal—Black bodies, sex workers' bodies, drug users' bodies. And the presence of a less powerful, less armed, "innocent" civilian population that is viewed as needing their protection further attests to their power. And yet anxiety about lack, about the fact that they do not actually possess this power over others even as they violently claim it, pervades police discourse about guns.

To name the gun as a phallic object is an insult, because it suggests this lack of power. It suggests that the masculine identity of the officer needs some kind of supplementation. The gun is only an accessory—it is not an immutable part of the officer. And so the lack remains. This is one of the insights of psychoanalysis—that this sense of power and control that is being chased can never be satisfied. As soon as a gun is purchased, the object of desire shifts. As soon as the body of the "Other" is momentarily possessed or controlled, new bodies appear as threats and objects of desire.

Heidi Nast argues that in the U.S., white male identification with industrial-machines-as-phalluses propped up a sense of pride and power throughout the industrial age.[44] Nast agues that deindustrialization threatens this phallic identification. And perhaps this is linked to a shift to increasing gun cultures and economies in deindustrialized areas, in which the gun meets a need for new objects of identification. Rather than pride in creation through industry, this pride is linked to the power to destroy. My fantasies and my clients' gun fantasies promise power and control. Rather than coming into relation with others and developing the capacity to imagine other people's subjectivities, guns orient people toward their power to destroy. And yet, listening closely to these fantasies and stories about guns reveals what police know and cannot know: the inevitable failure of these fantasies of power and autonomy.

Guns that Betray

Fantasies about guns often emerge in the process of police departments and individual officers searching for different, better guns. In these fantasies, guns constantly betray. Whether we refer to them as handguns or sidearms, they are accessories to the body of the officer that constantly threaten to turn against, to fail to protect, or to shift into a mark of shame.

In Baltimore, police have taken a substantial economic hit as a result of their decision not to sell their guns back to manufacturers. In 2013, they lost out on $700,000 they would have received from selling their used Sig Sauers to a wholesaler, and in 2011 they lost $500,000 in rebates when they declined to sell a stockpile of 9-mm handguns back to Glock. This decision is a result of a fear that guns might be used to break the law. At that time, Deputy Police Commissioner Bert Shirey asked, "If we put guns back on the street and they're used in a crime, do we bear some responsibility for putting them back into circulation?"[45] Shirey's question of responsibility suggests that the traces of the Baltimore Police Department remain in the guns even after resale, making the department in some way responsible for the guns' future actions. Not only are police identities shaped by their guns, but perhaps their guns are shaped in some way by the police that use them.

The question of responsibility isn't a hypothetical one. In 2011, Oklahoma police discovered that a former Baltimore service weapon—a Glock .40-caliber Model 22 semiautomatic—was used in the murders of two young girls. Since that time, Baltimore police have chosen to destroy their old guns—melting them down—or to sell them only to other police departments, rather than risk that these guns will later be used in ways that betray the police understanding of their acceptable use. Again, they are not doing anything to influence the legal availability of guns—but they are losing over a million dollars in legal gun sales to ensure that these specific guns cannot have an afterlife of crime.[46]

This fear of betrayal shows up not only after guns are retired; on the job there is tremendous anxiety that service weapons will fail to serve and protect. In a 1992 article about the move to 9-mm Glocks, the *New York Times* cites officer Robert James Evers, "a 19-year veteran who works an overnight shift in Brooklyn," discussing the weakness of the NYPD's previous standard-issue .38-caliber. He states that "guys . . . brazenly laugh in your face" and that the gun "has no impact on them."[47] In suggesting that a gun could have "no impact" on these laughing men, Evers's comment invokes the long historical imagination of Black bodies as less capable of feeling pain than white bodies, one that continues in present assumptions about Black pain.[48] Rather than accessorizing his ego, his gun, which he imagines as laughable and weak, heightens his feeling of powerlessness.

The betrayal fantasies highlight the fact that guns exist not only as a part of police identity, but also as things. Bill Brown states, "We begin to confront the thingness of objects when they stop working for us."[49] The thingness of guns makes visible the limits of heroic gun fantasies. Guns do not always fill their role as hero props. They stick, they jam, they do not always hit their targets. And when they do hit their intended targets, they still fail to deliver. They don't provide safety, or help us to be good. Sometimes, police officers might question their participation in the project of policing, recognizing the distance between the promise of "serve and protect" and the daily realities of embodying state violence. At other times, cops turn their suspicions to the technology of the gun—and they seek ways to address perceived failures through more forceful firearms.

Darren Wilson's Gun Fantasy

In Ferguson, Missouri, police officer Darren Wilson's gun was a .40-caliber Sig Sauer. One of the stories he tells about his 2014 murder of Michael Brown is a story of failure and betrayal by his gun. The gun could not stop the racialized monster he imagines while he shoots and kills Michael Brown. Christina Sharpe deconstructs Darren Wilson's grand-jury testimony describing his shooting of Michael Brown, noting that Wilson's "brutal mythical imagination" exaggerates Brown's strength and size, attributing superhuman powers to him.[50] In this narrative, Wilson cannot imagine Brown's fear or pain. Although he has the gun and the badge, Wilson tells a story in which he imagines that he doesn't have any power. Though the two men are a similar height and Wilson is older, the officer describes himself as weaker, smaller, and younger. Wilson stated, "I felt like a five-year-old . . ." Sharpe notes that Wilson is "transformed by his proximity to blackness to a 5-year-old child."[51] This tiny child self needs protection, needs power, and he looks for it in his gun.

It is in this moment in Darren Wilson's narration of the shooting that we see that he describes two fantasies: a monster fantasy projected onto Brown and an abandonment fantasy projected onto his gun. Both of these fantasies work to isolate him from the reality of his actions and present himself as a powerless victim. When he reaches for his gun, he is betrayed. In his testimony, Wilson describes how his Sig Sauer first abandoned him by failing to work. "It just clicked. I pull it again. It just clicked." He continues, "At this point, I'm like, 'Why isn't this working,' this guy is going to kill me if he gets ahold of this gun.'" In the moment, Wilson fantasizes a further betrayal— though the gun will not work for him, he imagines that it would shoot just fine if it is shooting at him. Darren Wilson then described the impact of the gunfire he directed at Michael Brown. Wilson states that when he hit Brown, Brown "flinched." He continues, "he was almost bulking up to run through the shots."[52] This horrific scene, in which Michael Brown is being shot and killed, again contains a narrative of betrayal of Wilson by his gun. Even as it was shooting Brown, it was too weak to protect him—in his described fantasy of what happened, the gun was having no impact.

This case example belies the idea that "cops and guns go together." Rather, Wilson's fantasies around why he killed Brown suggest a complex relationship with his gun. Rather than being the hero, he tells a story in which he is the child. The gun is the part-object that fails to protect him. It is a relationship of fear and anxiety, fraught with the potential that the technology could betray him at the moment he needs it most. It is also one of dependency. His relationship with his gun promised safety and allowed Wilson to step into the role of police officer. Imagining his encounter with Brown, Wilson tells a paranoid story in which death is outside of his control. He imagines his gun deciding whether the person to die was him or Brown, through its own agency and power.

This story may have been manufactured as a part of Wilson's legal strategy, crafted after the fact of the shooting to establish the legal basis for acquittal. And yet, the fantasy reflects an understanding of guns as lively things that his defense team judged to be compelling. The story conveniently inverts gun-as-protection into gun-as-threat at the moment of lethal violence, dropping any consideration of Michael Brown from the scene and staging a drama between Wilson and his gun. Wilson's defense team made the bet that this story would be compelling, that the grand jury would be captured by this story of innocence in the face of failed technology. Imagining the scene through this narration, the majority-white grand jury decided not to indict Wilson.[53]

Wilson's complex description of his relationship to his gun might seem strange beside his thin descriptions of Brown's motivations and actions. Yet many police training practices encourage this focus, on guns as complex, and on racialized suspects as simple. In video shooter simulations, the presence of the gun remains real, while the presence of the criminalized other is virtual, simply an image on a screen. The people being encountered on the screen don't take different actions based on the demeanor and engagement of the officer. Rather, they are preprogrammed to do the same thing every time: either attack or not. Once someone is identified as a threat, the proper response is to kill them. As a function of their material presence, the guns might act differently, though. Officers are in direct physical contact with them, and they might experience them as having a slow trigger or a fast trigger, of acting differently in response to how they are handled. The gun remains complex while the person is flattened.

   The Ferguson police department response to the shooting reinforced the idea that something was wrong with the equipment. One reaction of the department was to invest in "less-lethal" attachments to guns.[54] These are bright orange ping-pong-ball-looking attachments that are marketed with the claim that they make it less likely that the bullet will kill its target, instead delivering "blunt force trauma."[55] While Wilson feared his gun was not powerful enough, the department's actions suggest that the gun was simply a bit too "lethal" and could be adjusted. The fundamental elements of the scene remain unchanged. A police officer encounters a person they perceive—via a racialized gaze—as a threat.

   The response of some reformers to the shooting betrays a similar reliance on the promise of technology. Following the shooting, a call for body cameras emerged from those interested in police reform.[56] Susan Sontag has written that the camera is "a sublimation of the gun" that nonetheless follows the same logic. "To photograph people is to violate them [. . . ;] it turns people into objects that can be symbolically possessed."[57] These things are imagined as solving police violence, without having to shift ongoing police power.

   These responses follow the relational logic of the gun: one of power-over. They view police officers as unable to manage without guns, as needing to be technologically managed or supervised. In U.S. policing, a quest for better material technologies has served as one way to distract from the questions raised about the legitimacy of police power in the aftermath of police violence. New technologies arrive promising that they will prevent such events from ever happening again. Whether guns, new nonlethal weapons, or body cameras, these objects promise that police power can be made antiracist. Yet, as Bill Brown reminds us, things don't always do what we want them to.

   Even in the presence of a fixture to place over a firearm or a new technology to ride alongside it, police power has always been a force for state-sanctioned racialized violence. Rather than celebrating how "cops and guns go together," the construction of a heroic identity through participation in state-sanctioned violence can be named as a problem.

   Counselors, psychologists, and other mental health professionals have a choice. We can refuse to normalize police violence as cultural difference. And we can explore the present anxieties about embodying police power that cops bring into the consulting room. In doing so, we open up the possibility of imagining other life paths, other ways to build identity, and other ways to relate that refuse hero scripts. In refusing carceral psychology, therapists can recognize that people who work as police don't need to be told that police power is built on contradictions and false promises. Rather, they deserve therapists who are willing to listen as they explain and explore their situation. Therapists must be willing to look at police power, and refuse to condescend to their clients as unable to face the brutal truths of their work.

Guns aren't simple cultural artifacts—they are technologies for reproducing violent inequities, and they have a special role in maintaining U.S. white privilege. Those technologies are both shaped by and work to shape the fantasies, identities, relationships, and expectations of cops. Constantly carrying them has an impact on officers. No matter how well they may be paid for their work, or how much they like some aspects of the role, it is reasonable to raise the question of what it costs. Guns encourage the psychic operation of splitting—they are transitional objects out of relationality and into psychic combat with the other. Looking with a gun involves a gaze for the purpose of identifying threats.

Police psychologists suggest that there is nothing to see and no reason to discuss guns in therapy. They insist that guns must be treated as unrelated to violence. Winnicott recognizes the importance of the gun, and suggests that we cannot think together in its presence. And yet we must think about the violence that shapes our lives and our clients' lives. With my clients, that means figuring out how to name and think about the gun in the room.

Again and again in our sessions, Carl noted his fear of accidentally shooting someone in his home—of mistaking a loved one as an intruder. He recognizes that he takes the psychic impacts of police power home. This means that someday, he might accidentally assign someone he loves to the category of threat. These fearful fantasies emerge at home, in the space where he is supposed to be off the clock and free to engage in other types of relationships. He wants a barrier between his job identity and his family. He wants some distance between his life and his gun.

One day, Carl comes in with the familiar chai latte. Today it is iced. He has been on vacation, making some household improvements. He mentions that he's finally ordered a long-put-off purchase—a gun safe for at home. We've discussed it before, and it was always something he kept meaning to do and never getting around to actually doing. I'm curious about what prompted the change. He's unsure. While he is used to having his gun constantly beside him, he's decided to see how it feels when he puts it away.

CHAPTER 2

Statistic

Frameworks of Precarity in Policing

The afternoon sun is shining through the curtains of my office, creating a sunny square across the couch and rug. The window-unit air conditioner rumbles over the street noise. I am sitting in my chair, looking across at my client Sam as he settles into a spot on the corner of the couch.[1] He puts his coffee on the side table and starts the session by talking about his job. It's more than just a job to him. He has been working toward a career in law enforcement his whole life. He grew up wanting to be a cop, playing video games and watching cop dramas on television. He went to college and did what he needed to do to pass his classes. He applied to a department, passed the pre-employment screenings, and started work. Sam's whole life seemed right on track. It was a solid plan. But when he started the work, he started to feel ambivalence.

"I don't know how long I'll stick with it." He takes a sip of his coffee. "The night shifts are hard but I can handle them, I'm a fucking vampire anyhow." Another pause.

I wait, and he continues. "You deal with some sick shit. You really see the worst of people."

I am still listening, noting the shift of language to "you," a coping strategy to provide a bit of distance from the anxiety evoked by remembering the "sick shit" of his job. I think for a minute about the idea of the "worst" of people and the reassurance provided by dividing a chaotic world into categories and types. I think about the misery of this job, and how his once-certain life path is now opening up to new questions on multiple fronts.

He continues, "Did you know the average life expectancy on this job is like sixty years old? They are basically paying you to kill yourself. If some fuck doesn't kill you, they still get you when you retire."

49

He barks a short, bitter laugh, then pauses, looks down. He has this: a guarantee of early death and an expectation that he will encounter the worst. A sense of being alone and unsure of the future. And he's getting ready for his night shift. Sam reaches for his coffee and takes another long drink.

I reflect back his uncertainty about what the future holds. The work of our session turns to articulating the loss of a sense of sureness he once had. At the moment, I don't pick up the story he's told me about dying young. It returns to me in the days after our session, as I ponder how this story of expectant death fits in with the other pieces of his life. It's not the first time I've heard this statistic in session.

Almost every police officer I have worked with has told me the story of their inevitable untimely death. They do it in an offhanded way, professing how little they care. They mention it in the context of discussing how terrible the job is, after the most recent miserable interaction with someone who hated and feared them. Most often they do it before or after a sip of coffee. I find myself wondering how I could respond clinically. I note his detached and casual tone. "By the way, I'm going to die. No big deal." How do I make sense of what is being communicated to me in this moment? As his therapist, I think that my work is to try to figure out what this ever-present idea of dying does.

I want to understand how the story functions in his life. One immediate question I have is whether this story is better described as an actual or an imagined loss. Is it a brutal reality or a false fantasy of vulnerability? While both have a psychic reality, the difference between actual and perceived risk matters. It could harm my client to reinforce false perceptions of risk, and it could also harm them if I fail to validate their lived experience of precarity.

My question harks back to the early days of psychoanalysis, when Freud changed his mind about whether his "hysterical" patients had experienced abuse or anxiously fantasized about it.[2] While Freud's turn toward fantasy is credited as foundational to the field of psychoanalysis, sometimes it is also narrated as a profound betrayal of traumatized women.[3] Psychoanalysis offers tools to work with individual and collective fantasies, but it does damage when it underestimates the real impact of the traumas and losses we encounter in life. I don't want to rush ahead with interpreting fantasies of vulnerability, and in the process overlook real-world differences between my own experiences and those of my clients. I want to have a better sense if this is a distorted belief about vulnerability or an accurate one.

A different question I have is what to make of the detached affect around it. He tells me that he's going to die young like he's discussing the weather. Explanations for this affect run through my head: a young person feeling distant from risk, a performance of masculine toughness, an internalized sense of inevitability around the loss, or a passive invitation for me to rush in with concern and rescue. I wonder how to make sense of my client's simultaneous expression of and disavowal of intense personal danger. I wonder about his attitude about expressing vulnerability and fear. I consider that the story might function to prove his tough-guy status or affirm his membership in a special fraternity. As I contemplate these potential meanings, I decide to take a deeper look at the stories of premature death that circulate around policing. Thinking deeply with my client means being curious about this statistic: how it moves and what it does. I want to understand how stories of premature death function in U.S. policing.

Running the Numbers

The statistic quoted to me again and again is this: the average life expectancy for police officers in the United States is sixty-six years old, more than ten years below the national average. The statistic is a strange thing. It's a distillation, a generality drawn from lots of bodies that marks them all as vulnerable. It holds the weight of science, and when it is spoken it arrives with the force of authority. It is an easy, memorable fact. Putting a number on it makes the harm of doing the job real. Ten years of lost life: it hits like a punch.

The first time I hear it quoted to me, I am surprised by the claim. I wonder, "Is it really that dangerous to be a cop?" I type the question into Google and see what pops up. The sixty-six-year life-expectancy statistic shows up as a featured snippet.[4] I also find it cited in a range of popular press sources, including 60 Minutes and in the New York Daily News.[5] But as I dig deeper, that statistic loses its strength. The ten-year-lower life-expectancy statistic is drawn from a 1998 study of police officers in Buffalo, NY.[6] The study includes only white men who worked for at least five years as police officers between 1950 and 1990, and it finds that the average age of death for those men is sixty-six. The ten-year age gap has been calculated by comparing this number with contemporary life expectancies for white men. However, because it includes deaths over a wide range of time, the average calendar year of death in the study is 1973. The average date of birth is 1907. The ten-year difference in life-expectancy statistic compares current life expectancies for people at birth to those of people born up to a century earlier. Being born in different eras is a much clearer explanation for the difference in life expectancy than any occupational risk.

A 2013 paper reports even more extreme results, with 21.7 years chopped off cops' lives.[7] This study was published in a journal from the Omics International company. In 2019, this company was fined $50 million for running predatory journals. The *New York Times* reports that, rather than having typical rigorous peer-review standards for papers, Omics journals "often accept and publish them immediately, with a perfunctory review or none at all."[8] The life-expectancy research seems to suggest, more than anything else, that some researchers are invested in finding support for the idea that police are at much greater risk than the rest of the population. A 2010 study in California uses actuarial data and reports that cops have life expectancy after retirement similar to that of people who perform other state jobs.[9]

I decide to shift from life expectancy to a broader question: Is policing dangerous? If so, what makes it dangerous? To answer this question, I look to measures of occupational safety. The job category of "law enforcement workers" doesn't make the list of top-ten most-dangerous occupations compiled by the Bureau of Labor Statistics,[10] a list that includes people working in fishing, logging workers, aircraft pilots, roofers, and garbage/recycling collectors. Although they're not the most at risk, there is some evidence of increased risk. In 2014, police had almost four times as many fatal work injuries as the average for all occupations. A 2016 report documents between 79 and 146 officers dying from fatal work injuries every year in the period between 2003 and 20014.[11]

One area of increased risk is undeniable. Police claim the top spot in terms of suicide risk: police officers and security guards are the most at risk of suicide while at work. They are also one of the highest-risk occupations for suicide off the job.[12] My client worries about somebody "getting him" on the job, but according to these statistics, he himself may be the person most likely to pose a risk to his safety.

Multiple Precarities

The cops who tell me of their early death are living in one of the few industrialized countries of the world with decreasing life expectancy. From 2015 to 2017, life expectancy in the United States was declining, a rarity for industrialized countries.[13] While U.S. life expectancy rose slightly in 2018 and 2019, the small increases failed to keep up with significant increases in life expectancy in European countries over the previous decade, and the U.S. remains behind a number of much poorer countries in terms of life expectancy, including Cuba, Slovenia, and Costa Rica.[14] The COVID-19 pandemic caused a drastic drop in life expectancy in the first half of 2020, to the lowest level since 2006. This drop was especially pronounced for Latinx and Black populations.[15]

Economists Anne Case and Angus Deaton have tracked the rise of mortality in the U.S. through an increase in what they term "deaths of despair": alcohol-, drug-, and suicide-related deaths.[16] They describe these causes of death:

> They are drinking themselves to death, or poisoning themselves with drugs, or shooting or hanging themselves. Indeed, as we shall repeatedly see, the three causes of death are deeply related, and it is often hard for the coroner or medical examiner to classify a death; it is not always easy to tell a suicide from an accidental overdose. All the deaths show great unhappiness with life, either momentary or prolonged.[17]

Deaton and Case track a number of causes of death, including increasing inequality, substance use, lack of healthcare access, and increasing gun ownership. Some of these factors may apply to police, but others do not. Police are employed, in secure, highly unionized jobs, and are more likely to have access to healthcare than the general population.

However, these jobs bring them into another scene of despair—ongoing state-sanctioned violence. Over 1,000 people a year are killed by U.S. police, and a disproportionate number of those killed are Black, Latinx, or Indigenous. Premature death has emerged as a central concept for abolitionists in describing what is at stake in the battle against state-sanctioned racist violence. Ruth Wilson Gilmore defines racism as the creation of premature death—"the state-sanctioned or extralegal production and exploitation of group-differentiated vulnerability to premature death."[18] A 2015 study focused on the role of police in contributing to this premature death among people of color and found that deaths from "legal intervention" increased 45 percent from 1999 to 2013. The death rate from "legal intervention" is highest for Indigenous (American Indian and Alaskan Native) men, with disproportionately high rates for Black and Latinx men.[19] In addition, there may be further negative health outcomes from stress and poverty exacerbated by police and judicial actions. A 2017 CDC report states that Black people in the U.S. have four years lower life expectancy than white people due to "psychosocial, economic, and environmental stressors" that accumulate and lead to "premature aging and earlier health decline than whites."[20] The COVID-19 pandemic exacerbated these existing disparities, extending the life-expectancy gap to six years between white people and Black people in the U.S.[21] Unlike the police life-expectancy studies, these statistics are difficult to dispute.

U.S. police officers work in national conditions of increasingly deadly despair, in which they participate in deadly violence and contribute to premature death for Black, Indigenous, and Latinx people. Cops perceive that they are deeply harmed by doing this work, telling their own statistic about premature death.

I find myself pulled toward several different ways to think about what is happening when police quote this early-death statistic. These different frameworks appear and overlap in discussions of police work, and they inform the types of intervention strategies suggested by psychologists, politicians, police leadership, and activists.

One frame is that it is an act of denial and appropriation. Instead of recognizing their violence, cops pose as the true victims. A second framework is that police are traumatized by their work. The shocking violence they participate in impacts their mental health and puts them at risk, much like soldiers at war. Rather than choosing between the first or second framework, I suggest a third explanatory frame that acknowledges the daily misery of police work. The "failed-hero" framework argues that the shitty daily work and eroded interpersonal relationships that constitute policing accumulate and wear away people's mental and physical health. A felt sense of misery and precarity arises out of the brutal, bureaucratic, and antirelational nature of police work, as cops experience being repeatedly set up to fail at being a "good guy" or a hero.

According to the appropriation frame, cops' claims of precarity are a ruse to deny their own participation in violence. At best, their belief in their own risk is false, at worst it is a manipulative tactic to build sympathy for violent police forces and discredit their victims. This is a framework that can show up in abolitionist and critical prison studies accounts. In contrast, the first-responder trauma framework is the predominant model offered by police psychology and popular press accounts.[22] It is often employed to point toward individual psychological solutions for the psychic problems of police work. The failed-hero framework lines up with political theorist Lauren Berlant's concept of cruel optimism, in which the object of our desire makes us miserable.[23] The dream of being a hero is actually part of the structure that creates misery and a sense of deep personal vulnerability among cops.

Though they overlap, each of these frameworks offers a different way to understand what's happening when my client tells me that he thinks his job will make him die young. He could be buying into a lie, anticipating likely trauma, or describing how his lifelong dream has led him into a miserable, deadening situation. I look through each of these lenses for the possibilities that they offer in understanding this moment.

The Competing Vulnerabilities Frame

One possible response to the statistic quoted to me by my client is that it represents a false sense of vulnerability. Police claim victimhood while administering brutal violence to others. It could be that the claim of increased premature death and trauma for police is the ultimate act of appropriation—not only are police officers creating traumatic loss for others through their work, they are then claiming that loss as their own. Paula Ioanide describes this as an "astounding exercise of cognitive gymnastics" in which "whiteness symbolically and affectively appropriates the historical positionality of the marginalized and assign it to itself."[24]

The organizations that claim the phrase Blue Lives Matter are perhaps the clearest example to support this framework. On the Blue Lives Matter Facebook page run by the *Police Tribune*, the organization shares statistics and stories about line-of-duty death that suggest that police lives are precarious.[25] Urging people to take a stand with police officers, they suggest that their worth needs to be affirmed in a society that does not value them, and link police suicides directly to this lack of social value. They also share videos with graphic content of police officers, store clerks, and others shooting and killing people suspected of crimes, who are also often armed. While the posts celebrate white gun ownership, weapons held in Black hands are offered as justification for immediate murder.

The phrase "Blue Lives Matter" directly mimics the language of Black

Lives Matter. Unlike the statement "All Lives Matter," it doesn't argue against the recognition of uneven distribution of risk. Rather, it argues that police officers are the ones who really occupy the position of the precarious, vulnerable population.

While Blue Lives Matter is the most obvious example of denial and appropriation, a number of organizations focus on mitigating police officers' vulnerability. My visits to the National Law Enforcement Officers Memorial and the American Police Hall of Fame and Museum are suffused with this focus on police death. The Officer Down Memorial Page (ODMP) and the police advocacy organization Below 100 both present police as incredibly at risk.[26] Each month, ODMP lists statistics and stories about police who have died in the past month. Those who sign up for their mailing list or visit their website are subjected to repeated stories of on-the-job death. No similar networks exist for sharing stories of on-the-job deaths for higher-risk occupations such as cab-driving, truck-driving, logging, or construction.

Judith Butler refers to "the production of a hypervulnerability (of the nation, of masculinity)," which then "establishes a rationale for the containment of both women and minorities."[27] This hypervulnerable stance is linked to the denial of others' vulnerability—one way of stating this position is, "I'm being attacked the most, so everyone else should just stop complaining." Taking these vulnerability claims at face value could be potentially harmful—it would be validating and reinforcing a view of the world that leads to distorted relationships and violence. This is a substitution that insists police are the true victims.[28]

Police are not the only population to make this claim of true victimhood. Alyson Cole documents a shift in U.S. cultural politics starting in the late 1980s with conservative elements taking on the label of true victims.[29] Characterizations of victimized women, LGBTQ, and BIPOC people as "manipulative, aggressive, and even criminal" began to flourish, while a competing "Cult of True Victimhood" emerged to celebrate those predominantly white men who claim harm from efforts to redress individual and historic injustices. "True Victims"—Coles's term—are those harmed by "political correctness, affirmative action, hate speech codes, and similar manifestations of injurious victim politics." Cole writes "The True Victim is a noble victim. He endures his suffering with dignity, refraining from complaining or other public displays of weakness."[30] Statistics and stories of police death are used to make arguments around police officers as the true victims of policing, while simultaneously belittling or ignoring others harmed by police.

Thinking about my client, I reflect on the danger of colluding with this frame of appropriation and denial. While it's possible to confront people with evidence of others' vulnerability and precarity, the felt knowledge of police precarity embodied in these statistics and stories has an emotional weight for my client. This can fall into an impasse in which each side has its own version of the truth.

And yet, to continue with Butler's argument, "the discourse attests to what it denies"—denying vulnerability attests to vulnerability.[31] Talking about police precarity acknowledges that precarity is unevenly distributed. An acknowledgement of mutual bodily vulnerability can serve as an opening through which to challenge existing social relations. Butler emphasizes the ways in which our bodies inextricably position us in the social: "Part of what a body does . . . is to open onto the body of another, or a set of others, and for this reason bodies are not self-enclosed kinds of entities."[32] The discussion of my client's concern about their own well-being could be an opening into an encounter with the range of harms caused by policing. New possibilities arise when we link these two forms of precarity, and two assemblages of truths. I might want to challenge my client about his default into a victim stance and to call his attention back to the brutality in his everyday work life.

Thinking with this framework, my client's flat affect may be due, in part, to the fact that he doesn't actually feel that afraid. It's a story he's been told, but it doesn't totally match his distress. When he gruffly describes relationship struggles, I can see that he might benefit from getting more, not less, in touch with his vulnerability in his personal relationships. And yet it doesn't sit well with me to suggest that his invocation of the early death statistic is simple denial or appropriation. I can't buy into the idea that his claim is a conceit, because I see that he is distressed about his job. But I'm not sure that I'm seeing fear. It occurs to me that this distress might be better described as dread, frustration, or shame. The work is weighing on him.

The Trauma Framework

An alternate framework for thinking about my client's distress is that he is responding to constantly living with trauma. Police psychologists argue that "[e]xposure to trauma is inherent in police work."[33] Whether imagining their own dead body or encountering the bodies of others, dead bodies are ever-present in police work. Most mainstream reporting on the topic groups police with firefighters and emergency medical workers, describing the impact of first-responder trauma. Constant exposure to crisis situations involving grievous injury and death can wear on workers' mental health, leading them to develop posttraumatic symptoms. The flatness I see in my client's affect could be interpreted as a dissociative response to trauma.

Yet the framework of first-responder trauma seems to elide something particular about the work of policing. While there are commonalities between various first responders, the collation of emergency medical technicians and cops into the category of "first responders" can erase the unique role of police. Police aren't only first responders—they carry weapons and their work tools are primarily the threat and use of force. This is a different scenario from the medical technician or firefighter who works with the clear mission of saving lives. Working to save a life and failing is a vastly different emotional experience than entering an urgent situation with a gun and possibly shooting someone.

Police psychology accounts have drawn from military psychology, extending war-trauma models to police work. Criminologist and former cop Vincent Henry describes policing as "death work," due to the repeated exposure to death that is typical of the job.[34] Henry suggests that the primary traumas of police work are created when cops are called into scenes of death in their capacity as officers. Henry considers the trauma of being a first responder at scenes of violent death, of fear of being harmed in the line of duty, of seeing others killed, and of participating in what he calls "combat," as well as the institutional trauma of betrayal by your own leadership and departmental policies. Similarly, Kevin Gilmartin's *Emotional Survival for Law Enforcement* has trademarked and promoted his concept of the "Hypervigilance Biological Rollercoaster" that cops experience on the job. Gilmartin argues that it is not just gunfights that are traumatic for cops, but that police are also traumatized by the experience of working entire shifts with a sense of increased risk.

At times, trauma stories overlap with arguments about police officers' true victimhood—centering cops as victims while erasing other forms of violence. In Henry's discussion of "death work," there is no mention of the U.S. criminal legal system's creation of premature death.[35] Police are presented as the victims in the scenario of policing. Those who suffer from police violence are erased from these accounts.

Henry's concept of "death work" seems to capture something crucial about the emotional reality of the job. But it ignores something else—the violent work of the police. This splitting is repeated again and again in stories of policing, stories that claim "true victimhood" for police, while ignoring the traumatic impact of police violence. The psychological self-help guide *Deadly Force Encounters* is another example of this literature—it focuses on the risk of PTSD to officers who shoot people.

While the concepts of death work and first-responder trauma gesture toward the powerful emotional toll of police work, the trauma lens ignores the crucial insight that cops are not just exposed to trauma—they are tasked by the state with creating trauma for others through sanctioned use of force. The psychological literature on police trauma centers the bodies of police officers. Meanwhile, civilian deaths are reduced to triggers for cops' trauma.

I find myself musing on Gilmartin's choice of a "roller coaster" as a metaphor for the physiology of police work. A roller coaster creates a thrilling perception of danger, in a situation of relative safety. A roller-coaster ride reminds us that the perception of risk and actual risk are two different things. While constantly riding a roller coaster might be bad for one's health, there is a simple solution: get off the ride.

Media accounts of drone pilots suffering from PTSD have been criticized for humanizing drone pilots while continuing the erasure and dehumanization of people killed by drones.[36] Similarly, centering officer trauma serves to humanize officers who might otherwise be encountered as representatives of brutal state violence. In *Deadly Force Encounters*, Artwohl and Christensen argue,

> The law enforcement community has nothing to gain by presenting police officers as *Robocops*, efficient killing machines with perfect judgment and no feelings. This extreme view will only lead to false expectations of total perfection that will result in harsh condemnation of any officer who shows feelings or makes the smallest mistake.[37]

Here, presenting cops as having feelings is framed as a humanizing public-relations strategy. Informing the public about officer trauma may ease "harsh condemnations" of officers who make mistakes on the job. For Artwohl and Christensen, educational efforts around officer trauma provide protection from public scrutiny. Trauma discourses provide a frame for public relations, using psychological discourse to facilitate public acceptance of police violence.

Carceral psychology approaches would suggest that my client is being traumatized by his job. My goal as a therapist in this context would be to educate him about trauma responses, help him establish safety, process difficult experiences, and return to work. Screening for work-related PTSD, I might ask him if he is experiencing intrusive memories of work experiences, if he avoids thinking about work, or if he often feels jumpy or on edge. If he meets these criteria, I might work with him around specific memories of work events, to take the traumatic edge off them.

Carceral psychology evades the question of ethics. And yet all work around trauma involves ethics. It does not feel ethical to focus solely on returning people to functionality at a job that causes harm. Policing involves violence toward others, and further participation in that violence may harm my client further. I don't want to treat my client like a cog in a brutal machine. And at the same time, he has autonomy over his life and choices. These are not my life decisions to make—they are his. As he makes those decisions, I'm trying to think with him about the work and how it transforms him.

The Failed-Hero Framework

Questions about how policing impacts people's lives, and the risks it poses to them, point toward what the experience of policing is like. What exactly is it that makes policing miserable work?

Police work is miserable because it is what Micol Siegel describes as violence work: "work that relies upon violence or the threat thereof."[38] It demands that police embody the violent power of the state. It is work that places bureaucratic priorities over human relationships. Again and again, police officers cite the misery of the types of relationships police participate in. In their role as purveyors of state violence, people are often angry at or afraid of them. The job also has an impact on relationships outside of their work. My client is attached to the police role—he has a fantasy of a hero's life. And yet this fantasy, and all of the pleasures associated with it, has drawn him into a situation of total misery, in which he daily works in relationships of potential or enacted violence.

As I reflect on this conflict, I find myself thinking about Lauren Berlant's description of cruel optimism, "a kind of relation in which one depends on objects that block the very thriving that motivates our attachment in the first place."[39] My client's wish to be a hero, to be a good guy, has drawn him into a work life that promises him heroic moments but delivers endless asshole moments in their stead. He is attached to the idea of being a cop, but at the same time he knows that being a cop harms him. He has been set up to be a failed hero, and when he confronts the intractability of this situation, he feels frustrated, hopeless, and ashamed.

Police work is miserable in part because it combines bureaucracy with violence. Anthropologist David Graeber argues that "police are bureaucrats with weapons" who enforce regulations through the threat and use of physical harm. Graeber reminds us that although police are often imagined as primarily responding to crime, they more often enforce bureaucratic regulations such as the proper registration of cars and payment of administrative fees. He defines policing as "the scientific application of physical force, or the threat of physical force, to aid in the resolution of administrative problems."[40]

Former police officers who have described the work of policing agree with Graeber's assessment. Former police officer and philosopher Jonathan Wender describes policing as bureaucratic praxis, the "bureaucratic *problematization of human being*" (emphasis his).[41] Former Seattle police chief Norm Stamper reports that he was judged as a cop based on his arrest numbers, while the quality of his interactions with the public was not measured. "The people on my beat were, in a word, irrelevant."[42]

In pushing complex situations into systems of bureaucratic regulation, police confront systems of law that are unclear and that may even be impossible to comprehend. Looking at the actions of urban police in India during communal riots, Veena Das argues that "many of the functionaries of the state themselves find the practices of the state to be illegible."[43] The misreading of rules is not simply a mistake, it is a common practice structured into institutional functioning. Das writes,

The illegibility of the rules and also the human actions that embody these rules appear to be part of the way that rules are implemented. It is not that the mode of sociality to be found in the institutions of the state is based on clarity of rules and regulations and that these become illegible to the poor or the illiterate, but that the very persons charged with implementing the rules might also have to struggle as to how to read them.[44]

Police translate messy situations through unclear, illegible, or contradictory sets of laws, instructions, and regulations. For Das, the "signature of the state" is marked by the failure built into its communications through law, the ways in which it is both legible and inscrutable.[45]

In the U.S. context, the police are expected to simultaneously enforce law *and* order. This demand erases multiple conflicts between and within legal regulations and historical social orders. The imperative contained in the slogan "serve and protect" similarly places contradictory demands on police action. They are expected to provide "service," which suggests a relationship in which they are meeting civilian demands. At the same time, they are asked to protect, suggesting a paternalistic power over the same civilians they are serving. The commands to "serve and protect" and promote "law and order" serve as double binds in which two different communications are given that contradict one another and cannot be clarified.[46] In the face of conflicting demands, cops are left making decisions with little guidance beyond historical precedent and their felt sense of what they should do. No matter what they choose, they will fail.

German sociologist Max Weber argues that bureaucracy is marked by the element of "calculable rules" that eliminate "love, hatred, and all purely personal, irrational, and emotional elements which escape calculation."[47] Bureaucracy promises to eliminate the effect of emotion. Yet in practice, unclear and contradictory rules can set up bureaucrats' feelings as the deciding factor in decision-making. At the same time, bureaucrats are expected to be dispassionate, to refuse the perceived bias of empathic connection. The refusal of empathic connection and the disavowal of the law's contradictions create stress for those who embody legal bureaucracy. Police take on these stressors in order to maintain the appearance of the U.S. legal system as coherent, comprehensive, just, and rational, even when the cops themselves experience the systems as deeply flawed.

Bureaucratic emotional labor structures scenarios of refused recognition—encountering people as forms, criteria, stereotypes, and statistics. This is the emotional labor of constricting, not recognizing exceptions, and hewing to one interpretation of regulations despite emotional appeals—the labor of being an asshole. Policing combines direct encounter and threat of force. While social-service workers administering Section 8 housing programs are tasked with denying shelter to those who do not qualify, they are not charged with physically, forcibly evicting those whom they deny.[48] In contrast, police encounters pair administrative violence with the threat of physical violence.[49]

Cops describe this situation as one of being hated by the people they encounter. In an online article, "The 10 Worst Things About Being a Police Officer," former highway-patrol officer and police-academy instructor Timothy Roufa lists the worst parts of the job: (1) the excuses, (2) the attitudes, (3) the hours, (4) the stereotypes, (5) the myths, (6) the perception of cop culture, (7) the scrutiny, (8) the politics, (9) the pain, and (10) losing peers.[50] Notably, six of ten of these worst aspects result from some variation of poor communication and misunderstanding between communities and cops. The attitudes, excuses, stereotypes, myths, perception, and scrutiny all point to moments in which the people they're interacting with see cops as incompetent, ill-intentioned, unethical, or bad. While he also points to organizational politics and long hours, it's the sense of disconnection between a person's sense of self and other people's perception of them that is highlighted again and again.

The failed-hero framework has its own explanation for how police are harmed by the work. Berlant argues that people are pulled into speeding up their lifetimes as a way to get some form of relief from the daily awfulness of these particular manifestations of contemporary carceral capitalism, a concept Berlant terms "slow death."[51] Berlant uses the example of the worker who exercises the lateral agency of going to get a candy bar during a work break. This action does nothing to challenge vertical hierarchies of social power; the relief comes in the form of a time-loan: I get an emotional break now, but the cost of that break is a tiny increase in my risk of premature death. Over time, the coping strategies used to get through the day accumulate into their own sources of suffering. Living in the cruel optimism of wishing to be a hero, cops are constantly confronted with the impossibility of being a hero, and are tasked instead with administrative and physical violence. In this scenario, cops might blunt their despair in a million different ways.

Imagine a patrol cop, stopping off for a huge caramel latte from a corporate coffee chain. The officer is in the midst of a long shift, engaging with other people through the threat of violence. They are asked to promote law and order—two things that contradict one another at times and leave them with only wrong choices. In the middle of this headache, a brief reprieve arrives in the form of caffeine, sweetness, and a familiar brand, perhaps even a pleasant encounter with the coffee shop staff. The coffee break is an enlivening moment in the numbing death work of policing. It awakens the senses, but does little to create new possibilities for relational or structural change. The comforting treat simultaneously heightens an already-anxious state, as caffeine and sugar set the heart racing faster.

Moments of pleasurable escape can also be found in violence and aggression. Gilmartin notes the appeal of working in a job that feels dangerous and exciting. "[T]his state of alert interaction with the environment . . . feels rather good physically—at least for the first few years." An activated autonomic nervous system can make people feel "alive, quick witted, and able to handle any problems." Rather than being passively exposed to violence, many officers seek out "action" on the job, with the hope of being able to experience the thrill of "catching bad guys." For cops seeking some reprieve from shitty bureaucratic labor, the search for enlivening moments can bring faster forms of death. The quest to feel present might include dangerously fast driving, drinking alcohol or using other drugs, provoking intense interpersonal encounters—manic gestures toward a feeling of aliveness. This understanding challenges the "trauma narrative" in which cops are wounded bystanders to violence that they neither anticipated nor precipitated. Instead, these behaviors suggests a relationship of cruel optimism with violence, in which cops seek out moments of heroic "action"—which then serve to increase their sense of isolation and shame.

Bureaucratic emotional labor rewards depersonalization, a lack of empathic connection, and a refusal of emotions—a paranoid relating style that isolates and promotes the narrative that if I do not attack, I will be attacked. In that emotional world, it may be hard for some police to imagine non-destructive solutions to their distress. A predominant model of police suicide suggests that officers get locked into the emotional stance of their work as their only mode of dealing with stress, losing the ability to imagine other ways of being.[52] Rather than an individual psychological issue, this failure of imagination is a way of thinking promoted by the institutional context of the work. High rates of police suicide may be linked to the difficulty of living within the emotional restrictions of the cop role.

Policing is a form of work that promotes death in a variety of ways. Cops take on the shitty position of enforcing state violence. And they participate in destructive coping strategies to numb the experience of how awful the job is, which may also cause harm. The failed-hero framework suggests that my task with my client might be to develop some strategies to cultivate a different kind of feeling alive. I want to look for forms of agency that can enhance the possibilities for him to live and grow in complex relationships, outside of the cruel promise of being a hero.

Giving Up the Hero Role

Giving up the hero role is hard to do. In *Deadly Force Encounters*, police psychologists Artwohl and Christensen outline the split worldview that frames the daily world in which officers work.

> Early in your career, it becomes clear in your mind that there are good guys and bad guys. While different police agencies use different terms—suspect, perp (for perpetrator), crook, and a variety of more colorful terms—you can walk into any police agency and say "bad guy" and everyone will know whom you are talking about.

They describe this emotional position as structured by the work—part of the compensation of being a cop is being reassured that you are one of the "good guys." Artwohl and Christensen then go on to suggest that moments of violence break open this simple emotional framework.

> Sometimes it can be a little fuzzy whether the victim is totally good, but there is never any doubt in your mind that *you* are a good guy and it's your job to go out and catch the bad guys. Oversimplistic? Perhaps. But if you are like most officers, you will come to think this way because it's the world in which you work. Then when you have to kill someone, no matter how justified, the division between good and bad often becomes confused.[53]

According to these psychologists, the emotional aftermath of a police shooting has the potential to rupture the hero narrative. The emotional crisis that follows a shooting stresses the attachment to the hero narrative. It is the moment in which the cop becomes aware that he might be a "bad guy"—"the division between good and bad often becomes confused." This sentiment reveals the lie contained in the earlier statement that the officer "had" to kill someone. It acknowledges the possibility that the past could have been different. Maybe they didn't have to kill someone. Maybe the whole idea of being one of the "good guys" is a lie.

Artwohl and Christensen describe the inability of police-academy training to confront one's own terrible, destructive potential and other people's vulnerability. "No one tells you what it's like to thrust a gun at a human being, feel the steel explode in your hand, and watch the human crumple to the floor[. . . .] No one tells you what it's like to know that *you* caused that."[54]

The emotional crisis provoked by recognizing one's own capacity for harm may lead to feelings of guilt and a shifting relationship to ones' own destructiveness. And yet it is not until after someone has been killed that Artwohl and Christensen imagine police officers reckoning with their own capacity for destruction. And even then—they are more focused on the pain of disillusionment, about the loss of one's own heroic identity, than they are concerned with the other people harmed.

Of course, it is not necessary to physically harm another person to begin grappling with your own aggression and potential for violence. And some who do cause other people's deaths never experience that crisis. U.S. policing is riddled with examples of those who do not report any crisis around their own destructiveness, even in the aftermath of killing other people.[55] The process of psychotherapy provides other opportunities for transformative encounters with one's own destructiveness. This could be an opportunity for moving toward a position in which deaths are not justified as necessary or inevitable, but instead are grieved as a terrible thing.

The recognition of our potential to destroy others is what Melanie Klein marks as the entry into the depressive position.[56] This position involves an encounter with the other person's reality and a realization that we do not have control over them. We cannot destroy or restore them at will, and at the same time we are deeply dependent on them. Therefore, we must be careful with one another. Eve Kosofsky Sedgwick notes that this move into the depressive position "inaugurates ethical possibility—in the form of a guilty, empathetic view of the other as at once good, damaged, integral, and requiring and eliciting love and care."[57]

The depressive position abandons pleasurable fantasies of total goodness, in exchange for the pleasure of authentic human connection. In doing so, it lets go of both the fantasy of being an all-good hero and the cynical disillusionment that accompanies the inevitable realization that this fantasy is not reality. Integrity, here, is achieved not through an essential heroic nature, but from the hard work of trying to figure out how to be a good-enough ethical neighbor, friend, and person in each moment of encounter.

Within policing, early death and trauma are often framed as job guarantees, more certain than a pension. Every law enforcement officer I counsel tells me they expect to die young. They expect to be attacked, to be shot, or to destroy their bodies. They expect to see "sick shit," and they see it. They expect to use their weapons, and they imagine that outsiders—their family, community members, the media—will hate them when they do. These fantasies of being attacked distract from the state-sanctioned violence they embody. They expect to be fired, vilified, to live nightmares. They offer themselves up to the brutal hours of shift work, and to jump into sudden situations of extreme physical risk and exertion. But despite all this preparation for inevitable risk, they avoid grappling with how their relationship with violence is shaping their lives.

The trauma framework suggests that interventions need to be targeted toward recovering from scenes of death and grievous injury. A different approach is to see the problem as more pervasive. Not only do we see the violent power of the state in these spectacles of violence—we also confront it in the daily misery-making bureaucratic routines. These routines degrade relationships, suck resources, and kill hopes. Viewing police vulnerability solely through the lens of trauma or appropriation misses something. It misses that policing is structured as a form of cruel optimism—one in which its workers are sold a dream of heroism that will always fail. Statistics and stories of police death are the backbone to the idea of police as heroes—selflessly giving their lives for the public good. People buy into a promise: that they can be heroes for justice, always on the side of good, and promoting public safety. But on the job, they can find themselves moving further away from those things.

Back to the Office

My client has been living on a narrow path directed toward being a hero. Now he's suffocating a little in the airless script of the vulnerable protector, holding up this statistic and asking for some kind of help or sympathy. And what will I offer him?

I reflect on my notes. I realize that I've been distracted by the statistic. His comments started by gesturing toward another path. "I don't know how much longer I'll do it." For him, the statistic might not be a co-optation of other's suffering, but rather an expression of why he needs to stop. The next time, I am ready to pull on that thread.

As he begins talking about the shitty day at work, I reflect back the larger communication: "You're thinking of quitting."

"Yeah." He sighs, looks off into space. His face is full of grief, and I imagine that I can see his hero-cop dreams fading. He is silent. We sit in sadness for a few minutes. I try to avoid rushing. This grief has a different texture than the detached anticipation of future death. His life will be less simple than he had thought. I sit with him in this sorrow, resonating with the disappointment of not simply being good.

And then he turns to me. "I wonder what else I could do?"

CHAPTER 3

Guidebooks

Police Psychology at the Scenes of State Violence

Five days after the September 16, 2016, killing of Terence Crutcher by police officer Betty Shelby, the *New York Times* ran an article discussing the repeated failure of police to immediately administer first aid to Black people shot by police.[1] The article captures my attention. I've been disappointed with some of the tools my profession offers for thinking in the clinic about the psychic life of police power. In the article, titled "Why First Aid Is Often Lacking in the Moments After a Police Shooting," journalist Richard Pérez-Peña brings into view some of the other ways my field is engaging with policing as an institution.

Pérez-Peña notes public outrage at the lack of police effort to save Crutcher's life after he was shot. He also demonstrates a style of "both-sides" journalism that seeks to understand the police perspective. Pérez-Peña writes, "Experts in policing agree that the way officers respond, or fail to, is often a problem, but they say that such failures are not necessarily the fault of the officers, and that law enforcement agencies are starting to address them." He goes on to describe the role of trauma, lack of policies, and poor training in the failure of police officers to try to save the lives of people dying in front of them. While the journalist quotes some activists expressing anger at police negligence, he counterpoints this outrage with an appeal to "human nature" and trauma. "Yet others say that what looks like disregard for life may just reflect human nature. A person who has just shot someone is flooded with adrenaline, sometimes traumatized, and often not thinking clearly." The physiology of trauma is presented as an alternate explanation for racist behavior. It offers an alternative to being outraged at racist police violence, offering the reader a strategy to avoid condemning actions that seem like clear markers of disregard for Black life.

The *New York Times* article demonstrates one way that police department-ments are using psychological trauma research. Five days after a shooting, police leaders are using this research to encourage empathic understand-ings of police violence and to defuse calls for accountability. They individu-alize trauma, applying concepts to specific officers while ignoring the con-text of U.S. racist police violence. The individualized lens is applied selectively—the experiences of police officers are foregrounded, while the perspectives of Black people viewing or experiencing police violence are ignored. The police discussion of the physiology of trauma works to gener-ate public acceptance of dehumanizing actions that might otherwise elicit horror and outrage.

Psychological power is never neutral. It can be used to solicit compas-sion and empathy for some while erasing other life experiences. Critical psychologist Derek Hook draws on the work of French philosopher Michel Foucault to argue that all use of psychology is infused with power.[2] It repro-duces understandings of normal and abnormal that have been shaped by white supremacy, capitalism, and colonialism. In supporting the day-to-day operations of policing, police psychology interventions work to stabilize this current social order and strengthen state power.

In this chapter, I take a critical psychology approach to police psychol-ogy, exploring how psychological power is used to supplement police power. The chapter starts with a brief outline of police psychology for those unfamiliar with the field and its history. I then explore the connections between policing and psychology through an in-depth examination of the International Association of Chiefs of Police (IACP) guidelines for officer-involved shootings. A set of guidelines for managing situations of police violence that use psychological language and insights, they offer a window into how psychological power functions to support ongoing state violence.

Policing and psychology are deeply intermingled. Psychologists partner with police to offer screening, treatment, consultation, and trainings—all specifically aimed at supporting police departments. This work is referred to as the field of police psychology. Police psychology practices enact what Foucault has termed "biopower," "the administration of bodies and the cal-culated management of life."[3] These interventions ensure that the popula-tion of police officers is prescreened for psychological fitness, and that they are routinely evaluated if their behavior seems psychologically question-able; if they are disabled by psychological concerns, they are either treated and promptly returned to the workforce or declared unfit to work. These practices suggest that police officers are uniformly stable, rational, and able to dispassionately enforce laws. Further, the deployment of psychologists in a consulting role throughout police departments reassures the public that police practices are professional, ethical, reasonable, and in accord with practices that support mental health and well-being.

A Brief History of Police Psychology

Police psychology crafts itself as an apolitical and technical field. In the American Psychology Association division of public service, the section on police psychology defines itself through a list of the different things its members do:

> They are involved in the selection of employees, fitness for duty evaluations, critical incident stress debriefing, management of mental health programs, criminal investigative analysis (profiling) and hostage negotiations.[4]

Rather than being united through a set of coherent practices, the field is defined through its proximity to policing. Psychologists show up as helpers in the project of policing, bringing psychological knowledge to bear on a diverse set of aims. They screen officers for "psychological fitness" and support officers who experience trauma on the job. But they also step into a police role, lending insights into criminal behavior and assisting with interrogation and hostage negotiation.

One reason that policing needs the help of disciplines such as psychology is its need to enhance public perceptions of police legitimacy. Writing in 2020, Canadian police leader Daniel J. Jones argues that "[o]ne of the biggest challenges facing modern policing in recent years has been the lack of police legitimacy."[5] A perceived lack of legitimacy diminishes police power, as it makes the public less likely to cooperate with and support police. The history of policing involves constant attempts to increase perceptions of police legitimacy; as a result, the history of policing and incarceration is one of constant reform.[6]

Civic and police leaders work to legitimize police by introducing reforms that promise to limit their power and increase their skill. Uniforms and numbered badges were both first introduced as reforms to policing, ensuring that members of the public could identify specific police officers, observe whether they were working during their patrol shifts, and hold them accountable for actions while on duty.[7] Psychology was introduced to policing in the early twentieth century as part of this process of constant reform. In this case, the use of social science expertise promised to create an intelligent and emotionally stable workforce. The initial use of psychology within a few police departments through the first half of the twentieth century was followed by broader expansions in the postwar period.

The first psychological screening of potential police cadets was led by Lewis Terman, one of the founders of the field of intelligence testing. In 1916, Terman was commissioned to assess the intelligence of applicants to the San Jose, California, Police Department. This was the same year that he published *The Measurement of Intelligence*.[8] In this manifesto for testing, he spelled out the dangers of what he referred to as "feeble-mindedness"—a condition that blended intellectual, emotional, and moral inferiority.[9] Alexandra Minna Stern outlines Terman's use of intelligence testing in the service of eugenic policies in California. His intelligence testing was foundational in establishing the California Bureau on Juvenile Research, which researched the "causes and consequences of delinquency and mental deficiency" among children and teens.[10] Other eugenic efforts rooted in stamping out the threat of hereditary "feeble-mindedness" included the sterilization of young women, institutionalization, laws against interracial marriage, and racist immigration restrictions.[11]

In his involvement with the San Jose police hiring process, Terman administered an abbreviated version of his Stanford-Binet test to thirty applicants for police and firefighting positions in San Jose.[12] Terman suggested that those with an IQ of less than 80, whom he considered to be "feeble-minded," be automatically disqualified from police work. One third of the applicants were disqualified on this basis. The screening of police through IQ tests was a form of racial screening, designed to ensure that police forces remained intellectually superior in the face of immigrant applicants considered racially suspect. Terman subsequently partnered with the U.S. military on screening troops in World War I.[13] Critics point out that these screening practices encouraged white-supremacist hiring practices under the cover of scientific meritocracy.[14]

The next expansions of police psychology occurred in the years after World War II, when military testing practices to screen out "psychologically unfit" recruits moved back into police department use.[15] In 1954, the LAPD began using a series of personality tests to screen all new recruits. They included the Minnesota Multiphasic Personality Test (MMPI), a group Rorschach test, a tree drawing (also known as Koch's Baum Test), and a brief interview.[16] The MMPI is an inventory test that attempts to identify psychopathology. The testing purported to measure applicants' level of paranoia, depression, hysteria, introversion, anxiety, excitability, schizophrenia, hypochondriasis, psychopathy, and misalignment with traditional gender roles. The Rorschach test and the tree drawing are both projective tests, which use ambiguous cues in an attempt to uncover themes that may be outside of the subject's conscious awareness. Rather than screening on the basis of perceived intelligence, these tests sought to screen out people whose personalities were incongruent with policing, because of sadistic or psychopathic features. A number of urban police chiefs added psychological screenings in an effort to increase the professionalization of policing, but the majority of departments did not adopt the practice. By the early1960s, psychological testing for police applicants was used in approximately one-quarter of police departments.[17]

In 1965, President Lyndon B. Johnson called for the beginning of "a thorough, intelligent, and effective war against crime."[18] Expanded federal support for policing offered through his initiatives led to expansions in police psychology. The 1967 President's Commission on Law Enforcement and Administration of Justice report called for the development and use of psychological tests to determine the "emotional fitness" of applicants.[19] In 1968, the Omnibus Crime Control and Safe Streets Act passed, establishing the Law Enforcement Assistance Administration, which created funding for psychological initiatives within policing.[20] The increased demand for psychological services led to the rapid expansion of psychological professionals working to support police department operations in the 1970s and 1980s. Martin Reiser began working as a full-time police psychologist for the Los Angeles Police Department in 1968, providing in-house counseling to officers.[21] He published the first book on police psychology, *The Police Department Psychologist*, in 1972.[22]

In 1967, in response to the rebellions in Watts, Chicago, Detroit, Newark, and other under-resourced urban communities influenced by systemic racism, President Lyndon B. Johnson created a National Advisory Committee on Civil Disorders. Also known as the Kerner Commission, the committee issued its final report in 1968. The report was a sharp critique of white racism and the lack of resources in Black communities. The report also encouraged police reforms, including the use of psychologists to screen out potential officers who had "personal prejudices," including racism.[23] This recommendation was informed by the post-WWII boom in psychological explorations of prejudice, which included Adorno and his colleagues' 1950 study on the authoritarian personality.[24]

By 2003, Cochrane, Tett, and Vandecreek found that nearly 90 percent of police agencies in the U.S. used psychological testing as a part of their pre-employment screening.[25] Police-specific screening measures have been introduced, including the Inwald Personality Inventory, created in 1979, and the M-PULSE, released in 2008.[26] Although psychological screening was suggested as a response to concerns about racist policing, the implementation of the tests has been found to favor white male candidates in some instances. In an analysis of police hiring practices in Philadelphia from 2011 to 2014, the *Philadelphia Inquirer* found that the psychological screening pass rate for Black applicants was only 72.4 percent, while the pass rate for white candidates was 81.2 percent.[27] In 2015 in nearby Newark, New Jersey, members of the municipal council elected not to renew the contract of their psychological testing firm after finding racial and gender bias in police screening. The firm rejected 19 percent of women applicants and only 6 percent of men; it also rejected 10 percent of Black candidates, compared to 8 percent of Latinx and 6 percent of white candidates.[28]

Legal scholar Sujata Menjoge outlines the multiple ways that psychological testing can circumvent federal antidiscrimination laws. Testing allows employers to obtain information related to race, religion, gender, or national origin in ways that circumvent forbidden questions about those areas. It allows for the selection of personality traits similar to those of the existing workforce on the basis of a perceived "fit" with the organization. And the tests themselves are often standardized on white U.S. middle-class samples, leading to the identification of Black, immigrant, and economically disadvantaged applicants as "abnormal."[29] While presented as a professionalizing "check" on police enactments of racism, there is evidence that psychological screening in policing has helped sustain white-supremacist and patriarchal hiring practices. Further, psychological screening practices for police are an enactment of the "clinical approach" to racism in the institution of policing. Eduardo Bonilla-Silva defines this as "the careful separation of good and bad, tolerant and intolerant Americans."[30] These screening processes frame racist police violence as an individual psychological problem unrelated to police power.

Getting Organized

As police psychology proliferated in departments across the U.S., a demand for professional conferences and organizations emerged. According to police psychologists Peter Weiss and Robin Inwald, national organizing of police psychologists began with a meeting held at the 1973 International Association of Chiefs of Police (IACP) annual conference in San Antonio, Texas. At this meeting, a group of fifty-six psychologists and police administrators met to "improve communications between social/behavioral scientists" working in the field of policing. Weiss and Inwald credit this meeting as the space in which "the idea for a national police psychologists' group" began to grow.[31] Two years later, in 1975, the Society for Police and Criminal Psychology had its first conference, in Tucson, Arizona.[32] In 1982, a meeting of eleven police psychologists at the American Psychological Association (APA) annual convention led to the creation of the "Police and Public Safety" Section within Division 18 (Psychologists in Public Service) of the APA.[33]

Following a 1984 conference on police psychology at the FBI Academy in Quantico, a group of psychologists began discussing the need for an organization within the International Association of Chiefs of Police (IACP).[34] The Psychological Services Section of the IACP was officially founded on October 25, 1984, when the IACP Executive Board voted to approve their mission. Founded within a police professional organization, the Psychological Services Section requires three letters of recommendation from police chiefs or other leaders to become a member.[35] In its capacity as a professional police psychology organization, the Police Psychological Services section has issued guidelines for a number of police psychology practices. These include performing fitness-for-duty and pre-employment evaluations, consulting to police departments, setting up peer-support programs, and supporting officers' mental health in the aftermath of police shootings.

Part of the founding mission of the Psychological Services Section was "to promote the field of police psychology within the broad field of psychology."[36] This aspect of the Section's mission has been largely successful. Police psychology has its own professional publications, annual conferences, and a small number of graduate training programs.[37] In 2011, it was adopted as a specialty by the American Board of Professional Psychology, allowing psychologists to become board-certified Police Psychologists.[38] Within the American Psychological Association, Police and Public Safety Psychology was recognized as a specialty in 2013, and police psychology is a prominent section within the Division on Public Service.[39] The 2015 police psychology treatment handbook *Behind the Badge* opens with a foreword from the "father of cognitive therapy," Aaron T. Beck. Its cover contains an endorsement from Donald Meichenbaum, another influential figure in cognitive-behavioral therapy.[40] Similarly, Vincent Henry's *Death Work*, on the psychology of police trauma, begins with an introduction by noted psychiatrist and historian Robert Jay Lifton.[41] Respected academic psychology presses, including Guilford, Routledge, Oxford University, and NYU Press, have issued handbooks and monographs on police psychology.

While police psychology has done a good job of gaining institutional respect within the field, it has done a terrible job at ending racism in policing. The Kerner Commission vision that psychological screening might somehow reduce police violence has not been achieved. Indeed, reducing racism in policing is not even mentioned as an organizational goal by the IACP Psychological Services Section or as one of the problems addressed by the APA Police and Public Safety Psychology subspecialty.[42] And yet psychological intervention continues to be offered as a potential solution to police racism. Almost fifty years after the Watts uprising was sparked by the attempted arrest of Marquette Frye, an unarmed Black teenager named Michael Brown was shot dead on the streets of Ferguson, Missouri. The subsequent protests at Ferguson again prompted politicians to call for psychological solutions to police violence. In 2015, *The Final Report of the President's Task Force on 21st Century Policing* commissioned by President Barack Obama again called for increased integration of psychological expertise into law enforcement. This included integration of social psychology research on implicit bias into trainings for all officers.[43] In 2020, following the murder of George Floyd by Minneapolis Police, politicians, policy-makers, and pundits again suggested that psychological professionals might be able to help.

Following Floyd's murder, the president of the American Psychological Association Sandra L. Shullman issued a statement decrying the "racism pandemic." She outlines the devastating mental-health impact of daily exposure to racism. And then she pivots, to suggest that psychological research into policing could be a solution:

> Research shows, for example, that compared with whites, blacks feel more negative stereotype threats and more racial profiling when interacting with the police. However, psychological research also points to possible solutions. Studies find that when police act in a procedurally just manner and treat people with dignity, respect, fairness and neutrality, people are more likely to comply with their directives and accept any outcome, favorable or unfavorable.[44]

Stating that Black people "feel more" threatened and profiled, Shullman's language suggests that the problem of racism is one of "feelings" rather than physical threats. She then points to research about what might lead people to "comply" and "accept any outcome" in a police encounter, suggesting that the problem of the "racism pandemic" is one of a lack of Black compliance with police power. In a statement that is both a response to George Floyd's murder and sales pitch for psychology, the APA president argues that the field can help police get people to comply with and accept police power.

Critical psychologists Dennis Fox, Isaac Prilleltensky, and Stephanie Austin highlight that "mainstream psychology's underlying assumptions and institutional allegiances disproportionately hurt members of powerless and marginalized groups by facilitating inequality and oppression."[45] When the president of the American Psychology Association suggests that psychologists can teach police how to get people to "accept any outcome" of a police interaction, she is offering to facilitate the acceptance of inequality and oppression. Shullman probably means well, but her response is shaped by an unquestioning allegiance to the necessity of policing, and an underlying assumption that the problem is rooted in how Black people feel, rather than in how they are being harmed. While psychology strives to professionalize and improve policing, looking at the details of these practices suggests that they are creating new ways to rationalize and excuse racialized violence.

Both psychology and criminology strengthen police power by anchoring it within liberal discourses of reform.[46] Police psychology fits into the history of liberal reforms to the criminal legal system. Many of these liberal reforms have resulted in harmful expansions of state power. For example, progressive efforts to address the needs of imprisoned parents have led to the incarceration of children alongside their mothers.[47] Gender-segregated facilities are the outcome of feminist reform efforts at the turn of the century, which sought to protect women prisoners from sexual exploitation by placing them in an all-female environment.[48] Legislative attempts to end sexual violence in prison have increased forms of state sexual violence, such as remote video viewing of people in prison while they are using the toilet, showering, and in states of undress.[49] In the area of criminal law, the expansion of hate crimes laws, domestic violence reforms, and antitrafficking efforts have all been cited as liberal reforms that expand the carceral state.[50] Current reformers calling for increased psychological screening of police might consider the origin of these practices in racist and able-ist screenings for "feeble-mindedness," as well as current evidence of their gendered racist outcomes. Those advocating for psychologically informed practices to increase acceptance and compliance might consider the long histories of racist violence by police, and ask if acceptance and compliance are likely to lead to meaningful change.

Naomi Murakawa and Katherine Beckett have identified the penology of racial innocence, a framework that assumes that criminal legal policies and institutions are "innocent of racial power until proven otherwise."[51] In police psychology, we see the operation of a psychology of racial innocence—a framework that applies psychological principles and practices as if they are happening in a race-neutral context. Practices with racist impacts are only recognized as racist when they occur in situations of clear racist intent. "In its search for intent and causation, the penology of racial innocence neglects what we think of as the larger context and dimensions of racial power."[52] The historical context of racist state violence is ignored, and psychological interventions to support policing are treated as racism-neutral. Rather than meaningfully confronting racist state violence, these psychological interventions provide tips on how to manage it effectively.

This "psychology of racial innocence" is demonstrated in the IACP Psychological Services Section guidelines for responding to police officers' shooting of civilians.[53] Increased psychological involvement is promoted as a strategy to stop police violence. Yet the Psychological Services Section guidelines are concerned with managing this violence, not stopping it. They treat police shootings as though they are not connected to anti-Black racism, offering "colorblind" psychological expertise to assist purveyors of racialized violence.

Officer-Involved Shooting Guidebooks

Founded in 1893 by fifty police chiefs from across the U.S., the IACP is the largest professional organization for police, currently claiming more than

31,000 members in over 165 countries.[54] Its Psychological Services Section has access to police chiefs and leadership across the world. In 1988, the IACP Psychological Services Section issued its first guidelines for dealing with officer shootings. These guidelines have been regularly updated by the Section and are one of five major guideline documents available on their website, alongside two guides for psychological evaluations of officers, a document on peer support, and general guidelines for consulting with police departments. The officer-shooting guidelines, a twelve-page document most recently updated in 2018, contain suggestions for investigation and emotional support for the officer involved. They draw on trauma literature and critical-incident protocols, focusing primarily on supporting the mental health of police officers involved in shootings.[55]

The first guidelines, issued in 1988, represent an initial argument about what psychological knowledge can contribute to the issue of police shootings. They were the first protocols offered as a best-practice psychological model for responding to police shootings. Throughout this initial set of guidelines, officers' feelings are centered. These guidelines warn against "harsh" treatment of officers involved in a shooting, stating that such treatment can cause a "second injury" of "emotional trauma." They note that "[d]ue to such treatment, many officers have left law enforcement prematurely, as victims."[56] In naming the second injury, the guidelines do not define the first injury, which could only be the injury to the officer of shooting and killing someone.

While enacting violence can certainly be traumatizing, it is notable that the person who was killed is not mentioned as a victim in these initial guidelines. When they are mentioned, it is as an abstract, dehumanized object: "the body." Administrators are cautioned to "get the officer away from the body." In arguing that the officer needs to be protected from "the body," the human being killed by the officer is posed as potentially threatening, even after death. In other words, police psychology practices outlined in these protocols carefully consider police officer's potential trauma, while ignoring the death and trauma of community members.

In 2016, the IACP published a longer, forty-six-page guidebook on responding to officer-involved shootings with the grant support of the U.S. Department of Justice's Community Oriented Policing Services. The 2016 *Officer-Involved Shootings: A Guide for Law Enforcement Leaders* states in its introduction that it "is intended to provide guidance for preparing officers and departments prior to an officer-involved shooting[. It suggests] incident scene actions and procedures, recommend[s] procedures for conducting criminal and administrative investigations, [provides] suggestions for working with the media, and [offers] mental health and wellness considerations and procedures."[57] The guidebook offers guidance "prior" to a shooting, but the guidance is not intended to stop the shooting from happening. Rather, it recommends procedures for managing this anticipated event.

Perhaps the most striking feature of the IACP guidebook is that it exists at all, signaling an acceptance and expectation that officers will continue to shoot people. On the *Guidebook*'s back cover, a small summary describes the importance of the guidebook:

> As the authors of this guide note, an Officer-Involved Shooting (OIS) is probably the most traumatic event a police officer will ever experience in his or her career. If the reaction to such an event is not handled properly, it can not only take an emotional toll on the individuals involved, but spark anger in the community and create negative fallout for the rest of the department. To provide practical guidance for handling the wide range of challenges that follow an OIS, the International Association of Chiefs of Police (IACP) and the COPS Office collaborated to produce this detailed report. A must-read for all law enforcement agencies, it provides incident command and investigation procedures, guidance for selecting mental health professionals for post-shooting debriefings, suggestions for familiarizing officers with their rights, recommendations for working with the media, and expert advice in many other areas.[58]

The description begins with an acknowledgement of the traumatic impact of police shootings on officers. It suggests that managing this traumatic event poorly can be a trigger for community anger and negative consequences for the department. The guide is marketed to law-enforcement leadership as a way to manage the event, promising that there is a way that police shootings of civilians can be handled properly. It centers mental health concerns and draws extensively on the officer-involved shooting guidelines previously issued by the Psychological Services Section of the IACP. While the summary and introduction initially note the impact of the shooting beyond the individual officer(s) involved, the mental health guidelines within the book are all focused specifically on the individual officers at the scene.

The guidebook consists of an introduction, five different sections, and a list of resources. The first three sections are arranged chronologically, discussing how to prepare one's police department in anticipation of a shooting at some point in the future, how to respond at the scene of the shooting, and how to lead a "post-incident investigation." The fourth section addresses "Officer Mental Health and Wellness."[59] It is followed by a brief discussion of managing media in the aftermath of a shooting. Citing the language of trauma, the guidebook warns that "if managed improperly, the post-event investigation can even exacerbate officer trauma and misinformation."[60]

Officers as Victims

The protocols extensively describe the psychological supports that should be made available to officers and their families, including both peer counseling and professional counseling supports. They also recommend investigation practices that will not "exacerbate officer trauma."[61] For example, they recommend running tests to determine whether the officer was intoxicated at the time of the shooting, but acknowledge that this process may feel like an implicit communication of wrongdoing. Here, the officer's status as evidence is mediated by empathic attention to their experience of the process and its impact on their well-being.

The guidebook suggests that the police officer, who may have his gun seized as evidence, be given a new replacement gun as soon as possible. This new firearm is framed as a form of protection against feelings of vulnerability and a communication of trust. "Officers may feel vulnerable if unarmed. Since the department must collect the officer's firearm as part of the investigation, the department should replace it promptly, as a sign of support, confidence, and trust."[62] The guidelines rely on the materiality of the gun to promote feelings of safety in officers. The loss of a gun is framed as a potentially traumatizing injury. In getting a gun back into the officer's possession as soon as possible, the protocols cannot imagine the possibility of the officer feeling okay without a firearm.

Recognizing that this might be a moment when officers feel betrayed by leadership, the guidelines also encourage top officials to speak with the officer to express concern and sympathy. This point seems to reflect an awareness that critiques of institutional practices and leadership can emerge from a shooting. The psychological protocols work to ensure that this critique does not emerge, by reassuring the officer that leadership is on their side.

The IACP guidelines also mandate an officer's consultation with a psychological professional in the aftermath of a shooting:

> [T]he department should place any involved officer on administrative leave pending counseling by an agency-designated mental health provider. This meeting and any subsequent meetings that may be deemed necessary are not an evaluation of fitness for duty, but a conversation regarding the officer's mental wellness.[63]

Mental health counseling for officers after the shooting is explicitly designated as confidential and "not an evaluation of fitness for duty." This clarification is necessary, in part, because of the use of fitness-for-duty evaluations as screening tools that promise to prevent such scenes of violence. In addition, it counters police officers' perceptions that being forced to talk to a "shrink" is a disciplinary measure or part of an investigatory process. The guidebook insists on separating the responsibilities of a psychologist supporting an officer after a shooting and the responsibilities of a fitness-for-duty assessor.

The handbook outlines several different stages of officer reaction to shooting someone. They include immediate reactions, cognitive and emotional reactions, behavioral reactions, and then finally, "acceptance resolution." In the last stage, "the officer understands and accepts what happened."[64] There is no space in this healing trajectory for ambivalence, for staying with the troubling feeling that things could have been otherwise. Yet the report notes that even in the acceptance-resolution stage, "it is normal to have the occasional nightmare, flashback, and anxiety attack."[65] Even as the officers' dreams point to ongoing terror, the official narrative of "acceptance resolution" reassures them and their departments that everything is resolved.

An alternate reading of these symptoms might be that the nightmares, dreams, and anxiety attacks reflect ongoing distress related to participation in state-sanctioned violence. This distress indicates neither acceptance nor resolution, but an unconscious mind working to understand, to connect, and to repair in the aftermath of terrible harm. Though officers are counseled to ignore the nightmares, the nightmares continue. In these sleeping moments, they are powerless to stop the dreaded repetition of violence. These terrible dreams might indicate that some officers continue to feel ambivalent about their participation in state violence. In the dream, there may also be a wish: to recognize and protect the vulnerable other, even as you feel yourself at risk; to break through repetitive violence into something new, something otherwise.

Missing Victims

The victims of police violence and their communities are almost completely absent from the IACP guidelines for responding to officer-involved shootings. Their families are mentioned only once in the forty-six-page guide, which warns that "[f]amily members, as well as some community groups, may challenge the officer's decision to use deadly force, and in some cases may initiate civil litigation."[66] Rather than being considered as grieving victims, family members of those shot by police are encountered as potential litigants, dangerous to the officer who shot their loved one. The report makes no recommendations for informing victim's families of the shooting, or of offering apologies to victims.

The word "victim" is only used six times. The first two mentions are in the context of public responses to the shooting, which the IACP task force notes might be influenced by the "age and mental condition of the victim" and "the race of the officer and the victim." They don't expand on how public responses may vary based on race, or what histories might inform those responses. The final four references to victims are in the context of investigating them.[67] No suggestions are made for treating victims in a trauma-informed manner. Reading the guidebook as something that claimed to be informed by trauma psychology, I was surprised by the protocol that demanded that the victim's clothes be removed and seized for evidence. "Often the shooting victim's clothes can provide evidence of the shooter's proximity to the victim, the position of the victim's arms (either up or down), the distance and trajectory of the shots fired, or the entrance and exit points."[68] While the clothes are a part of a crime scene, there is no consideration of ways to ameliorate the potential secondary traumas caused by police stripping a shooting victim.

Michael Brown's family members and other community members have publicly spoken out about the traumatic impact of the police leaving his body uncovered in the street for hours. Although his body was left in the street, his mother Lesley McSpadden was not permitted to go to him. She was kept away from her son, because for police, his body's status as evidence trumped her right to be near and to grieve for her son.[69] Yet these considerations—of the traumatic impact of police regulations around the body and interactions with family—are absent. The guidelines issue no recommendations about respectful treatment of deceased victims or present friends and family members who have just witnessed their loved ones' deaths. Poet Claudia Rankine considers this scene, asking, "How must it feel to a family member for the deceased to be more important as evidence than as an individual to be buried and laid to rest?"[70]

In the best-practice guidebook, which seeks to ensure that broken protocols are fixed, and which will be the basis of training, there is no attempt to overcome whatever circumstances lead to absolute disregard for the dignity and integrity of some people's bodies, before and after their death. Issued "prior" to the shooting, there is no sense that the shooting could be stopped. Nothing is mentioned about putting new training or new protocols in place with the goal of ensuring that shooting victims receive immediate first aid. Nothing is mentioned about the tension between gathering evidence and reverence for the life of the person who was shot. The entire guide centers around a person being shot. It is present at the scene of their death. And yet, any consideration of their life, their dignity, or of the people who love them is absent.

The focus on trauma to officers and their families overshadows other traumas resulting from the scene of violence. These include the trauma of those shot and killed by police, the suffering and grief of their families, friends, and communities, and the terror experienced by those for whom the incident serves as a powerful reminder of their loved ones' and their own vulnerability. The language of psychological science is used within a narrative in which violent police officers are allowed complex subjectivities and the victims of their violence are flattened and de-centered. These practices only acknowledge officers as victims, while ignoring their role as perpetrators. This is a partial version of trauma therapy, which ignores that healing from this kind of trauma often involves grappling with questions about one's own violence. As the IACP protocols demonstrate, engagement with psychological health risks around policing can be used to reinforce a narrative of heroic police bodies in danger, framing police as vulnerable protectors even as the bodies of their victims lie bleeding on the ground.

Scripts in Action

While the protocols provide a script, specific scenes of police violence give examples of how these scripts are enacted. For example, the psychological language around trauma was mobilized by one police officer in the aftermath of his 2015 shooting of Quintonio LeGrier and Bettie Jones. Both Chicago residents were shot dead by police officer Robert Rialmo as he responded to a 911 call. The nineteen-year-old college student LeGrier was holding a baseball bat and was in a state of extreme emotional distress. Rather than helping to calm him and facilitate his connection to psychiatric emergency services, the responding officer shot both LeGrier and his neighbor Jones, who was standing in her doorway. Following the shooting, the families of both Jones and LeGrier filed lawsuits for wrongful death. A countersuit against the LeGrier family by Rialmo claimed that the officer had experienced "extreme emotional trauma" as a result of the shooting.[71] Challenging narratives that he was a perpetrator, Rialmo's lawyer portrayed him as a traumatized victim, stating "he is just tremendously, you know, upset that LeGrier forced him to take an action that caused this innocent woman's death."[72] This blame-the-victim response is supported by police psychological practices that focus on the officer's emotional state and ignore the emotions and perspectives of everyone else in the police encounter.

The wrongful death suit filed by Bettie Jones's family was settled for $16 million by the City of Chicago. In the LeGrier family's wrongful-death suit, the jury awarded a $1.05 million award, which was immediately overturned by the judge on a technicality, leaving the family with no compensation. The jury also found in favor of Rialmo's countersuit against the LeGrier, but did not award him any money. Placed on desk duty after the shooting, and then unpaid leave, Rialmo was involved in two additional instances of documented physical violence after the shooting, including punching two people in a bar in a dispute over a jacket. He was charged and acquitted of misdemeanor battery for that incident in the summer of 2018, then charged in another bar fight days later.[73] In November 2018, a judge ordered that the gun Rialmo used to kill LeGrier be returned to him, as no criminal charges had been filed against him.[74]

Consistent with the guidelines' focus on police as victims, Rialmo was the beneficiary of a GoFundMe fundraising campaign for his legal defense, as well as a May 2019 fundraiser held at the Chicago Fraternal Order of

Police that involved a gun auction.[75] He was finally fired from the Chicago Police Department in October 2019, and lost his subsequent lawsuit to get his job back. Speaking after his 2018 acquittal, Rialmo was asked if he was "just unlucky" for finding himself in so many situations of violence. Rialmo responded, "I can't say that I'm unlucky at all. I can say that I've been put in some pretty bad situations that many guys wouldn't have been able to get out of safely and I feel . . . I'm lucky for that matter."[76]

In the summer of 2018, Betty Shelby offered a continuing-education seminar for Oklahoma police officers on "surviving the aftermath of a critical incident."[77] In the two years since she killed Terence Crutcher while he was unarmed on the side of the road, she had resigned from the Tulsa Police Department, taken a reserve deputy position in a neighboring town, and taught at least one National Rifle Association firearms class.[78] In 2017 she had been found "not guilty" of first-degree manslaughter, and a U.S. Department of Justice civil rights investigation into the shooting was ongoing. (It was concluded without charges the following year.)[79] In the training, Shelby described herself as a victim of what she names "the Ferguson Effect," which she describes as "when a police officer is victimized by anti-police groups and tried in the court of public opinion." Shelby promises to help other police officers survive and thrive.

As I read about the training, I wonder if Shelby believes she has reached the "acceptance/resolution" stage described in the IACP Officer-Involved Shooting guidelines. Her story is the successful outcome promised by the guidelines: an officer who quickly recovers, unquestioning of their own goodness, uncritical of leadership, and ready to be back on patrol. In contrast, a critical psychological approach to police shootings does not offer an acceptance/resolution stage. Rather, it acknowledges the violence at the center of U.S. policing and the harm done to everyone at the scene of a shooting. A "return to normal" is a return to ongoing violence. Placing this as the goal is a disservice to all involved. It treats the current reality of policing as the only possible reality.

Refusing Resolution

Turning to an earlier setting reminds us that state violence is constantly shifting, and that psychological professionals can have different roles within those shifts. In the final chapter of *The Wretched of the Earth*, Frantz Fanon reviews two case studies of his work with European police inspectors stationed in Algeria. Both of these men are involved in torturing the freedom fighters who are resisting the colonial state. In these brief vignettes, Fanon takes a different approach to the psychic life of policing than the one offered by the IACP. He recognizes the links between state violence and psychic suffering. Fanon's critique of the colonial regime serves as a resource for his patients. He is willing to imagine them as having the capacity to move beyond their function in colonial state violence.

In the first case study, the patient immediately indicates his wish to leave the work, stating, "Doctor, I'm sick of this job. If you can cure me, I'll request a transfer to France. If they refuse, I'll resign." Fanon agrees to treat him, initially putting him on a medical leave from his work as a police inspector. In his brief clinical vignette, Fanon describes this patient's encounter with someone he had tortured in his capacity as an inspector. Both are receiving psychiatric treatment, and the officer comes face to face with his victim on the hospital grounds. Seeing his victim within a setting in which they are equal, and contemplating the suffering of his victim, the police officer experiences an anxiety attack. Fanon remarks that afterward the client "makes great progress." Perhaps his encounter with the person he had harmed has something to do with this clinical progress—the details of the case study are sparse. Yet the fact remains, that in his space of treatment, the police inspector is forced to confront his role as a perpetrator of violence. Whatever happened subsequently in the clinic, the officer is unable to continue in his role. The patient leaves his position in the colonial regime and returns to France.[80] His psychic well-being is improved by leaving his role as a police inspector.

The second police patient presents for treatment with Fanon when his brutal violence at work leads to increasing violence at home toward his wife and children. The patient both knows and refuses to know that his participation in colonial violence is the cause of his suffering. "This man knew perfectly well that all his problems stemmed directly from the type of work conducted in the interrogation rooms, though he tried to blame everything on 'the troubles.'"[81] This client cannot accept that it is in his psychic interest to stop the work of embodying colonial state power, perhaps because it is in his economic interest to continue. Instead, he blames the "troubles"— projecting the cause of his violence onto the Algerians. And he asks Fanon to make him a better torturer: "He asked me in plain language to help him torture the Algerian patriots without having a guilty conscience, without any behavioral problems, and with a total peace of mind."[82]

U.S. police power has made a similar request of the field of psychology. Police psychologists, counselors, and other psychology professionals have answered with a range of techniques, best practices, and protocols. While they assume a neutral stance, their "psychology of racial innocence" masks active participation in racialized violence. Through their participation in the IACP Shooting guidelines, these psychological professionals offer to teach police how to do what Fanon refused to do for his patient: to wield state violence with absolute peace of mind. A critical psychology approach to the psychic life of policing suggests a different path: supporting people to divest from their psychic and relational investments in state-sanctioned violence.

CHAPTER 4

Manual

The Nonperformativity of Implicit-Bias Training

The first thing we get in the training is a white binder. The hotel conference center is all set up for a three-day train-the-trainers on implicit bias, and at each place at the table is a thick binder full of training materials. The training participants are all police officers, and except for me and one other woman, all are men, mostly white men, mostly wearing khakis and polo shirts. They are learning to lead implicit-bias trainings for their departments, using the binders full of materials as a teaching guide. These binders serve as shields from accusations of bias or inequity. They are binders full of the science of implicit bias.

In recent years, implicit-bias trainings have emerged as a popular strategy for teaching people to understand and respond to present histories of racism in the United States. These trainings promise to apply contemporary psychological research on bias to reduce racism and other forms of prejudice. They are presented as an effective, research-based strategy for guiding people to encounter, reflect on, and ultimately shift their own potential for biased action. In particular, the trainings have been offered to police departments as an effective psychological intervention to reduce racist actions by officers. In February 2018, the New York Police Department announced plans to implement implicit-bias training for all officers over the course of two years.[1] While many local and national leaders have called for implicit-bias trainings in all police departments, some on the Right have stood up against this emerging consensus.[2] In September 2020, President Trump issued an executive order to ban trainings that teach that people are biased—challenging a core assumption of implicit bias. President Biden signaled his support for the trainings and rescinded Trump's ban on his first day in office.[3]

I am here at this training because I am curious about the possibilities and pitfalls of these kinds of trainings, which bring in psychological research to moderate police violence. I can see how implicit-bias trainings might serve as a point of entry for police to begin to confront their role in systemic racism. At the same time, I agree with antiracist scholars and activists who say that the trainings are falsely presented as a "fix-it-all" solution, that they focus too much on individual change, and that the time and money would be better spent elsewhere.[4] In my efforts to understand more about the problems and potential of these trainings, I reached out to one of the largest organizations on implicit bias in policing, which emerged to meet the demand for implicit-bias training.[5] This organization allowed me to observe their train-the-trainers session, review the curriculum, and review participant feedback forms for over thirty trainings. I also analyze local news accounts and interviews, and review popular accounts of implicit bias recommended by the trainers.

Many critiques of implicit-bias training from the Left concede that it may challenge individual racist attitudes, but argue that individually focused solutions are an ineffective use of resources. However, in my fieldwork I found that there were moments in the training in which participants were coached into mindsets and behaviors that actively reinforced anti-Black racism. In this chapter, I examine a series of moments from these trainings when people seem to be simultaneously stating a commitment to antiracism and reinforcing anti-Black racism. Police departments use training in implicit bias to demonstrate opposition to racism, but the trainings are rooted in a psychology of racial innocence that also works to reinforce racism. Like the "penology of racial innocence" outlined by Naomi Murakawa and Katherine Beckett, this use of psychology emphasizes lack of intent to suggest innocence of racism. Implicit-bias research that emphasizes lack of conscious intent in biased actions is used to suggest that criminal legal systems are innocent of anti-Black racism.

As people use popular translations of psychology research to try to address racism, they can do so in ways that inadvertently reinforce antiblackness and white supremacy. This includes work that defines racism as an individual, inevitable human neurological process; that presents arguments that elevate scientific research over specific historical, community-based, or cultural knowledge; and that treats individual bias, gender bias, heterosexism, and racism as parallel and interchangeable. Instead of challenging violent police behavior, at times the trainings assume white innocence and Black and Latinx criminality, soothe guilt and shame related to racism, create confusion and hesitation about behaviors that would work against racism, shift explicit racisms toward dog-whistle racisms, and ultimately reinforce the authority of privileged white people to name and describe the world.

Whatever the flaws of the actual trainings, some might argue that they are an important first step that performs a commitment to ending racism. It is true that the trainings themselves are things that speak. The speech act of stating "we are confronting our implicit bias" can be considered performative in the sense that J. L. Austin articulated in How to Do Things with Words.[6] By having a workshop, the department can be seen as enacting its opposition to racism. When a police chief shows up to introduce this training, they communicate to their officers that the department opposes racial bias. Reporting on the trainings in local media often follows this logic—the performance of the training is celebrated as proof that departments are tackling racism.[7]

Sara Ahmed's concept of nonperformative speech acts suggests a different understanding of how implicit-bias trainings might work. In nonperformative speech acts, "the failure of the speech act to do what it says is not a failure of intent or even circumstance, *but is actually what the speech act is doing.*" The failure is the function. Nonperformative speech acts are "taken up *as if* they are performatives (as if they have brought about the effects they name) such that the names come to stand in for the effects."[8] The act of training and the possession of training materials stand in for acts that could reduce state-sanctioned anti-Black violence, protecting police departments from calls that they be disarmed and defunded. Becoming more aware of these nonperformances helps us to understand how psychological knowledge operates to supplement police power in the U.S.

Defining Racism as an Individual, Inevitable Human Psychological Process

The training begins with the assertion that racism is a feature of the human brain. This message is consistent with some popular literature on implicit bias, which frames human neuropsychological processes as the cause of criminal-legal-system inequities. In his best seller Blink, Malcolm Gladwell describes police decision-making in the police shooting of Amadou Diallou as an example of the universal brain process of "thinking without think-ing."[9] In *Unfair: The New Science of Criminal Injustice*, Adam Benforado describes racist legal outcomes as a phenomenon that requires Americans to "look into the deep recesses of our brains." Benforado recognizes that there is "grievous unfairness in our house of law," which he blames on "human psychology."[10] While both Benforado and Gladwell identify racial injustice as a problem, they locate the problem in typical human brain processes.

Continuing within this frame, the training asserts that police depart-ments are prone to bias "because they hire humans." The first section of the implicit-bias training reiterates this perspective repeatedly, emphasizing the neurobiological basis of implicit bias. This message works to minimize white and/or police shame, through an argument that racism is normal and universal, a natural process of the human mind.

In his critique of color-blind racism, Eduardo Bonilla-Silva says that naturalization is one of its central frames. He writes, "By suggesting these preferences are almost biologically driven and typical of all groups in soci-ety, preferences for primary associations with members of one's race are rationalized as nonracial."[11] The naturalization of racism marginalizes peo-ple whose life experiences led them to avoid developing biases or helped them to unlearn them. These life experiences can include being a person of color. They can also include experiences such as being a part of interracial families, relationships, workplaces, communities, and friendships; active engagement with a variety of cultural expressions; or participating in politi-cal movements opposed to racism or other forms of oppression through an intersectional lens. Naturalization also suggests that being able to see and notice one's own bias is a strange, unusual skill, one that flies in the face of the behaviors determined by the "deep recesses of our brains."

In suggesting that "all humans" are characterized by implicit racial biases, implicit-bias training centers socially segregated white experience as the model for what counts as human. It does this, not because it is writ-ten by humans, but because those developing the curriculum do not engage with contemporary theories of intersectional racism. Scholars in critical race and gender studies have called for theorizing social power relations from the margin, highlighted the construction of the category of "human" through the exclusion of blackness, and drawn attention to the specific historical role of police in maintaining gendered racism.[12] Their work critiques the idea that "racism is human" or that police racism is caused by human neurological structures. For example, if one recognizes that police work pushes humans into bureaucratic systems, categorization may be understood as a product of bureaucratic systems rather than human nervous systems.[13]

Because it is grounded in this claim of universality among all humans, the implicit-bias training has difficulty addressing the specificity of contemporary U.S. police racism. It fails to substantially address the specific tasks and work environments of police, and how these specific factors intersect with racism. Further, it offers a hopeless take on racism, failing to imagine the possibility of social worlds not structured through the concept of race. A singular focus on neurological processes nonperforms antiracism, because it underrepresents the possibility of social change and the history of the idea of race, encouraging resignation to the "fact" of racially biased brains.

Assumptions of Criminality

After presenting the idea that bias is human, the trainers run through a brief overview of social psychological concepts about biases and stereotypes. They then present a short clip from the 2004 Paul Haggis film *Crash* as a way to start a conversation around biases. The clip features Anthony and Peter, two young Black men played by actors Chris "Ludacris" Bridges and Larenz Tate. Anthony is complaining to Peter about biased treatment in the restaurant they just left. Walking down the street, the two men notice as a white couple moves away from them and the woman pulls her jacket closely around her. Anthony continues his critique:

> [T]his white woman sees two Black guys, who look like UCLA students, strolling down the sidewalk and her reaction is blind fear. I mean, look at us! Are we dressed like gang-bangers? Huh? No. Do we look threatening? No. Fact, if anybody should be scared around here, it's us: We're the only two Black faces surrounded by a sea of over-caffeinated white people, patrolled by the trigger-happy LAPD. So you tell me, why aren't we scared?

Peter responds, "Because we have guns?" and the two proceed to carjack the white couple. At this moment in watching the scene, the police trainees laugh. They had expected to get lectured about biases, and the scene surprises them. A trainer reinforces the intended takeaway with an accompanying PowerPoint slide: "Sometimes, stereotypes are true."

The training reads that moment in *Crash* as evidence of the truth of anti-Black stereotypes: the young Black men were being stereotyped as criminals, and they were criminals. The reading of the clip encouraged by the training emphasizes the truth of Black criminality. Rather than challenging all stereotypes, or working to end disproportionate impacts of policing on Black communities, trainers appeal to the idea that fact-based policing can be misperceived as racist.

This is in line with the logic of predictive policing, in which statistical practices are mobilized to legitimize the heavy policing of Black communities. According to this logic, the police are not stereotyping—they are responding to the objective truth of increased crime in these areas. Critics of predictive policing have argued that in these practices, Black and Latinx people are never seen as innocent; instead, they are always already assigned "increased risk" as a result of historical and ongoing practices of racist criminalization by police, which the statistical predictions then replicate.[14]

The training goes on to discuss how, even when they are usually true, stereotypes can be dangerous. Yet the trainers have already endorsed the link between blackness and criminality as true. They do nothing to convey the dangers of flattening people's complex lives into stereotypic descriptions, except to note that *sometimes* the stereotypes are wrong. This overlooks how stereotypes portray people as objects (rather than subjects) of knowledge, flatten their experiences, and ignore their agency. Treating a person as a caricature is always untrue.

In this setting, a different text could open different conversations. Reading Gayl Jones's novel *Eva's Man*, literary scholar Hershini Young highlights the refusal of police and other legal discourse to engage meaningfully with Black women's complex lives. She discusses one Black woman's decision not to confess to a crime:

> Part and parcel of Eva's refusal to explain herself to the police are the clichéd explanatory responses that her actions would elicit, no matter what Eva might say about them. In other words, even if Eva were to speak, she would not be heard. The interpretation for her crime by the criminal justice system would diminish the complexity of her actions as a Black woman, always already infantilized, sexualized, and criminalized.[15]

Eva does not speak, because even when she does speak her voice is distorted by police expectations. Police choose the "easiest answer they could get" instead of trying to imagine the complexity of her life. Similarly, even as Anthony and Peter speak, their critiques of racial profiling are not heard. Instead, their revealed status as "criminals" is used to disqualify their authority on the criminalization of blackness. The laughter of the training group reveals their delight in "knowing" Anthony and Peter's status: black criminals whose behavior can be interpreted without engaging their words and worldviews.

Throughout the implicit-bias training, I also witnessed attempts to communicate the humanity of Black and Latinx people by suggesting that they might also be cops. In one story, trainers discuss an undercover cop getting shot by police; in another, they discuss an off-duty cop getting pulled over while on vacation upstate. This attempt to connect with cops through the possibility that the person they are encountering might be an undercover or off-duty cop seemed to be a strategic choice. It is an attempt to begin the process of unsettling racist expectations. However, it fails to address the idea that Black and Latinx people who are not cops deserve to be treated as criminals or killed. Rather, it divides people into populations of deserving and undeserving, linking expressions of Black culture to criminality and automatic guilt. Black cops are treated as occasional outliers to the assumed fact of Black criminality.

Giving Up Explicit Racisms for Dog-Whistle Racisms

One "case study" discussed in the training involved a 911 call in which the caller reported a suspicious person, whose only suspicious behavior was being a Black man sitting in a car in a white neighborhood—which they labeled a "race out of place" complaint. The trainers had just led a discussion of the danger of "profiling by proxy"—police responding to citizen complaints that are purely race-based. This seemed to be a clear place to state the absolute necessity of refusing to participate in the caller's assumption of Black criminality.

Yet in discussing how to respond to the call, the officers present were not willing to state "Just don't respond" or to name the call as "profiling by proxy." Instead, they discussed ways to coach the caller to identifying non-

race-based suspicious characteristics. They entertained the possibility of
sending a car to do a "drive-by" without stopping or explicitly questioning
the Black man, or perhaps checking in with the "suspicious" man to "see if
he was okay"—perhaps lying that he had been reported as unconscious in
his car. Rather than responding negatively to explicit racism, they brain-
stormed strategies to move their actions toward more "implicit" racism,
and thus perfectly innocent and excusable. Rather than challenging racist
practices, the exercise served to coach officers in how to shift expressions of
explicit racism into colorblind racist language, which would have a racist
impact but could be attributed to other factors.

A review of the training agenda suggests that the message "don't engage
in profiling by proxy" is the intended takeaway of this section of the training. The training materials serve as proof that they have learned about this
phenomenon. Yet in action, it transformed into a coaching session for
masking explicit racism. The impact of those racist police actions on the
person being profiled was not considered.

Disorganizing Antiracist Behavioral Prescriptions

Another way that the training nonperforms antiracism is through avoiding
clear behavioral directives. Instead, it offered mixed messages about potential behavior changes. Learning "the science" becomes the action taken,
rather than the action of refusing to engage in profiling, or shifting departmental control to the community, or disarming officers.

Part of the training curriculum contains a slowed-down encounter
between undercover police and a person they deem "suspicious." At the end
of the exercise, in which the officers were able to identify the "correct" set of
actions that avoided use of force, the trainers reveal that the case follows the
fact pattern of the Amadou Diallo shooting. The moral of the story, as presented by trainers, was this: slow down. They suggested that biased assumptions might be usefully overcome if officers were able to gather more information, as opposed to operating based on quick observations and
assumptions that tend toward bias. In this case example, the training acts
out Malcolm Gladwell's discussion of the Diallo case in *Blink*.

The next day, presenting the "new science" about implicit-bias tests, the
trainers stated that there is "a very interesting new study" coming out. They

described it as the "reverse racism effect" study, and explained that it is so new that it had not been included in the earlier sections of the training. The trainer reviewed the study's claim, which is that in shooter simulations, there was a slight delay in officers shooting Black suspects with guns.[16] The trainer summarizes the research by noting the threat to officers posed by this supposed new bias against shooting Black people: "This hesitation—may cost lives." Black people are described as getting an extra break—a few undeserved seconds of consideration that white suspects don't get. Replicating the biases of the study, the trainers suggest that these extra seconds translate into police deaths. The lives of Black people being shot by police are not considered.

One participant, clearly confused, asks, "But doesn't that go against what we learned yesterday?" He cites the "slow down" exercise. The trainer responds, "Well, we just want you to have the science. We'll be watching this and see what develops. Our goal is that you have the science."

One of the main messages of the training, "slow down, think about what you're doing, and question if it's linked to bias," has just been undermined. Instead, officers are given the opposite message: "Don't slow down to think, because then you might die." The muddle of conflicting "science" leaves officers with no clear message about how to actively avoid racist actions. At the same time, it tells them that their own racism is inevitable and natural.

I hear the participant's question as one concerning the larger point of the training—he appears to be trying to figure out how to translate his learning into action. In the face of this request, the trainers have no recommendations. This part of the training counteracted research findings about the benefit of engaging people with clear strategies to counter implicit bias.[17] In a 2012 study by Patricia Devine, Patrick Forscher, Anthony Austin, and William Cox, the "prejudice habit-breaking intervention" instructed participants in five strategies to use to reduce racial bias, including stereotype replacement, counterstereotypic imaging, individuation, perspective-taking, and increasing opportunities for positive contact, and found that engaging in them led to long-term reductions in racial bias.[18]

At this moment in the training, the trainers' spontaneous statement about the goal of the training shifts from the official goal of transforming implicit bias in behavior. The goal is stated instead as giving scientific authority to officers—"Our goal is that you have the science."

Alleviating Guilt and Shame around Racist Actions

The training functions according to the principle that shame and guilt are not helpful states for learning. It normalizes biased beliefs and actions, seeking to put participants at ease. According to feedback forms, it appears to succeed at this task. In participants' reviews of the trainings, the "guilt-free" nature of the training was emphasized. One wrote, "It was refreshing to discuss these topics without being told how bad cops are."[19] At one university police training, these views were repeated: "It was a no judgement zone. The way it was done promoted openness and prevented defensiveness." Part of how the trainings address guilt was through naturalizing bias throughout the population, as reflected by one review: "Deals with the root cause—human nature."[20] Another participant wrote that the training "explains how each person has bias in them even if they don't realize it." Another put it more simply, "I really thought this class was gonna suck. But it didn't suck!!!"[21] And others: "Wasn't what I expected"; "Didn't allow political correctness to hinder the training."[22]

Yet the pedagogical strategy of reducing shame may diminish people's motivation to take action. A recent research study found that a strong negative affect associated with awareness of one's previous biased behaviors predicts reduction of those behaviors. After being made aware that they had been stereotyping others, negative self-directed feelings such as guilt and shame motivated participants to work hard to avoid stereotyping.[23] This may seem intuitive—if we feel bad about doing something, we try hard not to do it again. This is one of the primary social functions of embarrassment and shame; feeling these emotions reduces the odds that we will do the same things again. In Melanie Klein's work, she highlights that the capacity to feel guilt is an accomplishment. It helps people move forward toward attempts at relational repair and allows them to live with an un-dissociated awareness of their capacity to do harm in the future.

By relieving feelings of guilt, the training may further demotivate participants to take antiracist actions. In the participant feedback form from one 2015 police department training, one participant wrote, "the fact that we could admit to some bias was actually a relief." This feeling of relief and comfort by participants is cited over and over again as a mark of success.

The Elevation of Scientific Knowledge

This implicit-bias training centers psychological experts and marginalizes communities of color. This marginalization makes it possible for participants to conclude that Black communities are ignorant of the scientific dynamics of racism, and that they have no specialized knowledge of how police racism operates. The training fails to grapple with the obvious: police have been sent to this implicit-bias training because of a pattern of racist police violence in the U.S. today. It distances participants from that reality.

The training omits any specific discussion of the role of police in maintaining contemporary racist inequalities, instead working hard to reinforce the idea that police departments are only racist "because they hire humans." There is some research basis for the claim that police officers are not more racist that other people in the U.S. For example, Joshua Correll found that, compared to police officers, community members had more racial bias in making decisions to shoot suspects in video game simulations.[24] However, highlighting this research in the absence of an in-depth discussion of the history and present racist impact of the criminal legal system offers no space for officers to grapple with ways that police power is specifically racist. This omission nonperforms anti-racism, obfuscating historical and community-based knowledge of police racism. The training curriculum's only admission of the historical realities of police racism was one slide, which showed a black-and-white photograph of cops with dogs attacking civil rights activists, followed by a picture of a news article about the Stonewall Riot. In talking about the slide, the trainer emphasized that historically, cops had supported racist Jim Crow laws in their role as law enforcers. The problem was posed, not as the specific use of police power against Black communities, but rather as the fact that police were historically tasked with enforcing unjust laws. The unjust past is contrasted with the colorblind present.

Far from situating police departments as especially involved in racism, the training leads some to the conclusion that police might have expert knowledge on antiracism.[25] Participants suggested that the training might usefully teach people in local communities about racism: "[T]his should be pushed out into the communities." Some police participants thought that Black community members might be less likely to accuse police of racism after being taught that implicit bias is universal and natural. "The class also teaches not to automatically accuse an officer of something. Let them explain it."[26] The training organization further reinforces this perception by leading "command-community" trainings in which community members, local NAACP officials, and police leadership are trained side by side in the science of bias. This training encourages the idea that "both sides" of police encounters need more education about racial bias. Rather than leading the training, the local NAACP leadership is positioned as needing to be educated about racism alongside police.[27]

Failures to Adopt an Intersectional Lens

In media accounts, the bias training was often presented as an antiracist initiative. Yet in the training, trainers rarely used the term "racism," interchangeably presenting examples of bias based on race, gender, sexual orientation, occupation, and personal taste, with no connection to differential social power or oppression. For example, one trainer spoke about the perception that she, as a woman police officer, would be more likely to be gay. She then shared that she was happily married to a man. Others spoke about the danger of assuming that women are less likely to be violent than men, sharing examples of times when petite women acted with surprising force in police encounters. The one training moment that addressed the historical reasons for fear of police presented both anti-LGBT and anti-Black policing as interchangeable. Showing slides of Jim Crow and Stonewall, the trainers suggest that both situations of police discrimination ended when the law changed. At one point, participants were encouraged to name biases against cops—that they all like donuts, or that they're all uneducated. In addition to treating different biases as interchangeable, this activity, like the example from the heterosexual officer unfairly assumed to be a lesbian, reinforces the idea that it is cops who are often the "true victims" of bias.

Discussing the NYPD implicit-bias trainings, trainer Noble L. Wray insists that "the 800-pound gorilla in the room is racial bias."[28] While racism may be the implicit main point of the training, the training's singular focus on the overarching concept of "bias" limits the discussion of racism. "Bias" is a term used to reflect individual prejudice. As a term, it can be unlinked from systems and specific historical contexts. It lends itself to a practice of discussing personal preferences divorced from social, economic, and institutional structures. In contrast, "racism" is a term that reflects the context of social systems organized by race. For example, Ruth Wilson Gilmore's definition of racism centers on its material impact on the lives and bodies of those it targets, as "group-differentiated vulnerability to premature death."[29] This definition highlights the violence of racism, its production and exploitation of vulnerability to death. Focused on racism as it impacts material bodies in political geographies, this definition contrasts sharply with definitions of bias that limit inquiry to individual thoughts and feelings.

Reinforcing the Authority of White People

At one point in the training, we broke into small groups around separate round tables. Participants took the opportunity to refill their coffee and grab a late-morning snack. I sat at a table with a small group of white men, their ages ranging from mid-twenties to mid-thirties. One officer turned to me, the observing grad student, with a question. "Have you or your friends ever experienced bias from cops?" We are both eating breakfast pastries. I sip on my coffee, feeling that the question is a test. It seems strange that this white man is asking me, a white woman, about my experiences of bias. This may be linked to the frame of bias, which shifts attention away from an explicit discussion of race toward any form of difference.

I tell him, truthfully, that I have not experienced racial profiling, and I note that police have always acted respectfully in their interactions with me. I also share that a friend has been repeatedly followed and questioned by a cop on the campus where she teaches, and it seems to be a fairly obvious case of racial profiling. She is Black, her white colleagues are not experiencing the same scrutiny, and only one officer is repeatedly profiling her. I expect him to acknowledge that the cop in question is being inappropriate, but to emphasize that this scenario is an exception—a "bad apple."

The interaction doesn't play out as I expect. The officer looks at me incredulously. "That's it? He's following her? That's his job." He presses for clarification, "Did he say something racist to her?" I explain that verbal disrespect isn't necessary for it to be harassment—he is clearly singling her out because of her race. Her white colleagues are not being followed. The officer scoffs, "But that's nothing. That's not a case." He ends the conversation abruptly, turning away to talk to his colleagues at the table.

The officer could not or would not understand the harms in the scenario

I was describing. Meanwhile, I couldn't make sense of his inability to see from my friend's perspective. At that moment, there was what psychologist Derald Sue has called "a clash of racial realities"—my friend had seen the racism, but the officer could not.[30] To him, the officer who harassed my friend was clearly innocent. He was imagining the "case" against that officer, noting its weaknesses. Throughout the implicit-bias training, he hadn't been asked to try to imagine things from my friend's perspective, what it was like for her to feel her body marked as suspicious in her daily place of work. In the course of two and a half days, he had only further consolidated his sense of expertise, his sense that his point of view was authoritative and that his actions would therefore be just.

It is significant that the facilitators are almost entirely current or retired police who hold positions of leadership within their departments. It is likely that everyone in the room during an implicit-bias training will be a police officer. This training structure is based on the idea of using credible messengers: police are assumed to be more open to learning challenging material when it is delivered by "one of them." Participants repeatedly cited the use of officers to facilitate as an important strength of the training. One participant commented that the training "would not be as well received from civilian instructors."[31] However, if the goal is learning how to consider the experiences of people who are racially and culturally different, the choice of police trainers and the police-only attendance provide limited practice in this relational skill. While trainers may be BIPOC, the majority of officers in the room are white. The training repeatedly flatters these officers' ability to serve as experts on racism, now that they have the science.

Implicit-bias trainings for police sound like a good idea—teaching police directly to confront their own unconscious racism. In practice, the training contained a number of moments that undermined this stated purpose, and even went against recent research in the field of implicit bias. The moments I have identified are a partial list of ways to nonperform antiracism. They emptied out the potential of the workshops to spark action, transforming the seminars into hollow monuments to institutional good intentions. Not just ineffective, these trainings can harm the project of stopping anti-Black police violence, working to strengthen police departments in the face of calls to defund and disarm. In terms of individual officers, they are encouraged to sink further into a sense of their own power and expertise, increasing their sense of themselves as unfairly maligned "good guys."

At one moment in the training, an officer pushes back against the frame being provided. On the final day, during a moment for questions, this participant awkwardly begins to speak, apologizing for the fact that his question might not be appropriate, but that he needed to ask it. He cites his interest in training models that elevate the sanctity of human life. He poses the question to the group, reflecting on his own explorations for a way to shift his department's violent culture and his own process of searching and not being sure. As he asks, he is hesitant, questioning, and anything but expert. He wonders if talking about ethics might provide answers and pathways to action that social sciences cannot. Maybe it's not about science, but about emphasizing how to treat other people, how to value their lives.

His questions hang in the air, unsettling the sense of closure and celebration. He has posed a question that the training, up to now, has elided: what is your stance on the value of other people's lives? In asking the question, he refuses the role of the expert that is being passed on to him, and highlights the emptiness of these binders. The trainers interrupt and redirect back to the implicit-bias literature, suggesting that this is a more effective path, because it's scientific. This was a brief moment of intense feeling and questioning, and the trainers offer quick solutions. Still, the feeling of uncertainty lingers.

CHAPTER 5

Museum

Heroic Fantasies at the American Police Hall of Fame

The American Police Hall of Fame and Museum (APHFM) in Titusville, Florida, is a short drive from Orlando. I zip down the highway in my rental car, enjoying light midweek traffic, Top 40 radio, and sunshine. I pass the exit to Disney World and continue on, following signs pointing toward the Kennedy Space Center. It's an American landscape: astronauts, Mickey Mouse, and open roads. As I approach the Space Center, Highway 405 becomes the NASA Causeway. The police museum is just off the highway. It is a large off-white complex surrounded by parking lots and palm trees.

I am visiting the APHFM to try to understand the growing phenomenon of police museums. The APHFM advertises itself as "the nation's first national police museum and memorial dedicated to law enforcement officers killed in the line of duty." For the United States's first, it is a young museum—founded in 1960.[1] Since that time, over 100 police museums have been established in forty-two U.S. states. Most have opened since 1980. They are located in geographically and demographically diverse sites: Hartford, Connecticut; Albany, Georgia; Burbank, California; Bangor, Maine; Denver, Colorado; Tampa, Florida; Detroit, Michigan; New York, New York; Honolulu, Hawaii; Des Moines, Iowa; and Cleveland, Ohio.[2] Expanding the frame to North America, there are museums in Vancouver, British Columbia (opened 1986); Toronto, Ontario (opened 1988); Montreal, Quebec (opened 1992); Winnipeg, Manitoba; Guadalajara, Jalisco; and two in Mexico City.[3] One recent addition to the wave of police museums is a national museum in Washington, DC, which opened in fall 2018 next to the National Law Enforcement Officers Memorial. While other police museums in the U.S. tend to focus on the history of individual police departments, reflecting a sense of policing as a local endeavor, the DC

The American Police Hall of Fame. Photo credit: Thomas Kelley/Alamy Stock Photo.

museum and the APHFM are both national museums, presenting a history of law enforcement across the country.

Police museums and memorials are sites where the expanding carceral state and expanding public memory practices intersect. They shape public perceptions of police work and reveal institutional narratives of police history and precarity. Affective relationships to policing are reflected in and shaped by the construction of the exhibits, and by the formal and informal rituals that occur at these sites. Police museums expanded rapidly over a time period in which police presence increased, prison populations grew astronomically, and police were outfitted with new military technologies. Their collections point toward the expansive reach of police culture, as well as its breadth.

Visiting the museum, I am immersing myself in its celebration of policing. In doing so, I am trying to understand more about how my own psychic world has been shaped by policing. The museum, like my consulting room, provides a material location for thinking about memory and feelings. But within the museum, these operations are not simple. Robert Buffington writes that Mexican police museums destabilize ideas about the role of museums in memory. Rather than reminding a forgetful present about a forgotten past, they "seek to obliterate a too-well-remembered past that troubles the present."[4] Within this Florida police museum, I am looking for the stories that are being told and omitted about police power—the fantasies about goodness, belonging, and heroism, and the ghosts that haunt its exclusions and erasures.

Organization of the Hall of Fame

At the entrance to the museum is a sign: "STOP: POLICE CHECKPOINT." It is the station to pay to enter the museum, staged as a police encounter. Though the museum is open to all, the checkpoint communicates a welcome to those who feel comfortable playing with the markers of police power. It is a space for those who can walk toward a police checkpoint without panic. At the checkpoint, the museum staff establishes what you owe. In 2020, the pricing structure was $13 for adults, $10 for military and senior citizens, $8 for children age four to twelve, $5 for law enforcement officers, $2 for surviving family members of officers who have died, and free for children under four.[5] The payment structure encourages all attendees to situate themselves in relation to what they've contributed to the project of policing. Police officers get a big discount because of their work, and this discount is extended even further to their surviving families after death. This likelihood, that police will die heroic deaths, is highlighted from the very moment of entry. Those with less proximity to police work pay more.

From the front entrance, I can see that the museum has several distinct components: exhibits, gift shop, memorial, and gun range. The small gift-shop area is to the left of the check-in counter. At the center of the main hall is the memorial, surrounded with hallways of exhibits. A small room is marked as the chapel. About thirty feet to the right of the entrance is a door that leads over to the indoor shooting range. You can both grieve a deceased officer and do target practice, a combination of activities encouraged through the pricing structures for the museum. For $40, visitors can purchase both museum/memorial admission and a visit to the on-site gun range. The website reassures, "Range Safety Officers are on hand to oversee that everyone stays safe—and to provide guidance and support when needed."[6] Visitors can mourn heroic cops in the memorial, learn about state technologies of violence in the museum, step into the role of the first-person shooter in the gun range, and buy products to mark their affiliation with and support for police power in the gift shop.

Within the museum are a variety of loosely organized exhibits. They include replicas of prison cells, execution tools, statistics about crime, information about famous criminals, and a wall containing "Officer of the Year" plaques. A number of exhibits blur the distinction between fantasy and reality. There are props from police movies alongside guns used in the field, educational displays about counterfeit money, and another display on how similar toy guns look to real guns.[7] A children's section features McGruff the Crime Dog, dress-up items, and puppets. Police department uniform patches from various cities are hung floor to ceiling in several different sections of the museum. They line the walls on the way to the bathrooms and hallways between the separate exhibits. A series of police vehicles includes both historical and contemporary cars and motorcycles. There are displays that highlight less-typical police transport: bicycles, snowmobiles, off-road vehicle, and boats. A dystopian fantasy future is also present—the police car from the movie *Blade Runner*.

In the museum gift shop is a range of products that name the museum or indicate support for law enforcement. I am drawn to a bin of rubber duckies. They are outfitted in a variety of police costumes—a highway-patrol cop ducky with a motorcycle helmet and reflective sunglasses; a cop ducky with a navy-blue shirt and a classic peaked cap; a state-trooper ducky with a mint-colored button-down shirt, brown tie, and brown-brimmed campaign hat. The SWAT-team ducky has a bulletproof vest, tactical helmet, and goggles. Like the "police checkpoint," these are tools for carceral fantasy. My favorite is the SWAT-team ducky—I am drawn to the stark contrast between a sweet rubber ducky and the terrifying image of a SWAT officer. It is a visual gag about military terror made domestic, bringing fantasies of inevitable violence into bath time, juxtaposing the racist histories of "cleaning up the streets" with the racist histories of hygiene campaigns. It casts the cop as an object of fantasy play.

Fantasies of Policing

The fantasies presented in this museum can help explain widespread attachment to U.S. police culture. Hollywood representations of policing technologies and the actual technologies of U.S. policing intermingle, encour-

Police rubber ducks. Photo credit: author.

aging attendees to engage with and think about policing through their own consumption of television and cinematic fantasy, anticipating dystopian futures and fantastic violence. Jacqueline Rose calls participation in fantasy the "psychic glue" that attaches people to the state.[8] Within the museum, different fantasies about state and interpersonal violence layer: there is a display of a gas chamber visible from between the memorial walls; displays describing serial rape and murder are followed by a police puppet and dress-up corner for children. Fictional cop characters such as Dirty Harry and RoboCop mingle with real historical criminals such as Al Capone and "Pretty Boy" Floyd.

Dirty Harry's signature gun from the movie franchise is on display. The gun is a Smith & Wesson Model 29 with a .44 Magnum cartridge. Dirty Harry refers to it in the film as "the most powerful handgun in the world." In the museum it is presented with a label that reads "GO AHEAD . . . MAKE MY DAY!" The movie prop and quote act as scripts for engaging in fantasies of police power. It is a script brought into the national political discourse through Ronald Reagan's use of the phrase, "Go ahead, make my day!" in celebrating his potential exercise of executive veto power.[9] It is echoed in Donald Trump's adoption of the flawed action-hero role; Trump jokes about shooting someone on Fifth Avenue and brags that he is "locked and loaded."[10]

The Dirty Harry fantasy is linked to a simultaneous disavowal and celebration of masculine white-supremacist power. American Studies scholar Michael Rogin notes that the "Make my day!" quote is from a scene in *Sudden Impact*, the fourth movie in the "Dirty Harry" franchise. In the movie, detective Harry Callahan invites a Black man to "go ahead" and shoot a white woman hostage, giving him justification to kill the man, which would "make [his] day." In the scene, Callahan's casual expression of his pleasure in killing calms the situation; the man releases his hostage and is arrested. In an article published seven years after the release of the hit movie, Rogin reports that among thousands of people that he questioned, only one person remembered the racial context of the scene. The absence of race and gender from people's memory of the scene points to a form of political amnesia, "a cultural structure of motivated disavowal."[11]

The white hero is remembered; the context that produced him is buried[. . . .] In the American myth we remember, men alone risk their lives in equal combat. In the one we forget, white men show how tough they are by resubordinating and sacrificing their race and gender others.[12]

The museum similarly reinforces the American myth of (largely white and male) police heroes risking their lives, whereas the disavowals lead to gaps in the museum. Missing from the displays are discussions of U.S. settler colonialism, racism, slavery, Jim Crow, and mass incarceration. Museum scholar Barbara Kirschenblatt-Gimblett writes that a museum is always "defined by gaps (gaps in the record, gaps in the collection, gaps in the narrative) and by leaps (intuitive leaps, poetic leaps, leaps of faith)."[13] The specifics of those gaps and leaps define the character of the museum. Racial thinking is both ever-present and unrepresented—it serves as the constitutive absence around which fantasies of state violence and individual heroism are oriented.

Psychoanalyst D. W. Winnicott makes a distinction between what he terms "fantasying" and the alternate activities of playing and dreaming. While dreaming and playing are engaged with life, fantasying exists as a form of dissociation, of not knowing or engaging with aspects of lived experience. In fantasying, omnipotence is retained, and "what happens happens immediately, except it does not happen at all." Unlike dreams, which are dynamic, the fantasies remain static, an isolated phenomenon. While dreaming and play can serve as a way of thinking, communicating, and exploring, fantasy runs on dissociated loops with scripts that do not change.

The phenomenon of fantasying in the museum is similar to what Marita Sturken has called the "tourist relationship to history." Sturken writes that this is a relational stance that "allows Americans to feel distanced from global politics and world events, and to see our role in them as separate and exceptional." This approach "disavows the impact of our often destructive and brutal policies, and maintains an innocence about them [and] provides the means for consumer-citizens to feel 'authentically' close to traumatic events while also feeling innocent and detached."[14] Throughout the museum, the story presented about policing mingles fantasy and reality, through invocations of fictional police characters and opportunities to pretend at policing. In addition to the gun range, interactive activities in the museum encourage people to take on a police role, making sketches of subjects or looking through night-vision goggles. In the play area, children can dress up in a variety of police uniforms and practice calling 911. The museum activates fantasy worlds around violence and safety. These worlds are partial; they have puzzling leaps in logic and missing information.

Anticipatory Memorial

The APHFM bills itself first as a "Hall of Fame"—a reference to the memorial. Unlike other halls of fame, which induct new members through a voting process among experts in the field, the American Police Hall of Fame can only be entered in one way: by dying in the line of duty. The memorial serves as the center and heart of the museum, with exhibits spinning out around it.

I walk through the cars to get to the memorial, and then realize that they're also a part of a memorial project. One white police car from the Fort Worth Police Department is covered in black sharpie signatures. A sign on the dash indicates that it is the Officer Hank Nava Memorial Car. A 2004 Ford Crown Victoria, it was the service vehicle of an officer killed in the line of duty in 2005. The vehicle was put on display following his death and covered with signatures from coworkers, community members, and family. The brief messages speak of grief, faith, and thanks: "Thank you for all that you have done"; "May God Bless You"; "R.I.P. Hank"; and a child's scrawl, "I whill miss you."

Walking into the memorial, I look up at the white stone entrance arch, emblazoned with the aphorism, "Good Men and Women Must Die, But Death Cannot Kill Their Names." I am struck by the present imperative. The quote suggests that there are more losses to come, and that these losses are neither optional nor problematic. "Good Men and Women Must Die." Police death is framed as inevitable. They've made the saying, which traditionally features only men, inclusive by adding in "women." The phrase "good men and women" links their goodness to a performance of gender. Police work promises a version of everlasting life—"death cannot kill their names."

The memorial begins with a marble half-wall featuring the APHFM crest. Resting on top of the wall is a box of tissues. The tissue box serves as a scriptive object: this is a place for crying. At the same time, it can suggest a prohibition on messy grief: clean yourself up. On each side extend marble walls engraved with the names of officers killed in the line of duty. The memorial architecture encourages visitors to pass through without long pauses. There are no benches or chairs for sitting and contemplating the names. I walk through it, my footsteps soft on the industrial carpet, scanning the thousands of names. Underneath their names, on the floor, are framed photographs of the officers or their families, along with poems and plastic flowers.

The names do not take up the same amount of space on all of the walls. Some cover about one-third of the available space, some a bit less. Names are being continually added to the walls, and there are large empty spaces on the walls underneath the names. This is the space for the "good men and women" who will die, whose deaths the memorial anticipates. During the mid-May Police Memorial Week, that year's fallen officers are recognized with a memorial service, roll call of their names, and twenty-one-gun salute.[15]

At the very center of the memorial is the Tomb of the Unknown Peace Officer. A marble slab shaped like a coffin is draped in an American flag. On the front of the marble is the inscription: "Dedicated to the unknown peace officer," and a Bible quote: "Blessed are the peacemakers, for they shall be called children of God." The marble coffin is ringed with funerary wreaths. In front of the flag-draped coffin, a statue of a police officer with his arms around a boy and girl presents the image of a fatherly protector—one who has presumably been lost. Rather than referring to the officer as "police," he is named as a "peace officer," suggesting a pairing with the military officer involved in the business of war.

The unknown peace officer clearly invokes the Tomb of the Unknown Soldier, a memorial at Arlington National Cemetery established to honor unknown soldiers from World War I whose remains could not be identified.[16] In his study of nationalism, Benedict Anderson writes that unidentified soldiers' tombs have been constructed in a number of countries as emblems of nationalism. "[V]oid as these tombs are of identifiable mortal remains or immortal souls, they are nonetheless saturated with ghostly national imaginings."[17] In grieving for the unknown lost soldiers, the nation is unified.

The Tomb of the Unknown Peace Officer sets the scene for a funeral or a viewing, encouraging visitors to fantasize about themselves at the funeral. If visitors are not yet grieving their own losses, they can imagine grieving heroic deceased officers, perhaps informed by beloved movie and television characters. Police are positioned as protectors of the imagined community of the U.S., protecting not against invading armies, but against an invasion of crime. The tomb suggests that policing is best understood as a service to the nation, rather than just a job. While other occupations—roofing, construction, landscaping, and farming—are more likely to lead to death, police death at work is presented as a sacrifice on the front lines of an endless national war against crime.[18] And yet the police memorial is distinct from the war memorial in its anticipatory nature. Every year, new names are added to the memorial. The coffin seems to stand in not so much for those who have died, but for all the deaths that are anticipated.

Alongside the tomb and the memorial, a "Prayer for Peace Officers" again stresses the vulnerability of currently serving police, asking God to watch over all officers:

Father in Heaven please give them the strength, courage, and perseverance to endure the unjust condemnation, danger, and physical abuse to which they are at times subjected. We recommend them to your loving care because their duty is dangerous.

The prayer anticipates that more will die, and presents them as already enduring a range of violence at the hands of unidentified perpetrators. This spectrum of violence includes "unjust condemnation, danger, and physical abuse." Anyone who participates in these activities, including condemning anti-Black police violence, is framed as contributing to officer death.

In addition to remembering and memorializing death, this space predicts harm and death. It is simultaneously a memorial and an "anticipatorial." The "ghostly national imaginings" about policing collapse time, and each police officer is overlaid with the aura of their future heroic death.[19] The space anticipates a continuing social order of ongoing death. The idea of looming "bad guys" has been identified as a pervasive component of police cultures. Sociologist Jerome Skolnick identified the common figure of the "symbolic assailant"—an imagined other who represents the potential for deadly violence, and whose shadow follows the officer through their work.[20] The perceived constant threat of danger from the symbolic assailants "requires the police officer [. . .] to live in a world straining toward duality, and suggesting danger when 'they' are around."[21] This split is reflected in language that divides the world into citizens and "dirt-bags."[22] While Skolnick defines police culture narrowly, the figure of the symbolic assailant is strong throughout U.S. political cultures. Michael Rogin refers to this phenomenon as political demonology—a political tradition "dominated by splitting, by anxiety about boundary breakdown, and by invasive, devouring exterminatory enemies."[23] The museum reflects this carceral imaginary, with the shadow of the assailant and the glowing halo of the hero projected over the everyday interactions of police work.

Throughout the memorial, the actual circumstances of officer death are missing. While the danger of the job is invoked, it's unclear why the job is dangerous. This absence allows for the continuation of a fantasy of violent attack. If cause of death were included, visitors might learn that the memorial includes officers who died during training exercises, as well as in car crashes while on patrol. While some died in violent encounters with suspected criminals, a large number of on-duty deaths are the result of accidents or illnesses. Of 1,582 line-of-duty deaths tracked by the National Law Enforcement Memorial Fund in the decade from 2009 to 2018, approximately one-third were from shootings.[24] Over half died from car/motorcycle crashes or job-related illnesses.

Questions about crumbling infrastructure, product safety, and healthcare fall out of the picture; these real sources of precarity are obscured by the shadow of the violent attacker. This framework within the memorial suggests that every police officer needs to be regarded as a future line-of-duty death. Because these officers sacrifice to protect the nation, members of the public are argued to have a duty to protect our vulnerable heroes from criticism and harm.

Administering Death

In the gaps between the memorial walls, I can see out to the rest of the museum. Near the flag-draped coffin, there is visible in the background a display about counterfeiting. In another spot, the gap between marble memorial columns reveals a glimpse of pale-green institutional walls—it is a gas chamber, transported from a prison. A wall plaque reads simply: "The Gas Chamber." Inside is a chair bolted to the floor, affixed with leather straps to hold the sentenced person in place.

Stepping out of the memorial to look at the gas chamber, I wonder at the connection between these two spaces. I had been contemplating lives lost. Now I am looking at a scene for the administration of death, with names or stories absent. Those killed in the gas chamber, unlike officers honored in the memorial, are not given names or photos. No marble coffin stands alongside the chamber to symbolize their missing bodies and names. Rather than as a continuation of tragic death, the gas chamber is presented as a solution to it, a way to avenge fallen heroes and neutralize lethal threats.

A wall plaque informs visitors that this gas chamber was previously installed in Maryland in 1956. It used cyanide gas to kill prisoners. Two accompanying photographs make visual jokes about the purpose of the chamber. In the caption for one photograph, dated 1956, the "architect of the gas chamber" is identified as James Brown. Later, I find that the *Baltimore Sun* identifies him in the photo as an architectural draftsman named A. Bennett Brown.[25] When I learn this, I wonder what to make of the slip. In the photograph, Brown is sitting calmly, in a suit and wide tie, strapped into a chair inside the chamber. Rather than being killed, he seems to be defying death. The image promises mastery over the tools of death, envisioning a one-way relationship in which these things only do what they're told.

A second photograph shows a caged pig inside the gas chamber; it is captioned "Pig used to test chamber." The caption continues: "The first guest of the execution chamber of the State of Maryland was a pig. This photo shows the pig in a cage sitting on top of the metal seat in the chamber." It is not clear if the picture is a before or after shot—the pig may be

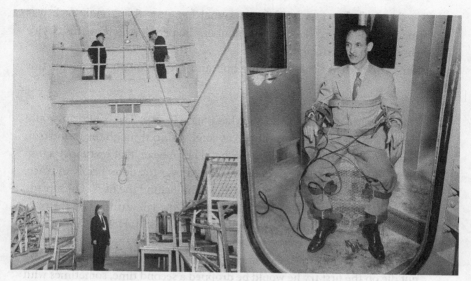

Archival photograph of gallows and gas chamber at Maryland Prison. The architect of the gas chamber, A. Bennett Brown, models the operation of the restraint chair inside the gas chamber. Photo credit: Bettman.

sitting in its cage or it may be dead. Even the pig is not described as "killed"—it is "used." It is not a victim, but a "guest." The use of a pig suggests that those being killed in the gas chamber are not human, or that some lives have little value. The two photos suggest two positions in relation to the gas chamber: confident architects and caged animals. The animals will be "guests" of the chamber, and architects have nothing to fear.

After I leave the museum, I learn that four people died from lethal gas in this pale green room. They were Black, and their names are Nathaniel Lipscomb, Carl Kier, Eddie Daniels, and Leonard Shockley. Shockley, killed in 1959, was seventeen years old at the time of his execution.[26] There is no mention of these people's lives or deaths in the museum.

The gas chamber is one of a number of tools for administering death or bodily punishment that spin out around the memorial. An electric chair, nooses, a guillotine, and dozens of guns and knives are on display. They are presented in a dispassionate, technical tone. Adjacent to the gas chamber stands a floor display case with a large metal bolt and a coil of thick rope. The rope is tied into a noose. The rope looks old, and the text indicates that it is a "device" that was used in an actual hanging. Someone's neck was snapped by this rope. Like the gas chamber, the people killed by this device are absent from the display.

The display card reads "hanging bolt and eye." Beneath this title is this text:

These devices were from the Maryland State Prison. The hangman would place the rope with 7 knots (not 13 as some claim) through the round iron circle. That in turn was attached to a hand hewn beam that was above a trap door. The person to be executed was placed over the door, firmly in place, and the noose placed over his head at a point behind the neck. Once ready the trap door was opened upon the signal of the jail warden and the prisoner fell about ten feet and was jerked to a standstill. Hopefully, the neck would be broken. If not the prisoner would dance in the air as the noose strangled him and movement stopped. Contrary to stories, if a prisoner did not die on the first try he would be dropped a second time, sometimes with someone pulling at his legs. Hopefully he would not be pulled hard enough to be decapitated. The rope kept the area shiny.

The affect of this card is one of removed, professional concern for "correct" procedure. There are two mentions of hope in this brief paragraph—the first that "the neck" will break and the other that the prisoner will not be decapitated. Hope here is for "just enough" punishment to the body to kill instantly, without creating a gruesome spectacle. This expression of hope suggests passivity in the midst of participation in extreme violence—only luck determines whether someone mutilates a body. There are also two mentions of inaccurate gossip about hangings. The text speaks in the voice of an expert hangman, one who knows the number of knots needed in the rope, and who distinguishes between an easy hanging and a difficult one. The rope is presented as a problem solver. In what strikes me as bizarre and confusing language, the rope is described as keeping the area around the gallows "shiny." The person dying by asphyxiation is described as "dancing in air," suggesting a pleasurable aesthetics of hanging.

The noose section of the museum also features photography of the hanging facilities, which ran in the Baltimore newspaper alongside the picture of E. Bennett Brown in the gas chamber. Beside the description of the noose and the photography is an even more technical description, "Executions by Hanging." It shares a brief history of hanging, once the most popular method of execution in the U.S., and notes that the last legal hanging was in 1996 in Delaware. Most of the display card adds technical details about how to ensure a good hanging. Carefully citing sources, the museum placard describes rehearsals with sandbags, and explains how to determine the length of the rope, how to prepare the rope through boiling and lubricating, and how to secure the "prisoner" in the noose. It serves as a how-to guide for the technical process of hanging a human being, and points toward additional sources for those interested in more information. They could be used as instructions for lynching.

The final item in the noose display case is a photograph, "Mass hanging in 1865." It shows the scene immediately preceding the hanging of four people for conspiring to assassinate Lincoln. This photograph of the mass hanging of white Confederate sympathizers serves to mark the exhibit on nooses as colorblind. It erases the use of lynching as a tool of racial terror through a display of hanging to support the Union. In the only photographic representation of death by hanging, the exhibit fails to acknowledge the historic links between nooses, lynching, slavery, and anti-Black racism. In doing so, it keeps the narrative of heroic cops safe from an encounter with the historic reality of police participation in lynching.

The photo caption notes that Mary Surratt, one of the co-conspirators, "became the first woman in American history to be hanged." I am suspicious when I read this, and later research bears my suspicion out. While Surratt, a white woman, was the first woman to be hanged as a result of federal sentencing, a number of women sentenced in state courts and targeted for mob justice had been killed by hanging. For example, just three months earlier, in March of 1865, an enslaved seventeen-year-old girl named Amy Spain was hung for treason for declaring herself free when the Union troops passed through her hometown of Darlington, South Carolina.[27] Other hangings of women are dotted across U.S. history. In 1855 in Missouri, an enslaved woman named Celia was hanged for killing the man who had begun raping her when she was fourteen. In 1863, Josefa "Chipita" Rodriguez was executed by hanging in Texas, following what was later recognized as an unfair trial.[28] Leaving these hangings out of the record, the APHFM exhibit on nooses erases the use of hanging as a means of maintaining a slavery-based economic system. It erases lynching. It erases state violence against Black and Latina women.

Throughout the display of the noose, there is no mention of race, slavery, or lynching. This absence suggests that the noose can be considered from a technological perspective without considering its function in state-enforced racial capitalism. This technical knowledge can be cited instead of the history of racialized violence. The display invites a reading in which "a noose is just a noose"—just another tool for a job. The excavation of racial meaning is necessary to maintain the affective economy of police-as-victim promoted in the memorial at the heart of the museum.

Lethal Violence Presented as a Moral Good

In addition to the nooses and gas chamber, APHFM also features an electric chair, a guillotine, and a wide variety of police guns. All are tools for the state creation of death—taking the lives of those deemed guilty or dangerous or disorderly. And yet, moving through the museum, the impact of this killing is absent. The few people impacted by state violence acknowledged in the museum are the most extreme cases: mass murderers, presidential assassins, and famous "gangsters." The majority of these exceptional criminals are white. In addition, the museum's focus on the death penalty suggests that state violence is mediated by due process. However, the death penalty is not responsible for the majority of state-sanctioned violent deaths. Twenty-five people were killed through the death penalty in 2018; in the same year, 1,164 people were killed by police.[29] These people were killed by being pepper sprayed, tased, shot, choked, or kicked by police officers; they were killed without trial, often without any evidence of criminal behavior.

The one exception for the otherwise unacknowledged people killed by the criminal legal system is Ted Bundy. A photograph of Ted Bundy's corpse is on the wall near the electric chair, again inviting visitors to thrill at the scene of a public execution. The photograph is accompanied by the caption "TED BUNDY: Mass Serial Murderer." The explanatory paragraph educates visitors about Bundy, and by extension all people who have been killed by the state. First, his crimes and alleged crimes are described:

> Ted Bundy is suspect of many un-solved [sic] crimes in which he made admissions. Law enforcement experts feel that Bundy may have killed over one-hundred women during his lifetime. . . . He was known as a serial killer. That is, someone who moves from place to place and kills. Because he moves and rarely knows his victims, the killers are hard to trace and convict.

The photograph caption then poses the question, "Did Ted Bundy deserve to die in the electric chair?" Rather than leaving visitors to sit with their own reflections on this question, it provides an answer:

> He was executed in February, 1989. He killed his first victim in 1974 in Seattle, Washington. A bright, well liked, well educated person, the gore of his murders make todays [sic] slasher movies tame. He confessed to at least twenty-eight killings just before his life was taken in what is known as "Old Sparky." Killers like Bundy have gone free after serving life terms and others have killed in prisons because society in that state does not carry out final judgment. When you look at this photo think of the women he raped and then killed in a frenzy, and ask yourself if this was enough punishment?

While his victims are unnamed, Bundy is referred to by last name, and the instrument of his death is given a familiar nickname. Viewers are encouraged to contemplate the spectacle of "frenzied" rape and murder, and to make decisions about "final judgment" from that moment of voyeuristic intensity. They are then rewarded with further voyeuristic details about his electrocution, a glance at Bundy's dead body, and a reassurance that this act is ultimately good.

The placard links Bundy's confessions to his electrocution—he confesses "just before" his life was taken. The electric chair is framed as producing truth that cannot be otherwise extracted from Bundy. The description also suggests that he would have killed again if allowed to live, suggesting an equation in which his death saves lives. This kind of calculation seems to run throughout the museum—that some must die so that others can live.

Within this framework, state actors' creation of death becomes a moral good. The willingness to carry out "final judgment" about who lives and dies is linked to safety, but it is suggested that sometimes that necessary task is not performed—"society in that state does not carry out final judgment." Alongside the pleasure in consuming Bundy's violence and then righteously celebrating his death, there is a political argument for the expansion of the death penalty. "Killers have gone free . . . and others have killed in prison." States with no death penalty are presented as creating more death through their failure to participate in the righteous violence of the death penalty. This argument extends beyond the death penalty, gesturing toward the possibility that even murder may not be "enough punishment." This seems to suggest that extralegal killing and torture may be necessary to keep people safe, and to encourage visitors to engage in pleasurable fantasies about these forms of violence.

Inevitable Violence and Vulnerable Heroes

Throughout the museum, the stories of violence suggest that it is inevitable. These include stories of a foolish public at risk and acting against its own interest, tricked by criminals, the press, and other mysterious forces. Just before the exhibit of guns and execution materials, there is a wall of newspaper clippings that features famous criminals, including bank robbers and Prohibition-era gangsters. The wall reflects public fascination with Bonnie and Clyde, Al Capone, and "Pretty Boy" Floyd. The description of Bonnie and Clyde notes that they were "not very successful criminals" but that "they were treated by the press with a lot of publicity." They were also an unsuccessful pairing, according to the placard: "Clyde Barrow was a homosexual, while his partner was known as a near nymphomaniac. They made an odd couple." A photograph shows Bonnie pointing a rifle at Clyde, the gendered meaning of the gun layering over the narrative of the pair's queerness.

The narrative of the power of the press continues: "Bonnie wrote poems and the poems were printed by newspapers all across the nation. They, too, became folk heroes made famous by the newspapers." The museum criticizes newspapers for creating "folk heroes" of criminals—and responds with the celebration of police as the real heroes. Against the moral good of policing, the press is described as siding with the bad guys, and putting police officers and good citizens at risk.

Around the corner from the execution exhibits is the American Police Hall of Fame Crime Clock. It is a large, electronic display that indicates how often different crimes are happening in the U.S. The display shows statistics from previous years and turns them into a prediction of the present and future. It condenses actions across the U.S. into one location. Listing offenses like theft and burglary alongside aggravated assault and rape, it reinforces the category of crime as something terrifying, and lumps together people who steal iPhones with those who sexually assault. The display presents a picture of constant danger—a rape every 5.8 minutes, a theft every 4.5 seconds. Just like police death, criminal violence is presented as constant and inevitable.

In the face of what they consider to be a hostile press and looming threats, the APHFM does its own work to tell the story of policing. Near the entrance to the memorial, one wall contains a series of plaques, one for each year, commemorating the "Officer of the Year." This represents the APH-FM's "annual search to locate one officer that they felt epitomized all law enforcement that year." I look over the plaques from recent years. The 2015 plaque honors Salt Lake City police officer Benjamin Hone. The plaque itself contains a representation of Hone and describes an incident in which he shot and killed a man who had stabbed a young woman during a home invasion. According to the plaque, "Officer Hone's quick actions and law enforcement training combined to make him a hero, to which he replied, 'I'm no hero, just an officer doing his job.'" The sentence proclaiming his heroism also contains Hone's own insistence that he is not a hero. This insistence suggests that all officers "doing their jobs" are heroes. The plaque suggests that killing the man was Hone's only option, and that in doing so he saved multiple lives. It also names two factors in his heroism: quick action and training.[30] The incident was subsequently featured on an episode of the true-crime series *Your Worst Nightmare*.[31]

Hone was the target of a subsequent federal civil-rights suit for releasing a K9 attack dog on Jackie Sanchez, who was at the time homeless and intoxicated. Sanchez suffered forty-two dog bites and was hospitalized for five days following the dog attack. The Utah district court found that his rights had been violated and awarded Sanchez $20,000 and attorney's fees. Hone's story suggests that the rescuing hero and excessive-force-using bad apple cop aren't two different styles of policing—sometimes they are the same guy.

"An unknown faceless group"

Looking over the wall of stories, I notice that the 2014 Officer of the Year plaque is different from those from other years, both before and after 2014. Rather than featuring one officer, it shows four: two white men, one white woman, and one Black man. Underneath them, instead of their names, the plaque honors "Law Enforcement Officers." Underneath the "name" is the location: "United States of America." The plaque explains:

> United States of America—2014 was a challenging year for law enforce-
> ment personnel across the nation. This challenge was created primarily by
> an unknown faceless group originating from social media and the drive by

media which directly and indirectly spawned what became known as "The War on Cops."

This special Officer of the Year Award goes to all Law Enforcement Officers across the nation who day in and day out continue to "Serve and Protect" while putting themselves in harm's way to protect those who would intentionally do them harm without warning or provocation.

All Law Enforcement Officers put their lives on the line, and for their continuous acts of bravery and for going above and beyond the call of duty, The American Police Hall of Fame is proud to bestow upon every Law Enforcement Officer in the United States and its territories its highest accolade to a living officer, the 2014 Law Enforcement Officer of the Year Award.

I ponder how the award defines the relationships here: officers put themselves in harm's way, and the critics intentionally do them harm. It is a hypothetical situation, discussing what "would" happen—yet somehow it's already known that there will be no warning or provocation; the term is used to express knowledge of the future. This is a persecutory fantasy in which they already know a betrayal is going to happen.

The fantasy in the Officer of the Year plaque is marked by a paranoid split between the all-good and the all-bad. "All Law Enforcement Officers" are honored as heroes, while those who oppose policing are marked as evil, engaging in a violence that is framed as ahistorical and impossible to understand: "without warning or provocation." Similar to Michael Rogin's political demonology, these enemies are presented through a frame of extreme splitting.[32] They could be made legible through a discussion of U.S. racism and anti-Black violence, but this is absent.

The plaque is dated June 30, 2015. There is no direct mention of Tamir Rice, Tanisha Anderson, Akai Gurley, Michael Brown, Eric Garner, Walter Scott, Freddie Gray, or any of the other high-profile deaths caused by police in the previous year. There is no mention at all of anti-Black racism. The Black Lives Matter movement is not named. Instead, the challenge for law enforcement is described as coming from "an unknown faceless group originating from social media" that is conducting "The War on Cops." In response to a movement that claims and names victims of anti-Black violence, the APHFM describes them as "unknown" and "faceless"—refusing to acknowledge their names or even that they have faces, instead describing the movement against violence as a war directed against cops.

Alicia Garza, Opal Tometi, and Patrisse Cullors, the founders of the

Black Lives Matter movement, have names and photographs that are pretty easy to find in a basic internet search.[33] Rather than a "war on cops," they founded Black Lives Matter as

> an ideological and political intervention in a world where Black lives are systematically and intentionally targeted for demise. It is an affirmation of Black folks' humanity, our contributions to this society, and our resilience in the face of deadly oppression.

Rather than engaging with a key argument of the movement—that police are treating Black lives as worthless—the plaque seems to confirm it by an insistent refusal to recognize them. Instead of legitimate concerns, those who would critique police actions in the media or social media are described only as "those who would intentionally do them harm without warning or provocation." Critiques of policing are treated as harm. Those who critique the police are distorted, defaced, and unacknowledged. In place of their actual names, faces, and voices, there is a projected idea of an irrational violent attacker.

The "bad guys" presented in the museum include activists, newspaper reporters, and people who break the law. All of these people are grouped together as promoting a continuum of violence. On one end of this continuum is questioning police power, or making the police look foolish. It includes actions that are perceived as taking the side of those marked criminal. Everything along this spectrum is presented as an attack that makes police officers' work more dangerous.

Action Fantasy on Repeat

The American Police Hall of Fame Shooting Center offers concealed-weapon trainings, the opportunity to rent a machine gun, a wide variety of firearms for sale in the pro shop, and admission discounts for police and corrections officers and their families. Putting scenes of action and adrenaline into a memorial for those who have been killed in the line of duty invites us to replicate their actions—to imagine ourselves running into danger. In my own use of the shooting range, described in chapter 1, I find myself pulled into this same set of fantasies. Contemplation and reflection are discouraged; the thrill of action substitutes. Part of this thrill is danger.

Like the noose display, the gun range encourages a technical relationship to violence, being able to handle a gun, and to administer the right amount of violence in the right direction. Violence is a skilled art, and it demands special abilities that take practice to learn and maintain.

Visitors can look at the names of the honorable dead, examine technologies for state violence against those described as monstrous, and then go to the gun range. There, the targets may have human shapes or be simple geometric shapes. The human shapes are either brightly colored outlines or monstrous zombies. I think of the description of Black Lives Matter as faceless, and the descriptions of criminals as monsters in the exhibits. The "bad guys"—those hunted and killed by police—can be killed again in fantasy in the shooting range. The shadows of symbolic assailants animate this museum as the understood reason for state-sanctioned violence as well as the cause of death for vulnerable protectors and innocents. The symbolic assailant is seen as the source of the presumed unchangeable fact of constant violence and death—which can be shifted only through their total extermination.

The American Police Hall of Fame is a space of fantasying. The fantasy encouraged by the museum resembles posttrauma play, which tends to be repetitive and fantasy-based and involve expression of a limited range of emotions.[34] A few scenes play over and over—terrible violence happens, the criminal tricks the public, the protector is betrayed, the protector is killed, and the criminal is killed. Visitors can imagine hanging, shooting, or electrocuting bad guys. The structures of this fantasy are hypervigilant and repetitive. The museum shares a carceral fantasy, but actually doesn't allow for dreaming or play. It creates spaces of pleasure around police power, including the pleasures of feeling familial belonging and the thrills of identification with "legitimate" violence. Winnicott states that "fantasying interferes with action and with life in the real or external world, but much more it interferes with dreams and with the personal or inner psychic reality."[35] Within the fantasy world, the traumas of U.S. state-sanctioned violence, including genocidal colonial violence, slavery, and current anti-Black police violence, disappear. And this disappearance impacts our ability to imagine beyond them.

The museum encourages a passive stance toward the future, including both a cynical embrace of fantasies of violence and a tourist distance from its real-life application. The stories told in the museum indicate contempt for those who don't grasp the message that violence is unending, and that the continuum of violence against our vulnerable protectors begins when citizens question authority. This stance allows for proximate feelings of pleasurable excitement and awe at current police power, while looking ahead to the terror of a world without them. These are successful state fantasies, as Donald Pease writes; they work "by inducing citizens to want the national order they already have."[36] Within these fantasies is a cultivated appreciation of the technical aspects of state violence. They celebrate the craft of policing, encouraging interest in the tools used to engage in the threat and practical application of state violence. The emotional pedagogy of the museum is to mourn and anticipate mourning our lost protectors, while thrilling at our proximity to their violent power. It orients people toward taking pleasure in fantasies of inevitable state-sanctioned violence, to enjoy the social order that we already have. Visitors can simultaneously engage from positions of innocence and celebration of violence, made possible by the motivated disavowal of the reality of U.S. anti-Black racism, which is present only as an absence in the museum.

The museum mirrors other sites in which stories of policing are told in the absence of historical and present perspectives on state-sanctioned violence. Television shows, movies, museums, books, news stories: these are all cultural sites where the fantasy of the U.S. hero cop emerges. Living in this fantasy can have its pleasures. But it pulls us away from other forms of creative exploration, other imaginations of how we might live, worlds we could build in which the idea that "good men and women must die" would not make any sense.

CHAPTER 6

Memorial

Blue Mourning at the National Law Enforcement Officers Memorial

On June 19, 2020, protestors gathered in Judiciary Square in Washington, DC, toppled the Albert Pike Memorial, the city's only monument to a Confederate general. Erected in 1901, the memorial has often been an object of protest. Civil War veterans lobbied against it before its creation.[1] One hundred and twenty years later, protestors pulled the statue down, rocking it off its base using long ropes. The crowd cheered as the statue fell to the ground. Some protestors then doused the fallen monument in accelerant and set it on fire.[2] The protest took aim at slavery and its afterlives: calling for an end to anti-Black police violence, people celebrated Juneteenth and took down a confederate memorial erected during the Jim Crow era. The base of the statue was draped with a banner reading "Defund the Police" and adorned with graffiti calling to "end white supremacy." After the statue fell, the crowd began chanting, "Black Lives Matter, Black Lives Matter."[3]

Located about a block away, the National Law Enforcement Officers Memorial (NLEOM) was not a primary focus of protest on that day. In addition to the national memorial, every state but one has a police memorial.[4] Most of these police memorials have been established since the rapid carceral expansion of the 1970s. Like Confederate monuments, police memorials have been constructed alongside a specific iteration of racist, state-sanctioned violence. Just as the construction of Confederate monuments surged during the consolidation of Jim Crow, police memorials proliferated during the rapid expansion of the criminal legal system in the period since 1970. While Confederate monuments honor those who fought for a slave state, police memorials honor those who die serving the carceral state. The NLEOM in Washington, DC, is the centerpiece of these memori-

The statue of Albert Pike was toppled by protestors near Judiciary Square in Washington, DC, on the Juneteenth holiday. Photo credit: ZUMA Press, Inc./Alamy Stock Photo.

als. As the national police memorial, it uses mourning practices to strengthen emotional attachments to a police power that sustains a heteropatriarchal white-supremacist social order.

The NLEOM is "the nation's monument to law enforcement officers who have died in the line of duty."[5] Federal legislation to create the monument was first proposed in 1972 by a member of the Police Benevolent Association. U.S. Representative and former New York City Police Department officer Mario Biaggi led the legislation's passage in 1984. The site was designed by Davis Buckley Architects and dedicated in 1991. The memorial is located on Judiciary Square, near the National Building Museum and the District of Columbia Court. A nearby National Law Enforcement Museum, designed "to tell the story of American law enforcement and make it safer for those who serve," opened in fall 2018.[6]

Proposed and built during the period of expansion of domestic policing and incarceration in the U.S., the memorial wall tells stories about policing in the U.S., about what creates safety, and about who belongs in our national narratives of heroism. The NLEOM site models a police-culture approach to grief work. I refer to this as "blue mourning," a style of articulating grief and grievability that strengthens police power.

Blue mourning works to shape feelings of belonging and pride in the carceral state and to craft heroic narratives around the work of state violence. Blue mourning practices are backed with the weight of the state, and they reinforce state power. The president and attorney general typically attend the national memorial's annual "Police Week" ceremony in which the previous year's names are added to the wall. These ceremonies repeat themes of heroic sacrifice and suggest that our heroic protectors are increasingly vulnerable.

Dismantling the legacy of Jim Crow involves a critical approach to Confederate memorials and symbols, many of which were reintroduced in the 1950s and 1960s.[7] Similarly, a critical approach to blue mourning can contribute to the project of thinking beyond the current iteration of police power. In this chapter, I engage with the NLEOM as a participant observer of police-related grief work, exploring how the work of mourning is also the work of world-building.

Structures of Grieving

National memorials are always involved in the deeply political questions of how death is narrated and which lives count as grievable. Judith Butler notes that these differential attributions of grievability shape social life.

> [G]rievability is already operative in life, and . . . it is a characteristic attributed to living creatures, marking their value within a differential scheme of values and bearing directly on the question of whether or not they are treated equally and in a just way. To be grievable is to be interpellated in such a way that you know your life would matter; that your body is treated as one that should be able to live and thrive, whose precarity should be minimized, for which provisions for flourishing should be available.[8]

Marking a set of lives as grievable shapes the social power that members of that group can wield in life. Mourning practices are also claims to power—they create and maintain social hierarchies and influence the distribution of resources.

The memorial serves to emphasize the grievability of police life, calling for displays of public mourning and gratitude to police. And yet despite the memorial's repeated calls to limit police precarity, it assumes ongoing death. Within blue mourning practices, the fact that police can die on the job orients people toward relationships with living police. The police memorial is built around the expectation of ongoing police death, and the ongoing need to honor the officers who are expected to die, protecting them from the death that has already been anticipated. In her book on the making of the police memorial, Connie Clark highlights the memorial's annual expansion.

> The National Law Enforcement Officers Memorial is different from every other memorial in our nation's capital in one specific way: It is a *living* memorial. Unlike, say, the Vietnam Veterans Memorial, which commemorates soldiers who lost their lives in a war that is now over, the Law Enforcement Officers Memorial stands for a war that goes on every day. Unfortunately, this "war" . . . has no end in sight. . . . Every year, the blood will be shed, the graves dug, the widows and children left behind.[9] [emphasis in original]

Clark writes that because the memorial has been built with the expectation of ongoing death, this makes it a living memorial. Its expansion is fueled by anticipated carceral expansion through the end of the twenty-first century. There are 128 panels in the memorial, with space for a total of 29,233 names. Clark calculates that, "assuming a rate of about 150 officers killed each year, the names of officers can be added to the Memorial until the year 2100."[10]

Clark's comparison with the Vietnam Memorial is instructive. The NLEOM mimics the Vietnam Memorial's simplicity of design and use of engraved names, and yet it differs significantly. The Vietnam Memorial refuses the sense of closure implied in most war memorials by refusing their aesthetic codes—choosing black marble instead of white stone, and modernist simplicity over representations that glorified war.[11] The NLEOM also works within a loss that defies closure. The design necessitates that the memorial grow, and anticipates that the event it memorializes will never end. Yet unlike the Vietnam Memorial, the NLEOM makes strong claims about the meaning of the losses it marks. While the Vietnam Memorial refuses to affix a singular interpretation to the war, the NLEOM interprets the meaning of deaths that have not even happened yet.

The memorial also demarcates a shift in national memorial practice.

While U.S. memorials have traditionally honored soldiers or political leaders, the NLEOM was the first nationally recognized memorial for nonmilitary workers. The NLEOM is the only such memorial located in the nation's
capital. The passage of legislation recognizing the NLEOM was followed by
federal recognition of memorials honoring firefighters and astronauts in
1990 and 1991, respectively. In the 2010s, a memorial was also constructed
for emergency medical services. In 2018, the National Memorial to Fallen
Educators was created to honor "Public or Private School, Pre-K through
12th Grade Educators (anyone who works in a school environment) who
have given their lives in the line of duty."[12]

The educator memorial's framework of "line-of-duty deaths" suggests
that military memorial practices serve as a template for all of the occupation-
based memorials. The sacrifices of these professionals are made visible only
through their sudden, violent death—legible as contributing to the nation
only in contrast to the actions of a violent criminal. They suggest a framework in which heroic good-citizen workers constantly live in a state of
domestic war, facing the threat of death in their everyday routines. The
police memorial serves to honor those who are imagined as most at risk in
this fantasy of the nation.

Visiting the Memorial

The memorial consists of gardens, a long reflecting pool, representational
statues of lions, and two curved 304-foot-long blue-gray marble walls.
Engraved on these walls are the names of law enforcement officers killed in
the line of duty, from 1786 to the previous year. The wall is several feet high
and curved inward. Across the paved path, there is a low, curved bench that
runs parallel to the wall. This long bench creates space for people to sit and
contemplate the names on the wall. Several large adult lions are perched on
the memorial wall, aligned with the fallen officers. The cubs play on the
bench, a parallel to those who are visiting.

Four quotations on the wall introduce and interpret the memorial. The
quotations align police power with American values, Christianity, and the
"natural order" of things. The first is from George H. W. Bush's dedication
of the memorial. "Carved on these walls is the story of America, of a continuing quest to preserve both democracy and decency, and to protect a
national treasure that we call the American dream." Bush refers to the

American Dream as being under attack and needing protection. Alongside the preservation of democracy is something else—decency—invoking the police function of maintaining social order and promoting state-endorsed values. Another quote is from the Roman historian and senator Tacitus: "In valor there is hope." Valor is defined as courage in battle, and the quote suggests that police are functioning as military in a domestic war. The willingness to fight bravely, to risk death, is framed as creating hope for the future. Together, the quotes suggest fighting to preserve current social orders.

A third engraved quote from a surviving spouse, Vivian Eney Cross, invokes heroism: "It is not how these officers died that made them heroes, it is how they lived." Just as this quote both centers and shifts attention away from "how these officers died," the circumstances of their death, a central focus of the memorial, is elided. They died at work, and how they died makes them eligible for inclusion and memorialization. In the case of Cross, her husband, Sergeant Christopher Sherman Eney, was shot in the back by another officer during a SWAT team training exercise in 1984. His death could be attributed to poor safety protocols in training, or to the practice of U.S. officers carrying loaded guns, or to the proliferation of military tactical training throughout U.S. police departments. The absence of specific details about his death subsumes his story into the memorial's prevailing framework of policing as domestic war.

The wall also contains a quote from Proverbs 28:1: "The wicked flee when no man pursueth: but the righteous are as bold as a lion." This quote links nation, religion, and natural order. The Christian religious imagery is from the Old Testament, emphasizing a strong split between good and evil, and characterizing good people as fierce lions. It references the four statuary groupings overlooking the memorial, which depict lions protecting their cubs.

The lion statues were created by American sculptor Raymond Kaskey. The memorial's website explains their meaning: "the statues symbolize the protective role of our law enforcement officers and convey the strength, courage and valor that are the hallmarks of those who serve."[13] The lion is perched above the wall with officers' names etched on it, while the cubs are relaxing on the visitors bench—clearly aligning those who visit with the role of cubs, children to be protected by the powerful lions. The cubs are a cute-animal form of what Lauren Berlant calls "the infantile citizen of the United States," in which democracies "produce a special form of tyranny that makes citizens like children, infantilized, passive, and overdependent

The National Law Enforcement Officers Memorial, Washington, DC. Photo credit: Alexandre Tziripouloff/Alamy Stock Photo.

on the 'immense and tutelary power' of the state."[14] Depicting the relationship between citizens and police as resembling that between lions and their cubs not only insists on the familial relation as a model for citizenship, it naturalizes this relation by framing this form of violent power as continuous across the animal kingdom. Rather than purely masculine, the state presented by the memorial is heteronormative—two male and two female lions are included among the statuary. This stands in sharp contrast to the observed behavior of actual lions, who live in prides rather than heterosexual pairs. (Male lions are not involved in raising cubs and may even attack and kill them.) The predatory nature of the lions' violence is also absent from the sculpture—there is no intergenerational attack or mutilated prey. The violence of the lions is presented instead as protective heteropatriarchal violence, while truly dangerous violence is imagined instead as an outside attack on the cubs.

The lion embodies the kitsch sensibility described by Marita Sturken in that it "convey[s] the message that this sentiment is one that is universally shared."[15] The baby cubs provide a rationale for why police death is necessary and natural, aligning it with the fantasy of loving parents who are absolutely dedicated to their children's well-being. Layered over the traditionally masculine metaphors of war, domestic policing is celebrated through domestic narratives of protective mommies and daddies.

Police Week

Every May, during "Police Week," the NLEOM Foundation hosts a ceremony honoring new officers added to the wall. The U.S. attorney general leads the candle-lighting ceremony at the memorial, and at the candlelight vigil, the names that have been added in the past year are read aloud, and family members of those who passed are recognized. The event incorporates the police work practice of roll call, referring to the list of those who died as "The Roll Call of Heroes." In 2019, this list included 158 people who died in 2018 and an additional 213 "whose stories of sacrifice had been lost to history until now."[16] Some of these were officers impacted by 9/11, but the list also included officers who died as long ago as 1786. The addition of police officers from the eighteenth and nineteenth centuries reflects the memorial's project to retroactively construct a narrative of police sacrifice as central to the history of the nation.

Bethlehem, Pennsylvania, police officer Russell Lande wrote of his experience taking a bus sponsored by his police union down to the "Police Week" ceremony in which new names are added to the wall, noting that it was at the memorial where he reached "my full understanding of how truly dangerous the job of a police officer really is."[17]

After a brief walk through the memorial, the emotion poured through my veins. When one is looking at wedding photos, childhood pictures, letters from children to their slain loved one, flower bouquets and newspaper articles accounting the incident—the memorial becomes very overwhelming[. . . .] The single most mesmerizing event was when I observed a photo of an officer . . . standing adjacent to the memorial on one of his prior visits. That officer's name was now etched on the wall, as he had become a statistic and fatality in the name of law enforcement.[18]

Lande confronted a powerful reminder of his own potential vulnerability—standing at the wall, he occupies the same role and the same space as the officer who died. It is "mesmerizing." He is invited into a powerful identification with that officer's death.

Lande writes that after this first experience, he returned annually to the Police Week celebration and organized buses of local officers to attend the ceremony from Pennsylvania. He describes a space of powerful camaraderie, forged through identification with sacrifice. Lande was so inspired by the experience that he initiated the construction of a police memorial in his hometown of Bethlehem, Pennsylvania. The memorial honors six local officers who died while policing in the previous century.[19]

Participation in the Police Week ceremony is a chance for political leaders to highlight their relationship to policing. Donald Trump attended and spoke at the ceremony in every year of his presidency, and he took the additional step of having the White House lit in blue lights during Police Week. Barack Obama attended on four of his eight years in office and issued statements on the years he did not attend, a pattern that was identified by some as flagging an ambivalence toward policing.[20] George W. Bush attended every year except 2009. At the 2017 ceremony, Attorney General Jeff Sessions delivered brief remarks. He ended by emphasizing the relationship of support and gratitude of citizens toward the police:

> And lastly, to all those serving here I have a simple message for each of you: We have your back and you have our thanks.
>
> I believe it is one of the highest callings of my job to call attention to your successes and encourage our fellow citizens to support you in your difficult and dangerous work. And as long as I am the Attorney General of the United States, the Department of Justice will have the back of all honest and honorable law enforcement officers.[21]

The theme of vulnerable protectors is central to Sessions's comments—demonstrating gratitude, he stresses the need for citizens to protect police. The metaphor of "we have your back" suggests a persistent fear of attack by the public. This is a metaphor that shows up repeatedly and across political parties, with Obama making a similar pledge to have the back of law enforcement in his 2016 open letter.[22]

Visiting the Memorial

The memorial wall shapes public interaction. The performance of memory practices is scripted, through choreographed events, a guided walking tour, and the on-site provision of grieving materials. The actions scripted by the memorial—placing wreaths (for sale at the gift shop), tracing names (paper provided), dialing into the walking tour (number listed on a nearby plaque), and participating in the annual candlelight vigil, promote silent reverence. Although people are encouraged to leave memorial offerings, these practices are highly regulated through memorial policies. In 2019, the NLEOMF Twitter account highlighted the practice of bringing decorated vehicle doors from police cruisers in honor of deceased officers, tweeting out a reminder to people to remove their decorated vehicle doors from the memorial when leaving DC.[23]

When I first visit the memorial in 2017, I call into the walking tour. An unfamiliar recorded voice tells me that it is visited by millions "who have come to show their appreciation and support" for law enforcement. As a visitor, I'm interpellated into the performance of "appreciation and support." It also states that the wall contains the names of over 19,000 law enforcement officers who have died in the line of duty. The number quoted on the call indicates that the walking tour hasn't been updated in a while, as there are currently more than 21,000 names on the wall.

The walking tour includes a collection of firsts in police death, including women and Black officers. In the description William Johnson, "the first African-American officer to die," in 1870, the tour notes that "for many years, African Americans were not accepted in the law enforcement profession; that began to change in the 1800s." There is no mention of the Civil War, slavery, or slave patrols. The tour tells a progress narrative, in which policing has become more diverse and democratic by including Black and women officers among the ranks of those who have died heroic deaths.

The tour also notes the exceptional deaths, including the youngest person to die in the line of duty (a seventeen-year-old struck by lightning) and the greatest number of officers to die on any one date (September 11, 2001). Correctional officers are recognized, with a special nod to the seven prison guards killed in the Attica uprising.[24] The majority of those profiled involve stories of violence: tales of bombs, prison uprisings, and physical attacks. This emphasis on violent death ignores the prevalence of accidental line-of-duty deaths, reinforcing the idea that police officers are dying in acts of heroic battle.

The NLEOM gift shop features a variety of NLEOM swag, including keychains, a calendar, water bottles, and coffee mugs. A stuffed "teddy bear" version of the memorial's lions, named Pudgy Lion, is available.[25] Other potentially scary aspects of policing are domesticated and made safe in the gift shop offerings: there are stuffed Rottweiler and German Shepherd police dogs, a bath-time-ready rubber duck outfitted in police gear, police hand puppets, and the children's book *Feeling Safe with Officer Frank*.[26] There are several shelves of books, including a short paperback on the construction of the memorial, DVDs about the memorial, and self-help psychology books on how to emotionally manage police work, including the spousal guide *I Love a Cop* and the trauma-informed recovery manual *CopShock*.[27]

The 2018 NLEOM calendar has a preface dedicated to "fallen heroes." Twelve deceased officers are pictured, one photograph for each month alongside brief captions describing the scenes of their deaths. Types of death include being shot in a pizza restaurant, being robbed at gunpoint while leaving a club and then shot in the head, being killed in a car accident pursuing a suspect, being hit by an inattentive driver while investigating an accident, being unintentionally shot while training, or dying in a plane crash on the way to a training. The message of these diverse death-stories is that cops are constantly at risk. One story—being shot in a robbery only after discovery of the police badge—stresses that cops are always at an increased risk. Wherever they go they are presented as more vulnerable because of their chosen work.

Whether in the audio tour, the memorial calendar, or during Police Week, the memorial practices often focus on individual officers. They encourage contemplation and awareness of the human story of the individual heroic officer. There is no discussion of the police power or its role in U.S. life. Policing is presented as a timeless, natural feature of human social life, a heroic and risky path that some choose, in order to make everyone else safer.

Policing Death

The story of policing told by the NLEOM does not include all police deaths on duty. The annual process of engraving new names on the wall reflects stringent policing of which officers' lives count as grievable; anyone whose story complicates the narrative of heroic fallen officers is not included. These policies belie the engraved sentiment that "it is not how these officers died that matters." Staff of the memorial fund research each death to ensure that it fits the criteria of who can be considered to have died in the line of duty. Duty is marked as something different than work. Some deaths that occur at work are excluded from the category of "line-of-duty deaths" because they don't correspond to behavioral expectations. Other deaths that occur in off-work hours are claimed as line-of-duty deaths, because they involve acts of heroism.

The policies of the NLEOM specifically exclude officers whose deaths are caused by suicide, alcohol or drug use, "the intentional misconduct of the officer," or "performing his or her duty in a grossly negligent manner at time of death."[28] Substance use, misconduct, negligence, and emotional distress combine into a category of death that cannot be honored—the death of the disorderly or distressed officer. Although death by substance abuse or suicide may be directly linked to the emotional toll of the job, this is not considered a memorializable death. The memorial erases the emotional distress caused by the demands of the job, as well as those who fail to meet the criteria of "hero."

Physical illness may count, but it is highly scrutinized. Death by disease may qualify as a "line-of-duty death" if the disease is contracted while on duty, as long as that disease is not linked to substance abuse. The memorial website explains their criteria:

> Each death caused by disease shall be reviewed by the Armed Forces Institute of Pathology or other medical personnel with similar skill and expertise. If it is determined that the officer died as a result of infectious disease contracted while performing official duties, or by exposure to hazardous materials or conditions while performing official duties, that officer is eligible for inclusion on the Memorial.[29]

A distinction is made between physical disease and emotional distress. While you can be honored at the memorial if you catch pneumonia on duty, you cannot be if you catch despair.

To include the large numbers of police officer suicides on the wall would be to highlight other crises—those not linked to the danger of the outside attacker. Police are at increased risk of suicide.[30] They also report high rates of substance use. There are few current data on police rates of domestic violence, but previous studies have reported a broad range, from 4.8 to 40 percent of police families having experienced it.[31] Yet some argue that the lack of research masks an epidemic of intimate partner violence within law enforcement.[32] Acknowledging deaths that highlight these issues would lead to different stories about U.S. policing. These are stories in which heroic aspirations are replaced with heartbreak and despair, or stories in which the cop is the villain, not the hero. Within the framework of blue mourning, these deaths are marked as ungrievable. To consider them would unravel public emotional investments in police power.

The Margins of Grievability

In 2013, the NLEOM made a controversial decision to exclude an officer who was shot while on duty. Jennifer Sebena was a Wisconsin police officer killed in Wauwatosa on Christmas Eve of 2012. She was ambushed leaving the police station and shot several times, first with her attacker's gun and then with her service weapon. Her name was initially refused by the memorial because she had a personal relationship with her murderer—he was her husband.

The memorial committee stated that Sebena's death was the result of domestic violence, which they saw as "death of a personal nature." As it was "personal," the murder was not linked to her police work, even though it occurred while she was on duty and involved her service weapon.[33] Public accounts of the shooting named Sebena's murderer as an Iraq war veteran, an ex-Marine who had served two tours in Iraq, suggesting that he was a "wounded" veteran whose military experience informed his violence against Sebena.[34] Only after protests from Wisconsin state police associations and Governor Scott Walker, whose neighborhood Sebena was patrolling at the time of her death, did the board reconsider. In a special meeting, they voted to include Sebena's name in the memorial.

The controversy around including Sebena's name is surprising, in part because the violent nature of her death aligns in many ways with memorial narratives of cops under attack from violent outsiders. Yet the hesitation about including Sebena's name suggests tremendous difficulty reconciling her murder with the memorial's implicit narrative of protective heteropatri-archal state violence. Acknowledging the harm done to soldiers in their enactment of state violence, and naming it as unacceptable, would suggest that state violence doesn't protect U.S. families. Rather, it puts them at risk. Naming intimate partner violence as posing a risk to officers similarly unravels the memorial's narrative of where harm resides.

Only when conservative male leaders such as Governor Walker stepped in to vouch for Sebena was she recognized as worthy of memorialization. The controversy around Sebena's inclusion reveals a crisis in heroic narratives of heteropatriarchal violence. While the wall limits the terms of debate to one of how women can seek inclusion within a carceral state, Sebena's story points out the risks when heteropatriarchal violence and state violence overlap.

Dirty Harry Narratives of Police Death

Police memorials hold a special place in U.S. police culture, as sites for blue mourning practices that emphasize heroic vulnerability. They suggest that a lack of citizen reverence for agents of state violence can be dangerous to these officers. This narrative was popularized in the iconic 1971 U.S. film *Dirty Harry*. The film begins with a long shot of deceased officers' names on a police memorial plaque. Reviewing the film in the *New Yorker* in 1972, critic Pauline Kael commented that it's a strange opening, as the movie is not about a police officer who dies.

> The tribute, however, puts the Viewer in a respectful frame of mind; we all know that many police are losing their lives. The movie then proceeds to offer a magically simple culprit for their deaths: the liberals.[35]

Dirty Harry presents a worldview in which police violence is justified by the unquestionably evil nature of criminals. Those on the Left who fail to understand this—liberal judges, politicians, and voters—are presented as putting cops at risk. In this story, the perceived vulnerability of cops is exacerbated by limits on police power. This constant attention to deceased heroes serves as a justification for expanding police powers and an argument for civilian subservience. The associated idea—that policing is a battle between good and evil—implies that this social order needs to be eternal.

Clint Eastwood, the actor for whom *Dirty Harry* was a defining role, is affiliated with the national memorial. He has filmed fundraising appeals for the memorial, and he began serving as the memorial's honorary chairman in 2011.[36] The national memorial was first proposed to Congress in the year after *Dirty Harry*'s release. Leaders of the NLEOMF repeat the *Dirty Harry* message that critiques of policing put police at risk. NLEOMF founding CEO Craig Floyd, who served from 1984 to 2018, writes in his biography that his work "is widely credited with changing America's attitude toward the law enforcement profession and saving officers' lives"—linking critical public attitudes with police death.[37] Former U.S. Attorney General John Ashcroft issued a statement on being named chairman of the board in September 2016:

> I am honored to serve as Chairman of the Board of the National Law Enforcement Officers Memorial Fund providing thought leadership and governance oversight at an important time in the organization's history. The recent growing disrespect for the rule of law demonstrated in some American communities troubles me greatly, and it should not be ignored.

He continues:

> Forty-one officers have been shot and killed already in 2016. Fourteen of those firearms-related deaths were the result of ambush attacks, including five in Dallas and three in Baton Rouge. We must end this senseless violence before more lives are lost. This effort is one of the Memorial Fund's top priorities, and it has my full commitment.[38]

The wall is framed as a necessary protection for police under attack. U.S. attitudes about police are described as entering a new state of crisis—"recent growing disrespect for the rule of law"— implicitly contrasted with an earlier era of respect for authority. Questioning police power is linked to deadly "ambush" attacks on police, as though any challenge to their authority is the same as a violent, surprise assault.

Blue mourning at the memorial de-centers the actual event of each officers' death, replacing it with a narrative of violent attack on law enforcement. Though its design invokes the specter of an outside assailant, the line-of-duty deaths memorialized at the NLEOM are not primarily caused by violence against law enforcement. Many are due to accidents, such as car accidents while racing to respond to a call, or friendly fire during training exercises. The memorial's mission—"to make it safer for those who serve"—again seems to suggest that the practices of the memorial do something to interrupt danger. The Memorial Fund's vision, "to inspire every citizen to value law enforcement," suggests that it is insufficient reverence for officers' importance that puts them at risk.

The data shared by the NLEOMF points toward other explanations for officer death: the most police officers per year were killed in the1930s (over 300 in 1930).[39] As prohibition was the most dangerous time for law enforcement, a historical perspective might argue that advocating for drug decriminalization and a shift toward treatment models for drug use would be one of the most important actions to avoid officer death. Another look at the historical data would note declines in total numbers of officer deaths since the 1970s, despite large increases in the police and prison workforce. Although the population of officers is growing, every year they are less likely to die on duty. Rather than a crisis of ongoing risk, the data suggest that those who work in policing are safer than ever before in U.S. history. The memorial does not mark a crisis of increased police precarity. Rather, it signifies a shift in national hierarchies of grievability that have elevated the agents of domestic state violence, emphasizing their vulnerability even as they are made safer than ever before.

Responding to Protest

How might the memorial's presentation of a hierarchy of grievability shift in the face of the current massive social movement, Black Lives Matter? On June 20, 2020, the day after the Albert Pike Memorial was toppled, the NLEOMF launched a new initiative on its website. The "community bulletin board" frames the memorial as a progressive voice on police reform, "intended to gather suggestions and examples of current programs that help bring together law enforcement and the communities they serve."[40]

The bulletin board is introduced as a response to unnamed "current events around the country." The memorial asserts their commitment to "diversity, fairness, respect, honor, and justice," without explaining how these terms might relate to the "current events." In terms of actions:

We will continue to focus on the history of law enforcement and, with every opportunity, introduce the public to the good men and women who sacrifice their lives to keep us safe. Likewise, we understand and will continue to acknowledge the history, complexities, and challenges that exist between American law enforcement and communities of color.

In this framing, the "history of law enforcement" is something distinct from "the history, complexities, and challenges . . . between law enforcement and communities of color." While their focus is on the former, they "understand and acknowledge" the latter, without questioning how it might interrupt the memorial's focus and orientation. The incoherence of the statement, in part, arises from the inability to think beyond the frame of police as vulnerable heroes.

Funded by the DuPont Corporation, the bulletin board frames the problem they are trying to solve as one of "disconnection" between police and communities. In the moderated bulletin board, they state, "We encourage positive and forward thinking ideas," and warn that "confrontational messages, political statements, and profanity will be swiftly removed from the bulletin board." Even within this platform, which seems to respond directly to the Black Lives Matter movement and associated international protests, the memorial draws attention to individual officers' vulnerability and heroic sacrifices—elevating their lives as particularly precarious. It supports a fantasy of cops dying heroically, and builds investment in the idea that a police power supported by ongoing police death is the necessary and right social order. Their response to pervasive violence is one of inclusion— offering to strengthen a protective connection to heteropatriarchal police power for "communities of color." Rather than shifting the social order, it works again to try to convince people, through fantasies of inclusive dialogue, to "want the national order they already have."[41]

Beneath the bulletin board, there is a quote by Sonia Pruitt:

As the Chairwoman of the National Black Police Association and a member of the Board of Directors at the National Law Enforcement Memorial and Museum I would like to emphasize that there is no turning back and that the work we and this organization must do is paramount to finding a path forward.

The memorial suggests an improved relationship in the future, one that will put an end to "current issues" while still allowing for a celebration of police history.

This initiative highlights how police reform is a constant part of policing. The reform effort insists on the ongoing role of the vulnerable protector, and it fails to name violence or shift the national hierarchy of grievability established at the memorial. It refuses the alternate approach to grief work enacted through the Black Lives Matter movement. Instead, it offers a promise of "connection" to police for those who remain "civil" in their comments.

This wall is a scriptive thing that gives instructions about how to understand death, and about which deaths count as heroic or even as recognizable. Within the framework of blue mourning, conspicuous absences include the nonrecognition of deceased officers who might be seen as less than heroic and the acknowledgement of those killed by police. The shadows of the memorial include the emotionally wounded cop; the harmful violent cop; the negative effects of heteropatriarchal, racist, and settler colonial violence; and those wounded and killed by police violence. These are structuring absences in the memorial. These absences allow visitors to understand police vulnerability as caused by insufficient public obedience and reverence.

The pleasures offered in the memorial are premised on a particular narration of police violence as necessary, familial protection. It marries conservative discourses on the family and the nation with "tough-on-crime" narratives of policing, presenting a vision of the future in which there is endless war against domestic enemies. Family violence and anti-Black violence in the U.S. history are erased. Instead, the naturalizing frame of a parental, protective state places citizens in the role of thankful children.

The National Law Enforcement Officers Memorial teaches an orientation toward the future, predicting a coming century in which the memorial wall is constantly increasing. It promises a different wage to those working as cops and prison guards—heroic death. The stated mission of the wall links history and safety, suggesting that public education about "the story of law enforcement" will reduce dangers to officers, perhaps through increasing public empathy for and understanding of police. These practices of blue mourning propose resolving questions of safety through ongoing war and increased militarization. They also give instructions on how to live in an increasingly policed country, one that inverts the logic of policing—the public are responsible for protecting the police through ongoing demonstrations of their respect for authority. Public safety is collapsed into police safety, framed as public acceptance of police power. This sets up a circular structure of demands, in which police are always vulnerable, and the public is never reverent enough.

Conclusion

Abolitionist Psychologies

Before I trained as a counselor, I worked with a community organization named Girl Talk. Led by Chicago activist Wenona Thompson in the aftermath of her own teenage experiences within the punitive legal system, Girl Talk worked to provide support for girls who were locked up in juvenile detention. Facilitating art workshops, movie nights, and conversations, I met preteen and teen girls whose experiences of systemic and interpersonal violence were multiplied by the added violence of incarceration.[1] And at the same time, they were much more than these painful experiences. The girls I met were not statistics—they were children and teenagers, trying to figure out how to have fun, connect with friends, figure out crushes, and navigate life. I resonated with some of their experiences. I knew that justice for them would create the world I wanted to live in, too.

I was in my early twenties when I worked with Girl Talk, and I learned and grew a lot in the community that Wenona Thompson created and the Black and feminist communities that surrounded and supported us. I felt my debt to the people who had invested in me. And at the same time, I could see that there were things that I didn't know how to talk about in our work, that were wound up with our experiences of violence, fear, and loss. I entered counseling school with the idea that I would learn some skills to give back, and also get a credential that allowed me to support myself and support organizing work outside of "the non-profit industrial complex."[2] In terms of different ways to respond to trauma and violence, I thought that becoming a counselor was the opposite of becoming a cop.

I'm not the only one who has made this opposition. The idea that cops are bad and counselors are good shows up in a number of advocacy campaigns. In 2016, a national campaign was launched under the name "Counselors not Cops."[3] The campaign works to shift school spaces into less highly policed zones.[4] Organizers demand that police be removed from schools, policies be changed, and mental health resources be increased. A 2019 American Civil Liberties Union report titled *Cops and No Counselors* similarly advocates for increased mental health funding alongside decreased police presence in schools.[5] When police are in schools, the authors note that they "do what they are trained to do—detain, handcuff, and arrest."[6]

These advocacy efforts push back against the broadening reach of police power, and they are right that cops and counselors bring different sets of tools and behavioral repertoires to their encounters. But their slogans can be deceiving. As I've learned in my own experience and research, cops and counselors are not always opposing forces. Working with cops as clients, I had to grapple with the fact that police power was not something outside of me. It wasn't only in my cop clients. It was something in which I was deeply enmeshed, as a U.S. citizen, a white woman, and a psychological professional. If I was going to raise questions about my clients' investments in police power, I also needed to question my own.

Psychology and counseling are deeply involved in the project of policing. They lend legitimacy to the institution through the widespread practice of fitness-for-duty screening, through consulting on policy and protocols, and through participating in ongoing police trainings. New therapeutic programs established in partnership with police and prisons often expand the scope and reach of police power. These include drug courts, therapeutic lockdown facilities, and specialized mental health units on police forces. The line between police and mental health professionals blends further when we consider that the psychiatric facility and the jail are often the same institutions—the largest psychiatric institutions in the U.S. are located in city jails.[7] And whether located within or outside of the jail, all psychiatric institutions can work according to carceral logics.[8] The carceral logics of counseling practice don't stop at the doors of inpatient treatment facilities. Counselors can also prop up police culture in their outpatient work: through punitive treatment modalities, coordination with police and prisons, and the daily assumption within their work that the current structure of policing is inevitable, necessary, natural, or good.

Even the work of grieving is tied up in our relationships to state-sanctioned violence. At the American Police Hall of Fame and Museum, the National Law Enforcement Officers Memorial, and other memory sites around the U.S., public recognition of lost life is also being used as a strategy to strengthen police power. Stories of heroic death teach hierarchies of grievability. They outline a vision of how people can act to protect their vulnerable heroes, demanding unquestioning loyalty to police power. These emotional investments in policing contribute to the complexity, persistence, and strength of U.S. police power.

Counseling and public remembering are powerful processes, capable of changing lives. For this reason, they are worth fighting for. While there is an active movement promoting police psychology and police "blue mourning" narratives, there is also a movement of people creating and sharing clinical practices that are abolitionist. Rather than framing counselors and cops as two mutually exclusive groups, recognizing our complicity creates opportunities for counselors to take action.

Mental health professionals can move to divest from police power in a variety of ways. One potential strategy might include challenging our professional organizations to stop legitimating police psychology. Institutional recognition and police-focused clinical certifications are not neutral—they actively support ongoing police power. Members of the APA have the capacity to raise challenges when the APA's organizational cover is used to excuse state violence—they have already done so with regard to psychologist participation in military interrogation. Other strategies for divesting from policing could include questioning how psychological professionals are recruited into an adjunct police role—including mandated reporting of child and elder abuse and our practices around involuntary commitment. Within our organizations, our clinical practices, and our educational efforts, this also means constantly questioning the idea that police power is race-neutral and making links to disavowed histories of white supremacist violence.

Abolitionist psychologies build our capacity to confront grief, to mark personal and collective histories, to empathize, and to build more just relationships. Counselors and psychologists can look to prison abolitionist scholars and activists. Angela Davis describes the work of abolitionists as trying to "to envision a continuum of alternatives to imprisonment—demilitarization of schools, revitalization of education at all levels, a health system that provides free physical and mental care to all, and a justice system based on reparation and reconciliation rather than retribution and vengeance."[9] Abolitionists seek out alternate modes of social and economic relation: strategies for responding to harm, distributing resources, and providing care. These new modes of relation also require psychic work to manage inevitable fears, anxieties, angers, and associated impulses to deploy state-sanctioned violence. Just as mental health skills are used to strengthen police power, they can be utilized to build abolitionist futures.

My own counseling practice has been enriched by my engagements with abolitionist thinking and intersectional feminist theory. Thinkers from these movements provide concrete tools for naming the dynamics of violence that shape our lives and figuring out how to live in a starkly unequal social world. For example, the Black Lives Matter movement models a theory of mourning through the manner in which lives lost to state-sanctioned violence are recognized. Organizers refuse to narrate victims' lives through the familiar terms of innocence or heroism. Instead, organizers highlight peoples' lives in relationship, routine, and community. Victims of police violence are claimed as valuable, not for their goodness, but for their everydayness: their relationships with mothers, brothers, children, coworkers, and friends; their love of ice cream or football or motorcycles; their hobbies; their losses; their mental health struggles; and their full range of experiences. This is a move into complexity. It evaporates fantasies about scary "criminals," not through presenting people as innocent, but through insisting that they be considered as whole. The movement has facilitated transformative encounters with losses that are simultaneously part of a long history and incredibly, painfully specific. Therapists have much to learn from this movement about the generative and creative power of staying present with grief.

Abolitionist psychologies are not new. Rather, they are a collection of organizations, processes, and practices across and beyond the disciplines of psychology, counseling, and mental health care. They include free counseling clinics, resources for survivors of violence (including state violence), treatment on demand, and the institutional commitments of mental health providers to avoid police involvement. For example, the Trans Lifeline support hotline has a policy not to call 911, even if they fear that their callers may harm themselves. This policy recognizes that police involvement is likely to put transgender callers at a greater risk of harm, and it requires that hotline counselors engage in conversations about client safety that do not revolve around police power. Other organizations provide models for what safety outside of punitive criminal responses can look like. The organization Stop It Now runs a helpline and provides resources to support people who are worried about other adults' behaviors toward children or about their own sexual urges.[10] They provide tools to stop sexual abuse before it starts, recognizing that sexual violence cannot be stopped through threats of state violence. This is not a passive approach to sexual violence—rather, it is an active prevention and early-intervention approach that isn't satisfied with punishing after the fact. It works to figure out what factors can stop harm from happening in the first place. Once harm has occurred, there are also models for transformative justice responses that seek to address interpersonal violence within a framework that acknowledges the impact of white supremacy, settler colonialism, heterosexism, and misogyny. The Creative Interventions project has released a toolkit to support community-based interventions to stop interpersonal violence, and has documented the success of some of these interventions through the Storytelling and Organizing Project.[11] The organization FreeFrom also works to end domestic violence. Its model for change is not through criminalization, but through supporting survivors of violence in getting the economic resources they need to leave dangerous situations permanently.[12] Each of these efforts works to shrink police power, and to decrease perceptions of the police as necessary for safety.

Psychologists and counselors can look to social work and clinical practice for further models of abolitionist psychology. Social workers provide leadership through their own challenges to their profession's complicity with policing. Rather than embracing the idea that social workers can simply replace or partner with police, these practitioners are calling for abolitionist and anticarceral social work.[13] Abolitionist psychology is also consistent with current best practices in the field of substance-use treatment. These practitioners highlight the harms of punitive approaches and outline alternatives. Harm-reduction initiatives in response to the opiate crisis have included the increased availability and distribution of naloxone, the creation of supervised consumption sites for drug users, drug-checking services to identify the contents of drugs bought through informal markets, and safe supply for substance users at risk of drug overdose or drug toxicity.[14] These interventions have saved lives by refusing the carceral response to substance use. Within counseling practice, motivational interviewing is often used as a strategy to connect with clients' values, and to ensure that clinical interventions are experienced as desired supports that increase clients' control over their lives, rather than shame-based policing. Originating in substance-use treatment, this approach has moved into general clinical practice. It is associated with better outcomes in eating-disorders treatment, and it is also integrated into first-line treatment for suicidality and self-harm.[15] Taken in sum, this suggests that an abolitionist approach to treatment has the potential to enhance the quality of clinical work.

Abolitionist psychology also aligns with a psychoanalytic lens, one that rejects surface narratives, considers unconscious processes, and adopts a practice of deep listening. Hatred, aggression, and envy can not simply be disavowed or repressed; to be meaningfully shifted, it is helpful to recognize and understand them. Abolitionist psychology requires a willingness to look for ghosts, and listen to them. It requires developing skills for grieving, and turning with curiosity toward new manifestations of the "cops in our heads and hearts."[16] In my clinical work, I've become more attuned to investments in the figure of the vulnerable hero; to the multifold ways in which police power is presented as natural, normal, or inevitable; and to fantasies of violence and rescue. Whether working directly with police or not, these themes present themselves in the clinic, as clients try to manage interpersonal conflict, respond to harm, and imagine danger. They are opportunities to try to understand the impact of police culture in all of our lives, and to imagine how it could be otherwise. At times, this might mean working with clients to grapple with their own participation in violence as they figure out how to see themselves as simultaneously capable of harm and worthy of existence. It can mean figuring out what accountability means to them, how to look at hard facts, and how to move closer to their values.

I continue to work as a therapist, but my own clinical career has taken me in new directions. In 2018, I moved back into a community mental-health setting. As one part of this work, I counsel in a voluntary program that supports children and teens in the aftermath of their own harmful sexual behaviors. My work is to accompany these clients and their families as they grow, learn, and heal in ways that help them avoid engaging in further harmful behavior. Adjusting our work to the specifics of each client's situation, I work with my clients and their families to strengthen relationships, ensure safety, manage emotions, and address behaviors. My clients are learning how to understand and manage strong feelings, how to notice and challenge beliefs that naturalize gender-based and sexualized violence, how to assume accountability, how to build a positive identity in the aftermath of their mistakes, and how to navigate sexual consent in the future. The counseling literature on sexual behavior problems reiterates the widespread finding that harmful behaviors are helped, not by punishment, but by access to mental health and community support to talk about what happened, to build skills, to engage with resources, and to connect with a feeling of hope.[17]

In my practice, I have found that there are a thousand answers to the question, "How can we build safer relationships and stop harm without police power?" Each answer is tailored to the specifics of that individual situation. They can involve getting families and communities involved, shifting cultures of violence, avoiding shame and labeling, teaching skills for accountability, and building positive attachments within just, equitable, and consensual relationships. They also involve refusing to split people into "all-good" and "all-bad," refusing the seductions of rescue and hero fantasies, and working instead to honor each person's experiences and desires for positive connection. These are the sets of tools that psychotherapists can bring to a problem. Often, they involve gaining awareness of the influence of intergenerational trauma and violence, and creating space to listen to stories and experiences that have been disavowed and denied. This is both a psychoanalytic process and an abolitionist one.

Abolitionist psychology is difficult work, because police culture is wide-ranging. It shows up in television, film, news, political debates, architecture, workplace rituals, and many other sites. It is all of the ways that police power is shown to be inevitable, normal, natural, necessary, and good. The figure of the vulnerable hero and a constant emphasis on the expectant death of cops support police power, and the current field of police psychology has normalized the role of psychologists as one that supports and strengthens U.S. police culture. Police culture tells a predictable story: that some people are cops and always will be. It tells us that some people are good guys and some are bad. It soothes anxieties about change by telling us that some relationships are fixed forever, they are and always will be the order of things. It tells us to accept an imagined world of constant attack and increasing death as the only possible world.

Throughout this book and in my counseling practice, I consider the losses that spring from a desire to be a hero, the inevitable failures in bureaucratized relationships that split humans into good and bad, and the psychic harm done to those who participate in and uphold violent power structures. Police culture is expansive, and it encompasses many aspects of contemporary life—economic and political structures, intimate and familial relationships, cultural production, and everyday actions. But this expansiveness also means that there are multiple points for intervention in trying to build a different sort of world. Policing is a set of institutions that can be destroyed—defunded, disempowered, and ultimately shuttered. It is a set of things that can have their ability to act on situations changed—melting guns down, repurposing vehicles, retiring and archiving manuals. It is a set of actions that people can cease doing—no longer threatening, fining, confining, or injuring. And it is also an understanding of the world that can be repudiated—creating psychic and social worlds that do not involve the violent extraction of resources and that do not create or condone premature death for some.

Throughout this book, my goal has been to model a process of self-reflexive exploration that can help differently situated readers identify aspects of their own emotional entanglements with police power. In *The Black Unicorn*, Audre Lorde writes against "the psychology of the oppressed / where mental health is the ability / to repress / knowledge of the world's cruelty."[18] Police culture posits that all loving and respectful relationships occur on one side of a thin blue line of state-sanctioned violence. Abolitionist psychologies refuse the assumption that state violence is a precondition for relationship. While some interpersonal conflict is inevitable, this is not the same thing as violence. Relationships can exist outside a context created by violence. We can build communities in shared grief and articulate an ethic of interdependence and care. Abolitionist psychologies shift emotional investments away from the figure of the vulnerable hero toward an understanding of every person's ability to both cause and repair harm. They support people in the process of confronting our histories, stopping harm, making reparations, considering multiple subjectivities, and trying to live in relationships that are gentle and just.

NOTES

Introduction

1. To preserve anonymity, I have changed client names and some details. All case examples are presented in compliance with the American Counseling Association 2014 *Code of Ethics*: "The use of participants', clients', students', or supervisees' information for the purpose of case examples in a presentation or publication is permissible only when (a) participants, clients, students, or supervisees have reviewed the material and agreed to its presentation or publication or (b) the information has been sufficiently modified to obscure identity." "2014 American Counseling Association Code of Ethics," American Counseling Association, accessed September 11, 2020, https://www.counseling.org/resources/aca-code-of-ethics.pdf

2. Stephen Mitchell, *Can Love Last? The Fate of Romance Over Time* (New York: W. W. Norton, 2002).

3. Code Switch Podcast, "A Decade of Watching Black People Die," *National Public Radio*, May 31, 2020, https://www.npr.org/2020/05/29/865261916/a-decade-of-watching-black-people-die

4. The *Washington Post* maintains a database of people killed by police shootings that has tracked 1,466 Black people shot and killed by police from 2015 to March 2021. The *Post* finds that Black people are twice as likely to be shot and killed by U.S. police as white people. "Fatal Force," *Washington Post*, https://www.washingtonpost.com/graphics/investigations/police-shootings-database/, updated March 28, 2021. Several of the people on this list were not shot by police, but died in police custody as a result of other forms of violence.

5. Mariame Kaba, "Yes, We Mean Literally Abolish the Police," *New York Times*, June 12, 2020, https://www.nytimes.com/2020/06/12/opinion/sunday/floyd-abolish-defund-police.html

6. David Hughes, "I'm a Black Police Officer. Here's How to Change the System," *New York Times*, July 16, 2020, https://www.nytimes.com/2020/07/16/opinion/police-funding-defund.html

7. For examples of this tradition of police ethnography, see Peter Moskos, *Cop in the Hood: My Year Policing Baltimore's Eastern District* (Princeton: Princeton University Press, 2008); Didier Fassin, *Enforcing Order: An Ethnography of Urban*

Policing (Cambridge: Polity, 2013); Steve Herbert, *Policing Space: Territoriality and the LAPD* (Minneapolis: University of Minnesota Press, 1996).

8. Fiona Probyn Ramsey, "Complicity, Critique and Methodology," *ARIEL* 38, no. 2–3 (2007): 65.

9. For more discussion of public emotional investments in state-sanctioned racist violence in the U.S., see Paula Ioanide, *The Emotional Politics of Racism: How Feelings Trump Facts in an Era of Colorblindness* (Palo Alto: Stanford University Press, 2015).

10. Josef Breuer and Sigmund Freud, *Studies on Hysteria*, trans. James Strachey. In *The Standard Edition of the Complete Psychological Works of Sigmund Freud, Volume II (1893–1895)* (London: Hogarth Press, 1955), XXIX–XXX.

11. Muriel Dimen, "Rotten Apples and Ambivalence: Sexual Boundary Violations Through a Psychocultural Lens," *Journal of the American Psychoanalytic Association* 64 (2) (2016): 361–73, 364; examples in this tradition include Sally Swartz, *Ruthless Winnicott: The Role of Ruthlessness in Psychoanalysis and Political Protest* (London: Routledge, 2019); Muriel Dimen, ed., *With Culture in Mind: Psychoanalytic Stories* (New York: Routledge, 2011).

12. Muriel Dimen, "Rotten Apples," 364.

13. Muriel Dimen, "*Lapsus Linguae* or a Slip of the Tongue? A Sexual Violation in an Analytic Treatment and Its Personal and Theoretical Aftermath," *Contemporary Psychoanalysis* 47, no. 1 (2011): 35–79, 39.

14. Carolyn Laubender, "Speak for Your Self: Psychoanalysis, Autotheory, and the Plural Self," *Arizona Quarterly: A Journal of American Literature, Culture, and Theory* 76, no. 1 (2020): 39–64.

15. Lauren Fournier, *Autotheory as Feminist Practice in Art, Writing, and Criticism* (Cambridge: MIT Press, 2021), 37.

16. Maggie Nelson, *The Argonauts* (Minneapolis: Graywolf, 2015). Nelson cites Paul Preciado's use of the term in *Testo Junkie: Sex, Drugs, and Biopolitics in the Pharmacopornographic Era* (New York: Feminist Press, 2013); Audre Lorde, *Zami: A New Spelling of My Name (Watertown, MA: Persephone, 1982)*; Gloria Anzaldua, *Borderlands La Frontera* (San Francisco: Aunt Lute, 1987). For discussions of the history of the term "autotheory" see the introduction to Lauren Fournier, *Autotheory as Feminist Practice in Art, Writing, and Criticism* (Boston: MIT Press, 2021); Robyn Wiegman, "Introduction: Autotheory Theory," *Arizona Quarterly: A Journal of American Literature, Culture, and Theory* 76, no. 1 (2020): 1–14.

17. Taylor, *The Archive and the Repertoire*, 27.

18. Laura Maruschak and Todd D. Hinton, "Correctional Populations in the United States, 2017–2018," *BJS Bulletin* (Washington, DC: Bureau of Justice Statistics, Department of Justice, 2016), https://www.bjs.gov/content/pub/pdf/cpus1718.pdf

19. "Crime in the United States, 2018," *FBI Uniform Crime Report*, https://ucr.fbi.gov/crime-in-the-u.s/2018/crime-in-the-u.s.-2018/topic-pages/persons-arrested

20. Charles Epp, Steven Maynard-Moody, and Donal Haider-Markel, *Pulled*

Over: How Police Stops Define Race and Citizenship (Chicago: University of Chicago Press, 2014), 2.

21. Frank Edwards, Michael H. Esposito, and Hedwig Lee, "Risk of Police-Involved Death by Race/Ethnicity and Place, United States, 2012–2018," *American Journal of Public Health* 108, no. 9 (2018): 1241–48; Paul J. Hirschfield, "Lethal Policing: Making Sense of American Exceptionalism," *Sociological Forum* 30, no. 4 (December 2015): 1109–17.

22. "Police and Detectives," Bureau of Labor Statistics, U.S. Department of Labor, *Occupational Outlook Handbook*, accessed February 22, 2019, https://www.bls.gov/ooh/protective-service/police-and-detectives.htm

23. "Security Guards and Gaming Surveillance Officers," Bureau of Labor Statistics, U.S. Department of Labor, *Occupational Outlook Handbook*, accessed March 12, 2019, https://www.bls.gov/ooh/protective-service/security-guards.htm

24. "Who We Are," Immigration and Customs Enforcement, accessed March 12, 2019, https://www.ice.gov/about

25. Steven W. Perry and Duren Banks, "Prosecutors in State Courts, 2007," Bureau of Justice Statistics—Statistical Tables (US Department of Justice, December 2011), available at https://www.bjs.gov/index.cfm?ty=pbdetail&iid=1749

26. "FBI Uniform Crime Statistics, 2013," Federal Bureau of Investigation, accessed March 12, 2019, https://ucr.fbi.gov/crime-in-the-u.s/2013/crime-in-the-u.s.-2013

27. United States Department of Justice, *Crime in the United States, 2010* (Washington DC: Federal Bureau of Investigation, September 2011), accessed December 20, 2016, https://ucr.fbi.gov/crime-in-the-u.s/2010/crime-in-the-u.s.-2010/tables/10tbl74.xls

28. Women are more likely to drop out of policing prior to promotion. Robin Haarr, "Factors Affecting the Decision of Police Recruits to 'Drop Out' of Police Work," *Police Quarterly* 8, no. 4 (2005): 431–53. For reporting on low rates of women in police leadership, see Kevin Johnson, "Women Move into Law Enforcement's Highest Ranks," *USA Today*, December 2, 2015. Ethnic minority officers in the United Kingdom are reported to have lower rates of retention and slower time to promotion; see Nick Bland, Gary Mundy, Jacqueline Russell, and Rachel Tuffin, *Career Progression of Ethnic Minority Police Officers* (Great Britain: Home Office, Policing and Reducing Crime Unit, 1999). Black women have been reported as having especially high rates of attrition from policing in the U.S.; see William G. Doerner, "Officer Retention Patterns: An Affirmative Action Concern for Police Agencies?" *American Journal of Police* 14, nos. 3/4 (1995): 197–210.

29. U.S. Bureau of Labor Statistics, "Union Members Summary," *Economic New Release*, January 1, 2020, https://www.bls.gov/news.release/union2.nr0.htm

30. Ron DeLord and Ron York, *Law Enforcement, Police Unions, and the Future* (Springfield, IL: Charles C. Thomas, 2017), 179.

31. Vicky Wilkins and Brian N. Williams, "Representing Blue: Representative Bureaucracy and Racial Profiling in the Latino Community," *Administration & Society* 40, no. 8 (2009): 775–98; Vicky Wilkins and Brian N. Williams, "Black or

Blue: Racial Profiling and Representative Bureaucracy," *Public Administration Review* 68, no. 4 (2008): 654–64.

32. Sean Nicholson-Crotty, Jill Nicholson-Crotty, and Sergio Fernandez, "Will More Black Cops Matter? Officer Race and Police-Involved Homicides of Black Citizens," *Public Administration Review* 77, no. 2 (2017): 206–16.

33. Timoney, John F. *Beat Cop to Top Cop: A Tale of Three Cities* (Philadelphia: University of Pennsylvania Press, 2010), p. x.

34. Kaba, "Yes, We Mean."

35. Robert Reiner, *The Politics of the Police*, 2nd ed. (London: Harvester Wheatsheaf, 1992), 19.

36. Mark Neocleous, *The Fabrication of Social Order: A Critical Theory of Police Power* (London: Pluto, 2000), 93.

37. Mark Neocleous, *The Fabrication of Social Order*, xii.

38. Historian Bryan Wagner points to the fundamental role of whiteness in police power in the U.S., noting that extralegal violence has often been enacted by whites. I would highlight that this violence was state-sanctioned in both implicit and explicit ways. Both in slavery and in its afterlives, whiteness functioned as a marker of how the power to enact violence was distributed. Bryan Wagner, *Disturbing the Peace: Black Culture and the Police Power after Slavery* (Cambridge: Harvard University Press, 2009), 7.

39. Egon Bittner, "Capacity to Use Force as the Core of the Police Role," in *Moral Issues in Police Work*, eds. Fredrick A Elliston and Michael Feldberg (New York: Rowman & Littlefield, 1985), 15–25.

40. Ruth Wilson Gilmore and Craig Gilmore explain that the state has "singular control over who may commit violence, how, and to what end." Gilmore and Gilmore, "Restating the Obvious," in *Indefensible Space: The Architecture of the National Insecurity State*, ed. Michael Sorkin (New York: Routledge, 2008), 141–62.

41. In *Black Marxism*, Cedric Robinson demonstrates that from its earliest iterations in Europe, capitalism has always involved the production and exploitation of racialized others. Cedric Robinson, *Black Marxism: The Making of the Black Radical Tradition* (Chapel Hill: University of North Carolina Press, 2000).

42. Jackie Wang, *Carceral Capitalism* (South Pasadena, CA: semiotext(e), 2018), 69.

43. Norm Stamper, *To Protect and Serve: How to Fix America's Police* (New York: Nation Books, 2016), 2–3.

44. Jonathan M. Wender, *Policing and the Poetics of Everyday Life* (Urbana: University of Illinois Press, 2008), 8.

45. Jean Paul Brodeur and Benoit Dupont, "Knowledge Workers or 'Knowledge' Workers?" *Policing & Society* 16, no. 1 (March 2006): 7–26; Richard Ericson and Kevin Haggerty, *Policing the Risk Society* (Oxford: Oxford University Press, 1997).

46. Laura Huey and Rose Riciardelli, "'This Isn't What I Signed Up For': When Police Officer Role Expectations Conflict with the Realities of General Duty Police Work in Remote Communities," *International Journal of Police Science & Management* 17, no. 3 (2015), 194–203.

47. Ruth Wilson Gilmore, "Globalisation and US Prison Growth: From Military Keynesianism to Post-Keynesian Militarism," *Race & Class* 40, nos. 2–3 (1999): 171–88.

48. Wagner, *Disturbing the Peace*, 12.

49. Wagner, *Disturbing the Peace*, 6.

50. Saidiya Hartman, *Lose Your Mother: A Journey Along the Atlantic Slave Route* (New York: Macmillan, 2008), 6.

51. Naomi Murakawa and Katherine Beckett, "The Penology of Racial Innocence: The Erasure of Racism in the Study and Practice of Punishment," *Law and Society Review* 44, no. 3–4 (2010): 695–730.

52. Jackie Wang, *Carceral Capitalism*, 263.

53. Eve Tuck and K. Wayne Yang, "Decolonization Is Not a Metaphor," *Decolonization: Indigeneity, Education & Society* 1, no. 1 (2012): 10.

54. Alyson Cole, *The Cult of True Victimhood: From the War on Welfare to the War on Terror* (Palo Alto: Stanford University Press, 2007).

55. Diana Taylor, *The Archive and the Repertoire: Performing Cultural Memory in the Americas* (Durham: Duke University Press, 2003), 143.

56. Micol Siegal, *Violence Work: State Power and the Limits of Violence* (Durham: Duke University Press, 2018), 14.

57. I am using Diana Taylor's concept of scenarios here, which are "meaning-making paradigms that structure social environments, behaviors, and potential outcomes" through set-up and action. Taylor, *The Archive and the Repertoire*, 28.

58. Alison Reed, "Caption This: Police in Pussyhats, White Ladies, and Carceral Psychology Under Trump," *Abolition Journal*, September 24, 2017, https://abolition journal.org/caption-this/

59. Siegal, *Violence Work*, 14.

60. Paula Rojas, "Are the Cops in Our Heads and Hearts?," in *The Revolution Will Not be Funded*, eds. INCITE! Women of Color Against Violence (Boston: South End Press, 2009), 197–213.

61. Walidah Imarisha, Alexis Pauline Gumbs, Leah Lakshmi Piepzna-Samarasinha, Adrienne Maree Brown, and Mia Mingus, "The Fictions and Futures of Transformative Justice," *The New Inquiry*, April 20, 2017, https://thenewinquiry .com/the-fictions-and-futures-of-transformative-justice/

62. Elizabeth Bernstein, "Militarized Humanitarianism Meets Carceral Feminism: The Politics of Sex, Rights, and Freedom in Contemporary Antitrafficking Campaigns," *Signs: Journal of Women in Culture and Society* 36, no. 1 (2010): 45–71.

63. Mimi Kim, "From Carceral Feminism to Transformative Justice: Women-of-Color Feminism and Alternatives to Incarceration," *Journal of Ethnic & Cultural Diversity in Social Work* 27, no. 3 (2018): 219–33.

64. Erica Meiners, *Right to Be Hostile: Schools, Prisons, and the Making of Public Enemies* (New York, Routledge, 2010); Erica Meiners and Maisha T. Winn, "Resisting the School to Prison Pipeline: The Practice to Build Abolition Democracies," *Race Ethnicity and Education* 13, no. 3 (2010): 271–76;

65. Judah Schept, Tyler Wall, and Avi Brisman, "Building, Staffing, and Insulating: An Architecture of Criminological Complicity in the School-to-Prison Pipeline," *Social Justice* 41, no. 4 (138) (2014): 96–115.

66. Dorothy Roberts, *Shattered Bonds: The Color of Child Welfare* (New York, Civitas Books, 2009); Dorothy E. Roberts, "Prison, Foster Care, and the Systemic Punishment of Black Mothers," *UCLA Law Review* 59 (2011): 1474.

67. Erica Meiners and Charity Tolliver, "Refusing to Be Complicit in Our Prison Nation: Teachers Rethinking Mandated Reporting," *Radical Teacher* 106 (Fall 2016): 106–14, 107.

68. Angela Davis, *Are Prisons Obsolete?* (New York, Seven Stories, 2003), 114.

69. 8 to Abolition, "Why," accessed September 19, 2020, https://www.8toabolition.com/why

70. Andre Gorz, *Strategy for Labor* (Boston: Beacon Press, 1967); The concept of "non-reformist reforms" was adopted to the argument for prison abolition in Thomas Mathiesen, *The Politics of Abolition* (New York: John Wiley & Sons, 1974).

71. On colonialism in psychoanalysis, see Ranjana Khanna, *Dark Continents: Psychoanalysis and Colonialism* (Durham: Duke University Press, 2003); on the figure of the primitive in psychoanalysis, see Celia Brickman, *Aboriginal Populations of the Mind: Race and Primitivity in Psychoanalysis* (New York: Columbia University Press, 2003); on disavowed gendered racial content in psychoanalytic case studies, see Emily Green, "Melanie Klein and the Black Mammy: An Exploration of the Influence of the Mammy Stereotype on Klein's Maternal and Its Contribution to the 'Whiteness' of Psychoanalysis," *Studies in Gender and Sexuality* 19, no. 3 (2018): 164–82; for a discussion of Freud's patriarchal views on gender, see Juliet Mitchell, *Feminism and Psychoanalysis: A Radical Reassessment of Freudian Psychoanalysis* (New York: Basic Books, 2000); for a review of the conservatism of U.S. psychoanalysis around race and gender, see Alexandra Woods, "The Work Before Us: Whiteness and the Psychoanalytic Institute," *Psychoanalysis, Culture & Society* (2020).

72. Derek Hook and Ross Truscott, "Fanonian Ambivalence: On Psychoanalysis and Postcolonial Critique," *Journal of Theoretical and Philosophical Psychology* 13, no. 3 (2013): 155–69, 157.

73. Ranjana Khanna, *Dark Continents: Psychoanalysis and Colonialism* (Durham: Duke University Press, 2003), xii.

74. Steven Reisner, "From Resistance to *Resistance*: A Narrative of Psychoanalytic Activism," in *First Do No Harm: The Paradoxical Encounters of Psychoanalysis, Warmaking, and Resistance*, eds. Adrienne Harris and Steven Boticelli (London: Taylor and Francis Group, 2010), 107–41; Elizabeth Hegeman, "Institutional Betrayal and the Case of the American Psychological Association," in *Psychoanalysis, Trauma, and Community: History and Contemporary Reappraisals*, eds. Judith Alpert and Elizabeth Goren (London: Taylor and Francis Group, 2016), 214–30.

75. Reisner, "From Resistance to Resistance," 107–8.

76. "Timeline of APA Policies and Actions Related to Detainee Welfare and Professional Ethics in the Context of Interrogation and National Security," Ameri-

can Psychological Association, accessed September 15, 2020, https://www.apa.org/ne
ws/press/statements/interrogations; James Risen, "American Psychological Association Bolstered C.I.A. Torture Program, Report Says," *New York Times*, April 30,
2015, https://www.nytimes.com/2015/05/01/us/report-says-american-psychologic
al-association-collaborated-on-torture-justification.html; James Risen, "Three
Leave Jobs over Psychologists' Involvement in Torture," *New York Times*, July 15,
2015, https://www.nytimes.com/2015/07/15/us/politics/3-leave-jobs-over-psychol
ogists-involvement-in-bush-era-interrogations.html; for a position paper on refusing to participate in all interrogations, including police interrogations, see Jeffrey
Janofsky, "Lies and Coercion: Why Psychiatrists Should Not Participate in Police
and Intelligence Interrogations," *Journal of the American Academy of Psychiatry and
Law* 34 (2006): 472–78; for a discussion of the harms of psychologists colluding
with law enforcement to exploit mental health vulnerabilities of suspects, see Jeffrey
Janofsky, "Reply to Schafer: Exploitation of Criminal Suspects by Mental Health
Professionals Is Unethical," *Journal of the American Academy of Psychiatry Law* 29,
no. 4 (2001): 449–51 (PMID: 11785618).

77. "Subject: Member Letter," email sent by APA president-elect Susan H.
McDaniel, PhD, and Past President Nadine J. Kaslow, PhD, ABPP to all APA members, Aug. 14, 2015, https://www.apa.org/independent-review/member-letter

78. "IARPP 2019—Tel Aviv," International Association for Relational Psychoanalysis and Psychotherapy, accessed September 15, 2020, http://iarpp.net/confere
nce/iarpp-conference-2019-tel-aviv/

79. Statement from the Palestinian Union of Social Workers and Psychologists,
PUSWP Facebook page, posted October 1, 2018, https://www.facebook.com/PUS
WP.Palestine/posts/902274599967730

80. "Don't Go," USA-Palestine Mental Health Network, accessed September 15,
2020, https://usapalmhn.org/about-dont-go/

81. Steven Kuchuk, Dan Friedlander, and Tami Dror-Schieber, "Eyes Wide
Open: Report from the 2019 Tel Aviv Conference Committee," International Association for Relational Psychoanalysis and Psychotherapy, accessed September 15,
2020, http://iarpp.net/article/imagining-with-eyes-wide-open-report-from-the-20
19-tel-aviv-conference-committee/

82. Dorothy Evans Holmes, "Culturally Imposed Trauma: The Sleeping Dog
Has Awakened. Will Psychoanalysis Take Heed?" *Psychoanalytic Dialogues* 26, no.
6 (2016): 641–54.

83. Dorothy Evans Holmes, "Culturally Imposed Trauma," 645.

84. Jacques Lacan, *Ecrits*, trans. Bruce Fink (New York: W. W. Norton, 2002),
75–81.

85. Judith Butler, *The Force of Non-Violence* (New York: Verso, 2020), 42–43.

86. Diana Fuss, "Interior Colonies: Frantz Fanon and the Politics of Identification," *Diacritics* 24 (1994): 19–42.

87. Frantz Fanon, *Black Skin, White Masks*, trans. Richard Philcox (New York:
Grove Press, 2008).

88. Fanon, *Black Skin, White Masks*, 93.

89. George Yancy, *Look, a White! Philosophical Essays on Whiteness* (Philadelphia: Temple University Press, 2012), 3.

90. Fanon, *Black Skin, White Masks*, 93.

91. Fanon, *Black Skin, White Masks*, 93.

92. Geeta Gandbhir and Blair Foster, "A Conversation with My Black Son," *New York Times*. March 17, 2015, https://www.nytimes.com/video/opinion/1000000035 75589/a-conversation-with-my-black-son.html

93. Lynne M. Jacobs, "Learning to Love White Shame and Guilt: Skills for Working as a White Therapist in a Racially Divided Country," *International Journal of Psychoanalytic Self Psychology* 9, no. 4 (2014), 297–312, 304.

94. Jacobs, "Learning to Love White Shame and Guilt," 307.

95. Neil Altman, *White Privilege: Psychoanalytic Perspectives* (New York: Routledge, 2021), 32.

96. Altman, *White Privilege*, 32.

97. Eve Kosofsky Sedgwick, *Touching Feeling: Affect, Pedagogy, Performativity* (Durham: Duke University Press, 2003), 37.

98. Jessica Estepa, "President Trump Thanks 'Deplorables' for Helping Him Win the 2016 Election," *USA Today*, November 8, 2017, https://www.usatoday.com/story/news/politics/onpolitics/2017/11/08/president-trump-thanks-deplorables-helping-him-win-2016-election/844744001/

99. Paula Ioanide, *The Emotional Politics of Racism: How Feelings Trump Fact in an Era of Color Blindness* (Stanford: Stanford University Press, 2015), 6.

100. Klaus Theweleit traces the psychology of fascism through an analysis of memoirs written by the *Freikorps*, German paramilitary groups active after World War I. Klaus Theweleit, *Male Fantasies, Volume 1: Women Floods Bodies History* (Minneapolis: University of Minnesota Press, 1987), 56–57.

101. Klaus Theweleit, *Male Fantasies, Volume 2: Psychoanalyzing the White Terror* (Minneapolis: University of Minnesota Press, 1989), 227.

102. Critics have noted that colonialism and racism are also central to an analysis of state violence in the context of the *Freikorps*, as these men often first became involved in state violence in colonial contexts. See Kevin Amidon and Dan Krier, "On Rereading Klaus Theweleit's *Male Fantasies*," *Men and Masculinities* 11, no. 4 (2009): 488–96.

103. Michael Rogin, *Ronald Reagan, The Movie: And Other Episodes in Political Demonology* (Berkeley, University of California Press, 1987).

104. Melanie Klein, "Notes on Some Schizoid Mechanisms," in *Envy and Gratitude and Other Works 1946–1963* (New York: Free Press, 1975).

105. Melanie Klein, "A Contribution to the Psychogenesis of Manic-Depressive States," in *Love, Guilt, and Reparation and Other Works 1921–1945* (New York: The Free Press, 1975), 262–89.

106. Tyler Wall, "The Police Invention of Humanity: Notes on the 'Thin Blue Line,'" *Crime, Media, Culture: An International Journal* (September 17, 2019).

107. Klein "Notes on Some Schizoid Mechanisms."

108. Sedgwick, *Touching Feeling*, 123.

109. Tanisha "Wakumi" Douglas, comments at "Abolitionist Social Work: Possibilities, Paradox, and Praxis," online panel hosted by Haymarket Books, February 25, 2021, https://www.haymarketbooks.org/blogs/284-abolitionist-social-work-po ssibilities-paradox-and-praxis

110. Naomi Murakawa and Katherine Beckett, "The Penology of Racial Innocence: The Erasure of Racism in the Study and Practice of Punishment," *Law & Society Review* 44, no. 3–4 (2010): 695–730.

111. Saidiya Hartman, *Scenes of Subjection: Terror, Slavery, and Self-Making in Nineteenth-Century America* (Oxford: Oxford University Press, 1997).

112. Andre Lepecki, "Choreopolicing and Choreopolitics; or, the Task of the Dancer," *TDR* 57, no. 4 (Winter 2013), 20.

Chapter 1

1. To preserve anonymity, I have changed client names and some details. All case examples are presented in compliance with the American Counseling Association 2014 *Code of Ethics*: "The use of participants', clients', students', or supervisees' information for the purpose of case examples in a presentation or publication is permissible only when (a) participants, clients, students, or supervisees have reviewed the material and agreed to its presentation or publication or (b) the information has been sufficiently modified to obscure identity."

2. D. W. Winnicott, *Playing and Reality* (London: Routledge Classics, 2005), 8.

3. Winnicott, *Playing and Reality*, 9.

4. Chelsey L. Kivland, "The Magic of Guns: Scriptive Technology and Violence in Haiti," *American Ethnologist* 45, no. 3 (2018), 354–66, 364.

5. D. W. Winnicott, "Hate in the Counter-Transference," *International Journal of Psychoanalysis* 30 (1949), 69–74.

6. Winnicott, *Playing and Reality*, 123.

7. Winnicott, *Playing and Reality*, 123.

8. Winnicott, *Playing and Reality*, 125.

9. Winnicott, *Playing and Reality*, 123.

10. Claudia Rankine, *Citizen: An American Lyric* (Minneapolis: Graywolf Press, 2014), 18.

11. Rankine, *Citizen*, 18.

12. María Lugones, *Pilgrimages/Peregrinajes: Theorizing Coalitions Against Multiple Oppressions* (Lanham, MD: Rowman & Littlefield, 2003), 73.

13. Shannon Sullivan, *Good White People: The Problem with Middle-Class White Anti-Racism* (Albany: SUNY Press, 2014).

14. Ellen Kirshman, Mark Kamena, and Joel Fay, *Counseling Cops: What Clinicians Need to Know* (New York: Guilford Press, 2014).

15. Kirschman, Kamena, and Fay, *Counseling Cops*, 17.

16. Derald Wing Sue, Patricia Arredondo, and Roderick J. McDavis, "Multicultural Counseling Competencies and Standards: A Call to the Profession," *Journal of Counseling & Development* 70, no. 4 (1992): 477–86, 479.

17. Kirschman, Kamena, and Fay, *Counseling Cops*, 17.

18. Jonathan Metzl, *Dying of Whiteness: How the Politics of Racial Resentment Is Killing America's Heartland* (New York: Basic Books, 2019), 77.

19. Sigmund Freud, "An Outline of Psychoanalysis," *International Journal of Psychoanalysis XXI* (1940), 77.

20. Rick Noack, "Five Countries Where Most Police Officers Do Not Carry Guns—And It Works Well," *Washington Post*, July 8, 2016, https://www.washington post.com/news/worldviews/wp/2015/02/18/5-countries-where-police-officers-do -not-carry-firearms-and-it-works-well/

21. See, for example, the Chicago Police Department policy, "Department Approved Weapons and Ammunition," Chicago Police Department, directive issued February 28, 2020, http://directives.chicagopolice.org/directives/data/a7a57 be2-12ce0ca3-81d12-ce0c-aae3aeb1a519d78b.html

22. Ashley Southall, "New York Police Department Is Retiring the Revolver," *New York Times*, May 31, 2018, https://www.nytimes.com/2018/05/31/nyregion /new-york-police-revolver.html

23. Jay Stuart Berman, *Police Administration and Progressive Reform: Theodore Roosevelt as Police Commissioner of New York* (Westport, CT: Greenwood Press, 1987), 89–90.

24. Handguns are classified by the type of bullet cartridge they have and by the size of their bullets. Handguns can be revolvers or semiautomatic, and are distinguished from long guns such as shotguns and rifles in that they can be used one-handed and carried more easily on a person. Caliber is the term that describes the internal diameter of the gun barrel. A .40 caliber barrel is 0.40 inches across on the inside. When caliber is discussed in metric, the word "caliber" is typically dropped and the name often simply states "millimeter." For example, people might discuss a .40-caliber or a 9-mm—both are talking about gun barrel size, the size of the bullets that they shoot. With shotguns, each gauge has a specific caliber—a 12-gauge shotgun has a caliber of .729 inches (18.53 mm), shooting a bullet with just over twice the diameter of a 9-mm handgun. "Glossary of Basic Firearms Terms," *The Range 702*, accessed September 19, 2020, https://www.therange702.com/blog/glossary-of -basic-firearm-terms/

25. Jane Fritsch, "Gun of Choice for Police Officers Runs into Fierce Opposition," *New York Times*, May 31, 1992, https://www.nytimes.com/1992/05/31/nyregi on/gun-of-choice-for-police-officers-runs-into-fierce-opposition.html

26. Doug Wylie, "9 mm vs. 40 caliber: How Do the Cartridges Stack Up?" *PoliceOne*, February 2, 2017, https://www.policeone.com/police-products/firearms/art icles/286263006-9mm-vs-40-caliber-How-do-the-cartridges-stack-up/

27. Dave Bahde, "7 Reasons Why Cops Choose the 9mm Over the .40," *Tactical Life*, June 26, 2018, https://www.tactical-life.com/firearms/handguns/7-reasons-co ps-choose-9mm-40/

28. For example, the Chicago Police Department requires annual qualification. "Annual Prescribed Weapon Qualification Program and Taser Recertification," Chicago Police Department, directive issued January 13, 2016, http://directives.chicag opolice.org/directives/data/a7a57be2-12b458ab-85a12-b45a-3d21647cad2b24db.html

29. Kirschman, Kamena, and Fay, *Counseling Cops*, 17.

30. Vron Ware, *Beyond the Pale: White Women, Racism, and History* (New York: Verso Books, 2015).

31. "Apply for a Firearms License," New York State website, accessed September 20, 2016, https://www.ny.gov/services/apply-firearms-license

32. Alec Wilkinson, "The Dark Presence of Guns," *New Yorker*, December 22, 2012, https://www.newyorker.com/news/news-desk/the-dark-presence-of-guns

33. Norm Stamper, *Breaking Rank: A Top Cop's Exposé of the Dark Side of American Policing* (New York: Nation Books, 2005), x.

34. Metzl, *Dying of Whiteness*, 76.

35. Metzl, *Dying of Whiteness*, 76.

36. Lacan, *Ecrits*, 581.

37. Judith Butler, *Gender Trouble: Feminism and the Subversion of Identity* (New York, Routledge, 1990), 44.

38. Patricia Gherovici, *Transgender Psychoanalysis: A Lacanian Perspective on Sexual Difference* (New York: Routledge, 2017), 31.

39. Hortense Spillers, "Mama's Baby, Papa's Maybe: An American Grammar Book," *diacritics* 17, no. 2 (1987): 65–81.

40. Fanon, *Black Skin, White Masks*, 157.

41. Angela P. Harris, "Gender, Violence, Race, and Criminal Justice," *Stanford Law Review* 52 (1999): 777.

42. Frank Rudy Cooper, "Who's the Man? Masculinities Studies, Terry Stops, and Police Training," *Columbia Journal of Gender and Law* 18 (2008): 671.

43. Andrea Ritchie, *Invisible No More: Police Violence Against Black Women and Women of Color* (Boston: Beacon, 2017), 14–15.

44. Heidi Nast, "The Machine-Phallus: Psychoanalyzing the Geopolitical Economy of Masculinity and Race," *Psychoanalytic Inquiry* 35 (2015): 766–85.

45. Jessica Anderson, "County Police Move to Keep Their Old Guns Off the Street—But at a Cost," *Baltimore Sun* September 25, 2013, https://www.baltimoresun.com/maryland/baltimore-county/bs-md-co-new-guns-20130913-story.html

46. Anderson, "County Police Move to Keep Their Old Guns."

47. Fritsch, "Gun of Choice."

48. See for example K. M. Hoffman, S. Trawalter, J. Axt, and M. N. Oliver, "Racial Bias in Pain Assessment and Treatment Recommendations, and False Beliefs about Biological Differences between Blacks and Whites," *Proceedings of the National Academy of Sciences of the United States of America* 113, no. 16 (2016), 4296–4301.

49. Bill Brown, "Thing Theory," *Critical Inquiry* 28, no. 1 (Autumn 2001): 4.

50. Christina Sharpe, *In the Wake: On Blackness and Being* (Durham: Duke University Press, 2016), 82.

51. Sharpe, *In the Wake*, 83.

52. Terrence McCoy, "Darren Wilson explains why he killed Michael Brown," *Washington Post*, November 25, 2014.

53. Monica Davie and Julie Bosman, "Protests Flare after Ferguson Police Officer Is Not Indicted," *New York Times*, November 25, 2014, https://www.nytimes.com/2014/11/25/us/ferguson-darren-wilson-shooting-michael-brown-grand-jury.html

54. Sam Frizell, "Ferguson Police Are Testing 'Less-Lethal' Attachments for Guns," *Time Magazine*, February 4, 2015, http://time.com/3695435/ferguson-police -michael-brown-guns/

55. "How It Works," *Alternative Ballistics*, accessed August 31, 2020, http://www .alternativeballistics.com/en/how-it-works/how-it-works

56. Ben Miller, "Data Pinpoints Moment When Police Body Cameras Took Off," *Government Technology*, January 28, 2019, https://www.govtech.com/data/Data-Pi npoints-the-Moment-When-Police-Body-Cameras-Took-Off.html

57. Susan Sontag, *On Photography* (New York: Farrar, Strauss, and Giroux, 1977), 14.

Chapter 2

1. This vignette is a composite in which some identifying details have been changed.

2. Sigmund Freud, *Dora: An Analysis of a Case of Hysteria* (New York: Touchstone, 1967).

3. Judith Herman, *Trauma and Recovery: The Aftermath of Violence—From Domestic Abuse to Political Terror* (New York: Basic Books, 2015), 13–14.

4. "Police Life Expectancy," Google search results, October 20, 2015.

5. "The Cleveland Division," *60 Minutes*, May 15, 2015, cbsnews.com/news/cle veland-police-60-minutes-bill-whitaker-2/; Stanley Crouch, "Some Lessons about Why Cops Have the Blues," *NY Daily News*, September 8, 1996.

6. John Violanti, John E. Vena, and Sandra Petralia, "Mortality of a Police Cohort: 1950–1990," *American Journal of Industrial Medicine* 33, no. 4 (1998): 366–73.

7. John Violanti et al., "Life Expectancy in Police Officers: A Comparison with the US General Population." *International Journal of Emergency Mental Health* 15, no. 4 (2013): 217.

8. Gina Kolata, "The Price for 'Predatory' Publishing? $50 Million," *New York Times*, April 3, 2019.

9. California Public Employees Retirement Fund Actuarial Office, *CalPERS Experience Study*, April 2010, https://www.calpers.ca.gov/docs/forms-publications /calpers-experience-study-2010.pdf; see also R. A. Raub, *Police Officer Retirement: The Beginning of a Long Life* (Illinois State Police, Division of Administration, 1987).

10. Bureau of Labor Statistics, "2017 Census of Fatal Occupational Injuries Summary," news release, Dec. 18, 2018, available at https://www.bls.gov/news.release /pdf/cfoi.pdf

11. Bureau of Labor Statistics, "Illnesses, Injuries, and Fatalities: Fact Sheet, Police Officers," August 2016 https://www.bls.gov/iif/oshwc/cfoi/police-officers-20 14.htm

12. With 24.2 suicides per 100,000 workers in 2015, police officer deaths by suicide were almost double the rate of on-the-job deaths. See Hope M. Tiesman, "Workplace Suicide," NIOSH Science Blog, April 13, 2015, https://blogs-origin.cdc .gov/niosh-science-blog/2015/04/13/workplace-suicide/

13. National Center for Health Statistics. *Health, United States, 2017: With Special Features on Mortality* (Hyattsville, MD: US Department of Health and Human Services, 2018), https://www.cdc.gov/nchs/data/hus/hus17.pdf

14. J. Q. Xu, S. L. Murphy, K. D. Kochanek, and E. Arias, *Mortality in the United States, 2018*, NCHS Data Brief, no 355. (Hyattsville, MD: National Center for Health Statistics, 2020); Kenneth D. Kochanek, Jiaquan Xu, and Elizabeth Arias, *Mortality in the United States, 2019*, NCHS Data Brief No. 395, December 2020 (Hyattsville, MD: National Center for Health Statistics, 2020); Sabrina Tavernise and Abby Goodnough, "American Life Expectancy Rises for First Time in Three Years," *New York Times*, January 30, 2020, https://www.nytimes.com/2020/01/30/us/us-life-expectancy.html

15. Elizabeth Arias, Betzaida Tejada-Vera, and Farida Ahmad, "Provisional Life Expectancy Estimates for January through June, 2020," *Vital Statistics Rapid Release*, February 2021, https://www.cdc.gov/nchs/data/vsrr/VSRR10-508.pdf

16. Ann Case and Angus Deaton, *Deaths of Despair and the Future of Capitalism* (Princeton: Princeton University Press, 2020).

17. Case and Deaton, *Deaths of Despair*, 38–39.

18. Ruth Wilson Gilmore, *Golden Gulag* (Berkeley: University of California Press, 2006), 28.

19. Joanna Drowosa, Charles H. Hennekens, Robert S. Levine, "Variations in Mortality from Legal Intervention in the United States—1999 to 2013," *Preventive Medicine* 81 (December 2015): 290–93. The study also found extreme variations in the death rate depending on geographic location, with southwestern states showing the highest rates of death by legal intervention.

20. Timothy Cunningham, Janet B. Croft, Yong Liu, Hua Lu, Paul I. Eke, and Wayne H. Giles, "Vital Signs: Racial Disparities in Age-Specific Mortality among Blacks or African Americans—United States, 1999–2015." *MMWR. Morbidity and Mortality Weekly Report* 66, no. 17 (2017): 444.

21. Elizabeth Arias et al, 2021.

22. See, for example, Keith Phaneuf and Jenna Carlesso, "Senate Revives, then Adopts Deal on PTSD Benefits for First Responders," *The CT Mirror*, May 30, 2019, https://ctmirror.org/2019/05/30/senate-democrats-gop-revive-deal-on-ptsd-benefits-for-first-responders/; Mary Sanchez, "Opinion: Police Suicide Reflects Toll of Unaddressed PTSD," February 19, 2019, *Atlanta Journal-Constitution*, https://www.ajc.com/news/opinion/opinion-police-suicide-reflects-toll-unaddressed-ptsd/zuurEjzYIdDzQ6FcDPlYjI/

23. Lauren Berlant, *Cruel Optimism* (Durham: Duke University Press, 2011).

24. Paula Ioanide, "Defensive Appropriations," in *Antiracism Inc.: Why the Way We Talk about Racial Justice Matters*, eds. Felicia Blake, Paula Ioanide, and Alison Reed (Santa Barbara: Punctum, 2019), 85.

25. "Blue Lives Matter" Facebook page, accessed September 20, 2020, https://www.facebook.com/bluematters/; the *Police Tribune* website, accessed September 20, 2020, https://bluelivesmatter.blue/about-the-police-tribune/

26. Officer Down Memorial Page, accessed September 20, 2020, www.odmp.org; Below 100, accessed September 20, 2020, www.below100.org

27. Judith Butler, *Notes Toward a Performative Theory of Assembly* (Cambridge, MA: Harvard University Press, 2015), 146.

28. Alyson Cole, *The Cult of True Victimhood: From the War on Welfare to the War on Terror* (Palo Alto, CA: Stanford University Press, 2007).

29. Cole, *The Cult of True Victimhood*.

30. Cole, *The Cult of True Victimhood*, 5.

31. Butler, *Notes Toward a Performative Theory of Assembly*, 146.

32. Butler, *Notes Toward a Performative Theory of Assembly*, 149.

33. Frank Dowling, Gene Moynihan, Bill Genet, and Jonathan Lewis, "A Peer-Based Assistance Program for Officers with the New York City Police Department: Report of the Effects of Sept. 11, 2001," *American Journal of Psychiatry* 163, no. 1 (2006), 151–53.

34. Vincent Henry, *Death Work: Police, Trauma, and the Psychology of Survival* (Oxford: Oxford University Press, 2004).

35. I am using Ruth Wilson Gilmore's definition of racism as the "the state-sanctioned or extralegal production and exploitation of group-differentiated vulnerability to premature death." Gilmore, *Golden Gulag*, 28.

36. Claudette Lauzon, "Drones Gone Wild, and Other Unruly Bodies of War: A Contemporary Art History," lecture at the Vancouver Institute for Social Research, November 14, 2016.

37. Alexis Artwohl and Loren W. Christensen, *Deadly Force Encounters: What Cops Need to Know to Mentally and Physically Prepare for and Survive a Gunfight* (Boulder, CO: Paladin Press, 1997).

38. Micol Seigal, *Violence Work*, 9.

39. Lauren Berlant, quoted in "Lauren Berlant on her book Cruel Optimism," *ROROTOKO*, June 4, 20102, http://rorotoko.com/interview/20120605_berlant_lauren_on_cruel_optimism

40. David Graeber, *The Utopia of Rules: On Technology, Stupidity, and the Secret Joys of Bureaucracy* (Brooklyn: Melville House Press, 2015), 73.

41. Wender, *Policing and the Poetics of Everyday Life*, 8.

42. Norm Stamper, *To Protect and Serve: How to Fix America's Police* (New York: Nation Books, 2016), 2–3.

43. Veena Das, *Life and Words: Violence and the Descent into the Ordinary* (Berkeley: University of California Press, 2007), 169.

44. Das, *Life and Words*, 172.

45. Das, *Life and Words*, 163.

46. The double bind is described in Gregory Bateson, *Steps to an Ecology of the Mind: A Revolutionary Approach to Man's Understanding of Himself* (Chicago: University of Chicago Press, 1972), 271–78.

47. Max Weber, *From Max Weber: Essays in Sociology* (Oxford: Oxford University Press, 1946), 216.

48. Robert Garot, "'You're Not a Stone' Emotional Sensitivity in a Bureaucratic Setting," *Journal of Contemporary Ethnography* 33, no. 6 (2004): 735–766.

49. Dean Spade discusses administrative violence in Dean Spade, *Normal Life*:

Administrative Violence, Critical Trans Politics, and the Limits of Law (Boston: South End Press, 2012).

50. Timothy Roufa, "The 10 Worst Things About Being a Police Officer," *The Balance Careers*, May 7, 2019, https://www.thebalancecareers.com/the-10-worst-things-about-being-a-police-officer-974911

51. Lauren Berlant, *Cruel Optimism* (Durham: Duke University Press, 2011), 137.

52. John Violanti, "Suicide and the Police Role: A Psychosocial Model," *An International Journal of Police Strategies and Management* 20 (1997): 698–715.

53. Artwohl and Christensen, *Deadly Force Encounters*, 5.

54. Artwohl and Christensen, *Deadly Force Encounters*, 3.

55. Ryan Grim and Aida Chávez, "Minneapolis Police Union President: 'I've Been Involved in Three Shootings Myself, and Not One of Them Has Bothered Me," *The Intercept*, June 2, 2020, https://theintercept.com/2020/06/02/minneapolis-poli ce-union-bob-kroll-shootings/

56. Melanie Klein, "Some Notes on Schizoid Mechanisms."

57. Sedgwick, *Touching Feeling*, 137.

Chapter 3

1. Richard Pérez-Peña, "Why First Aid Is Often Lacking in the Moments After a Police Shooting," *New York Times*, September 21, 2016, https://www.nytimes.com /2016/09/22/us/why-first-aid-is-often-lacking-in-the-moments-after-a-police-sho oting.html

2. Derek Hook, *Foucault, Psychology, and the Analytics of Power* (New York: Palgrave MacMillan, 2007), 2.

3. Michel Foucault, *The History of Sexuality: Volume 1*, trans. Robert Hurley (New York: Vintage, 1990), 140.

4. "Police and Public Safety," American Psychological Association, accessed August 31, 2020, https://www.apadivisions.org/division-18/sections/police/index ?_ga=2.242336130.18830214.1591473166-1403395913.1591473166

5. Daniel J. Jones, "The Potential Impacts of Pandemic Policing on Police Legitimacy: Planning Past the Covid-19 Crisis," *Policing: A Journal of Policy and Practice* (June 2020).

6. For more on the emergence of the carceral state as an outgrowth of liberal reform, see Naomi Murakawa, *The First Civil Right: How Liberals Built Prison America* (New York: Oxford University Press, 2014).

7. Eric Monkkonen, "History of Urban Police," *Crime and Justice* 15 (1992): 547–80.

8. Lewis Terman, *The Measurement of Intelligence* (Houghton, Mifflin and Company, 1916).

9. Terman, *Measurement of Intelligence*, 8.

10. Alexandra Minna Stern, *Eugenic Nation: Faults and Frontiers of Better Breeding in Modern America* (Berkeley: University of California Press, 2015), 79.

11. Angie Kennedy, "Eugenics, 'Degenerate Girls,' and Social Workers During the Progressive Era," *Affilia: Journal of Women and Social Work* 23, no. 1 (February 2008): 22–37.

12. Lewis Terman, Arthur Otis, Virgil Dickson, O. Hubbard, J. Norton, Lowry Howard, J. Flanders, and C. Cassingham, "A Trial of Mental and Pedagogical Tests in a Civil Service Examination for Policemen and Firemen." *Journal of Applied Psychology* 1, no. 1 (1917): 17.

13. Lewis Madison Terman, "The Use of Intelligence Tests in the Army," *Psychological Bulletin* 15, no. 6 (1918): 177.

14. John L. Rury, "Race, Region, and Education: An Analysis of Black and White Scores on the 1917 Army Alpha Intelligence Test," *Journal of Negro Education* 57, no. 1 (1988): 51–65.

15. Peter Weiss and Robin Inwald, "A Brief History of Personality Assessment in Police Psychology," in *Personality Assessment in Police Psychology: A 21st-Century Perspective*, ed. Peter Weiss (Springfield, IL: Charles C. Thomas, 2010), 5–28; Curt R. Bartol and Anne M. Bartol, "History of Forensic Psychology," *The Handbook of Forensic Psychology* (1999): 3–23.

16. All of these tests continue to be used by police departments in making hiring decisions. William U. Weiss, Kevin Buehler, and David Yates, "The Psychopathic Deviate Scale of the MMPI in Police Selection," *Journal of Police and Criminal Psychology* 10, no. 4 (1995): 57–60; Peter Weiss and Robin Inwald, "A Brief History of Personality Assessment in Police Psychology," in *Personality Assessment*, ed. Peter Weiss, 5–28.

17. Martin I. Kurke and Ellen M. Scrivner, eds., *Police Psychology into the 21st Century* (Hillsdale, NJ: Lawrence Erlbaum Associates, 1995), 10.

18. Elizabeth Hinton, "'A War within Our Own Boundaries': Lyndon Johnson's Great Society and the Rise of the Carceral State," *Journal of American History* 102, no. 1 (June 2015):, 100–112.

19. President's Commission on Law Enforcement and Administration of Justice, *The Challenge of Crime in a Free Society* (Washington, DC: US Government Printing Office, 1967), https://www.ncjrs.gov/pdffiles1/nij/42.pdf

20. Weiss and Inwald, "A Brief History of Personality Assessment in Police Psychology: 1916–2008," *Journal of Police and Criminal Psychology* 33 (May 2018): 189–200, 190.

21. Steve Chawkins, "Martin Reiser Dies at 87; LAPD's First Staff Psychologist," *LA Times*, April 16, 2015, https://www.latimes.com/local/obituaries/la-me-martin-reiser-20150417-story.html

22. Martin Reiser, *The Police Department Psychologist* (Springfield, IL: Thomas, 1972).

23. Kerner Commission, "National Advisory Commission on Civil Disorder" (Washington, DC: US Government Printing Office, 1968).

24. Adorno, Theodor, Else Frenkel-Brenswik, Daniel J. Levinson, and R. Nevitt Sanford, *The Authoritarian Personality* (London: Verso Books, 2019); Ellen Herman, *The Romance of American Psychology: Political Culture in the Age of Experts* (Berkeley: University of California Press, 1995).

25. Cochrane, Robert E., Robert P. Tett, and Leon Vandecreek, "Psychological Testing and the Selection of Police Officers: A National Survey," *Criminal Justice and Behavior* 30, no. 5 (2003): 511–37.

26. Weiss and Inwald, "A Brief History."

27. Tom Avril, "Blacks Fail Philly Police Psych Screening More than Whites," *Philadelphia Inquirer*, December 16, 2015, https://www.inquirer.com/philly/health /20151216_Blacks_fail_Philly_police_psych_screening_more_than_whites.html

28. Dan Ivers, "Bias Claims Against Psych Testing Firm Could Delay Newark Police Hires," nj.com, August 4, 2015, https://www.nj.com/essex/2015/08/bias_clai ms_against_psych_testing_firm_threaten_ne.html

29. Sujata S. Menjoge, "Testing the Limits of Anti-Discrimination Law: How Employers' Use of Pre-Employment Psychological and Personality Test Can Circumvent Title VII and the ADA," *North Carolina Law Review*. 82 (2003): 365.

30. Eduardo Bonilla-Silva, *Racism without Racists: Color-blind Racism and the Persistence of Racial Inequality in Contemporary America* (Lanham, MD: Rowman & Littlefield Publishers, 2014), 15.

31. Weiss and Inwald, "A Brief History," 191.

32. Weiss and Inwald, 191.

33. Weiss and Inwald, 192.

34. Psychological Services Section, "Section History," International Association of Chiefs of Police, accessed August 1, 2020, https://www.theiacp.org/sites/default /files/2019-12/Psychological%20Services%20Section%20History.pdf

35. "Police Psychological Services Section: Membership," International Association of Chiefs of Police, accessed September 10, 2020, https://www.theiacp.org/wor king-group/section/psychological-services-section

36. Psychological Services Section, "Section History," International Association of Chiefs of Police, accessed August 1, 2020, https://www.theiacp.org/sites/default /files/2019-12/Psychological%20Services%20Section%20History.pdf

37. "Educational Opportunities in Police and Criminal Psychology," Society for Police and Criminal Psychology, accessed September 11, 2020, http://www.policep sychology.org/Education

38. David M. Corey, Michael J. Cuttler, David R. Cox, and Jaime Brower, "Board Certification in Police Psychology: What It Means to Public Safety" *Police Chief* 78 (August 2011): 100–104.

39. "Psychologists in Public Service," American Psychology Association, accessed September 20, 2020, https://www.apa.org/about/division/div18

40. Sharon M. Freeman Clevenger, Laurence Miller, Bret A. Moore, and Arthur Freeman, eds., *Behind the Badge: A Psychological Treatment Handbook for Law Enforcement Officers* (New York: Routledge, 2015).

41. Henry, *Death Work*, vii–viii.

42. "Police and Public Safety Psychology," American Psychology Association, last updated August 2020, https://www.apa.org/ed/graduate/specialize/police

43. President's Task Force on 21st Century Policing, *Final Report of the President's Task Force on 21st Century Policing* (Washington, DC: Office of Community Oriented Policing Services, 2015).

44. Press release, "'We Are Living in a Racism Pandemic' says APA President," American Psychological Association, issued May 29, 2020, available https://www.apa .org/news/press/releases/2020/05/racism-pandemic

45. Dennis Fox, Isaac Prilleltensky, and Stephanie Austin, "Critical Psychology for Social Justice: Concerns and Dilemmas," in *Critical Psychology: An Introduction*, eds. D. Fox, I. Prilleltensky, and S. Austin (Thousand Oaks, CA: Sage Publications, 2009), 3–19, 3.

46. Judah Schept, Tyler Wall, and Avi Brisman, "Building, Staffing, and Insulating: An Architecture of Criminological Complicity in the School-to-Prison Pipeline," *Social Justice* 41, no. 4 (138) (2014): 96–115, accessed September 11, 2020, http://www.jstor.org.proxy.lib.sfu.ca/stable/24871277

47. Lynne Haney, "Motherhood as Punishment: The Case of Parenting in Prison," *Signs* 39, no. 1 (Autumn 2013); Lynne Haney, *Offending Women: Power, Punishment, and the Regulation of Desire* (Berkeley: University of California Press, 2010).

48. Estelle Freedman, *Their Sister's Keepers* (Ann Arbor: University of Michigan Press, 1981).

49. Jessi Lee Jackson, "The Necropolitics of Prison Rape Elimination," *Signs* 39, no. 1 (Autumn 2013).

50. Regarding domestic violence laws, see Elizabeth Bernstein, "Militarized Humanitarianism Meets Carceral Feminism: The Politics of Sex, Rights, and Freedom in Contemporary Anti-Trafficking Campaigns," *Signs* 40, no.1 (2014). Regarding sex trafficking, see Elizabeth Bernstein, "Carceral Politics as Gender Justice? The 'Traffic in Women' and Neoliberal Circuits of Crime, Sex, and Rights," *Theory and Society* 41, no. 3 (2012): 233–59. Regarding hate crimes, see Dean Spade, *Normal Life: Administrative Violence, Critical Trans Politics, and the Limits of Law* (Boston: South End Press, 2011); Eric A. Stanley, Dean Spade, and Queer (In)Justice, "Queering Prison Abolition, Now?" *American Quarterly* 64, no. 1 (2012): 115–27; and Joey L. Mogul, Andrea J. Ritchie, and Kay Whitlock, *Queer (In)Justice: The Criminalization of LGBT People in the United States* (Boston: Beacon, 2011).

51. Naomi Murakawa and Katherine Beckett, "The Penology of Racial Innocence: The Erasure of Racism in the Study and Practice of Punishment," *Law and Society Review* 44, no. 3/4 (2010): 695–730.

52. Murakawa and Beckett, "The Penology of Racial Innocence," 701.

53. "Officer-Involved Shooting Guidelines, 2018," Psychological Services Section, International Association of Chiefs of Police, https://www.theiacp.org/sites/de fault/files/2019-05/Officer%20Involved%20Shooting%20Guidelines%202018.pdf

54. "About," *International Association of Chiefs of Police*, accessed November 13, 2020, https://www.theiacp.org/about-iacp

55. "Officer-Involved Shooting Guidelines, 2018."

56. "Administrative Guidelines for Dealing with Officers Involved in On-Duty Shooting Situations," *IACP Psychological Services Section, 1988 Annual Section Meeting*, Alexandria, VA: International Association of Chiefs of Police, 1988.

57. International Association of Chiefs of Police, *Officer-Involved Shootings: A*

Guide for Law Enforcement Leaders (Washington, DC: Office of Community Oriented Policing Services, 2016), 1.

58. International Association of Chiefs of Police. *Officer-Involved Shootings*, cover copy.

59. International Association of Chiefs of Police, 23.

60. International Association of Chiefs of Police, 7.

61. International Association of Chiefs of Police, 7.

62. International Association of Chiefs of Police, 26.

63. International Association of Chiefs of Police, 26.

64. International Association of Chiefs of Police, 25.

65. International Association of Chiefs of Police, 25.

66. International Association of Chiefs of Police, 7.

67. International Association of Chiefs of Police, 18.

68. International Association of Chiefs of Police, 22.

69. David Hunn and Kim Bell, "Why Was Michael Brown's Body Left There for Hours?" *St. Louis Post-Dispatch*, September 14, 2014; Julie Bosman and John Goldstein, "Timeline for a Body: 4 hours in the middle of a Ferguson Street," *New York Times*, August 23, 2014.

70. Claudia Rankine, "The Condition of Black Life Is One of Mourning," *New York Times Magazine*, June 22, 2015, https://www.nytimes.com/2015/06/22/magazine/the-condition-of-black-life-is-one-of-mourning.html

71. Jeremy Gorner and Gregory Pratt, "Cop Who Shot Quintonio LeGrier and Neighbor Sues Teen's Estate, Claiming Trauma," *Chicago Tribune*, February 6, 2016, http://www.chicagotribune.com/news/local/breaking/ct-robert-rialmo-quintonio-legrier-20160206-story.html

72. David Schaper, "Claiming Emotional Trauma, Chicago Officer Countersues Victim's Estate," *NPR Morning Edition*, February 10, 2016, http://www.npr.org/2016/02/10/466250515/claiming-emotional-trauma-chicago-officer-countersues-estate-of-victim-he-shot

73. Dan Hinkel, "Benefit for Robert Rialmo, Cop Who Fatally Shot Teenager and Bystander, Will Raffle Gift Certificates for Guns," *Chicago Tribune*, May 2, 2019, https://www.chicagotribune.com/news/ct-met-chicago-police-union-shooting-robert-rialmo-raffle-guns-20190502-story.html

74. "Judge to CPD: Return Gun Back to Robert Rialmo," *WGN News*, November 28, 2018, https://wgntv.com/news/judge-rialmo-gets-his-gun-back/

75. Dan Hinkel, "Benefit for Robert Rialmo"; "Cop Who Shot LeGrier, Jones Starts GoFundMe to Pay Legal Bills," *NBC5 Chicago News*, January 27, 2018, https://www.nbcchicago.com/news/local/robert-rialmo-gofundme/154071/

76. Sam Charles, "Days After Acquittal, Robert Rialmo Involved in Another Bar Scuffle," *Chicago Sun-Times*, July 13, 2018, https://chicago.suntimes.com/2018/7/13/18327514/days-after-acquittal-chicago-cop-robert-rialmo-involved-in-another-bar-scuffle

77. Isaac Stanley-Becker, "She Fatally Shot an Unarmed Black Man. Now She's Teaching Other Police Officers How To 'Survive' Such Incidents," *Washington Post*,

August 28, 2018, https://www.washingtonpost.com/news/morning-mix/wp/2018
/08/28/she-fatally-shot-an-unarmed-black-man-now-shes-teaching-other-cops
-how-to-survive-such-incidents/

78. Stetson Payne, "Former Tulsa Police Officer Betty Shelby to Teach Basic
NRA Pistol Course with Husband," *Tulsa World*, April 24, 2019, https://
tulsaworld.com/news/local/former-tulsa-police-officer-betty-shelby-to-teach-
basic-nra-pistol-course-with-husband/article_0380c8b4-fdd3-5a59-80f9-
b4bd2ec9ce40.html

79. Associated Press, "DOJ: No Civil Rights Charge in Police Shooting," *AP
News*, March 1, 2019, https://apnews.com/article/e8b98d48130a4426b193a514280
320d5; Faith Karimi, Eric Levenson, and Justin Gamble, "Tulsa Cop Not Guilty in
Fatal Shooting of Unarmed Black Man," *CNN*, May 17, 2017, https://www.cnn.com
/2017/05/17/us/tulsa-police-shooting-trial/index.html

80. Frantz Fanon, *The Wretched of the Earth*, trans. Richard Philcox (New York:
Grove Press, 2004), 196.

81. Fanon, *The Wretched of the Earth*, 198.

82. Fanon, *The Wretched of the Earth*, 199.

Chapter 4

1. Laura Dimon and Rocco Parascandola, "NYPD to Start 'Implicit Bias Training,'" *PoliceOne*, February 18, 2018, https://www.policeone.com/patrol-issues/articl
es/470642006-NYPD-to-start-implicit-bias-training/

2. Implicit-bias trainings are one of the major recommendations of the President's Report on Twenty-First Century Policing produced in the aftermath of the
Ferguson protests. See President's Task Force on 21st Century Policing, *Final Report
of the President's Task Force on 21st-Century Policing* (Washington, DC: Office of
Community Oriented Policing Services, 2015). In June 2016, the Department of
Justice mandated department-wide training in implicit bias for all employees,
including all FBI agents, DEA agents, ATF agents, and U.S. Marshals. See Department of Justice, "Department of Justice Announces New Department-Wide Implicit
Bias Training for Personnel," 2016, https://www.justice.gov/opa/pr/department-jus
tice-announces-new-department-wide-implicit-bias-training-personnel

3. President Joseph Biden, "Executive Order on Advancing Racial Equity and
Support for Underserved Communities Through the Federal Government," January 20, 2021, https://www.whitehouse.gov/briefing-room/presidential-actions/20
21/01/20/executive-order-advancing-racial-equity-and-support-for-underserved
-communities-through-the-federal-government/

4. Kimberlé Crenshaw and Andrea Ritchie argue that "the problem is not
[...] whether the police officers in question [...] had been exposed to implicit
bias trainings." Rather, the problem is that "police relations reinforce the structural marginality of all members of Black communities in myriad ways." Kimberlé Williams Crenshaw and Andrea J. Ritchie, *Say Her Name: Resisting Police
Brutality Against Black Women* (New York: African American Policy Forum,

Center for Intersectionality and Social Policy Studies, 2015); Destiny Peery, "Implicit Bias Training for Police May Help, But It's Not Enough," *Huffington Post*, March 14, 2016, http://www.huffingtonpost.com/destiny-peery/implicit-bias-training-fo_b_9464564.html

5. This organization has been awarded competitive contracts with national and local police agencies.

6. J. L. Austin, *How to Do Things with Words*, 2nd ed. (Cambridge: Harvard University Press, 1975).

7. For example, see "Lovejoy Hosts Seminar on Impartial Policing, Seeks to Address Bias," *Clayton News-Daily*, April 23, 2017, https://www.news-daily.com/news/lovejoy-hosts-seminar-on-impartial-policing-seeks-to-address-bias/article_8d1079f1-d8f3-55f6-a369-effaadad2721.html; Kelli Linville and Cliff Cook, "Here's What Makes a Successful Partnership between a Police Department and a Community," *Bellingham Herald*, January 4, 2017, https://www.bellinghamherald.com/opinion/op-ed/article124398014.html

8. Sara Ahmed, *On Being Included: Racism and Diversity in Institutional Life* (Durham: Duke University Press, 2012), 117.

9. Malcolm Gladwell. *Blink: The Power of Thinking without Thinking* (New York: Little, Brown, and Company, 2005).

10. Adam Benforado, *Unfair: The New Science of Criminal Injustice* (New York: Crown Publishers, 2015).

11. Eduardo Bonilla-Silva, *Racism without Racists*, 76.

12. bell hooks, *Feminist Theory: From Margin to Center* (London: Pluto Press, 2000); Sylvia Wynter, "Unsettling the Coloniality of Being/Power/Truth/Freedom: Towards the Human, after Man, Its Overrepresentation—An Argument," *CR: The New Centennial Review* 3, no. 3 (2003): 257–337; Jael Silliman, Anannya Bhattacharjee, and Angela Yvonne Davis, eds., *Policing the National Body: Sex, Race, and Criminalization* (Boston: South End Press, 2002).

13. Former Seattle police chief Norm Stamper has highlighted the role of bureaucratic mandates in shaping police behavior. "In a Bureaucracy, What Gets Counted Counts," *To Protect and Serve: How to Fix America's Police* (New York: Nation Books, 2016), 2–3.

14. Joshua Scannell, "Broken Windows, Broken Code," *Real Life*, August 29, 2016, http://reallifemag.com/broken-windows-broken-code/

15. Hershini Bhana Young, "Inheriting the Criminalized Black Body: Race, Gender, and Slavery in 'Eva's Man,'" *African American Review* 39, no. 3 (2005), 385.

16. For part of the study, researchers used domestic violence scenarios with race-matched black and white heterosexual couples. Although described by researchers as reverse racism, the findings could alternately be attributed to gendered racism. The delay captured in the study could be described as a hesitation in responding to black women's victimization, compared to quick responses to white women being victimized. Lois James, Stephen James, and Bryan Vila, "The Reverse Racism Effect: Are Cops More Hesitant to Shoot Black than White Suspects?" *Criminology & Public Policy* 15, no. 2 (2016).

17. Patricia Devine, Patrick S. Forscher, Anthony J. Austin, and William TL Cox, "Long-Term Reduction in Implicit Race Bias: A Prejudice Habit-Breaking Intervention," *Journal of Experimental Social Psychology* 48, no. 6 (2012): 1267–78.

18. Devine et al., "Long-Term Reduction in Implicit Race Bias," 1270–71.

19. Reviews from Supervisors' Training held April 2015.

20. Reviews from training, August 2015.

21. Reviews from training, July 2015.

22. Reviews from training, July 2015.

23. Mason D. Burns, Margo J. Monteith, and Laura R. Parker, "Training Away Bias: The Differential Effects of Counterstereotype Training and Self-Regulation on Stereotype Activation and Application," *Journal of Experimental Social Psychology* 73 (2017): 97–110.

24. Joshua Correll, Bernadette Park, Charles M. Judd, Bernd Wittenbrink, Melody S. Sadler, and Tracie Keesee, "Across the Thin Blue Line: Police Officers and Racial Bias in the Decision to Shoot," *Journal of Personality and Social Psychology* 92, no. 6 (2007): 1006–23.

25. Police at the University of Iowa have invited the public to attend implicit-bias trainings that they are leading. Chantelle Navarro, "UI Police Invites Public to Attend Implicit-Bias Training Next Week," Friday, July 6, 2018, *KCRG-TV*, http://www.kcrg.com/content/news/UI-Police--487548671.html

26. Fair and Impartial Policing, reviews from Elon University PD training, July 2015.

27. For an example of these types of trainings, see Oscar Gamble, "Montgomery County Police, Community, and NAACP Attend Training on Fair, Unbiased Policing," *Times-Herald.* April 11, 2017, https://www.timesherald.com/news/montgomery-county-police-community-and-naacp-attend-training-on-fair/article_d49eb05a-d482-594f-8161-b12eba5ed4f5.html

28. Al Baker, "Confronting Implicit Bias in the New York Police Department," July 15, 2018, *New York Times*.

29. Ruth Wilson Gilmore, *Golden Gulag* (Berkeley: University of California Press, 2006), 28.

30. Derald Wing Sue, *Microaggressions in Everyday Life: Race, Gender, and Sexual Orientation* (New York: John Wiley & Sons, 2010).

31. Reviews from Supervisors' Training held April 2015.

Chapter 5

1. "About," American Police Hall of Fame, accessed August 31, 2020, https://www.aphf.org/about

2. See list on http://www.ipa-usa.org/?page=Museums, searched August 2017.

3. "About Us," Vancouver Police Museum and Archive, accessed August 31, 2020, https://vancouverpolicemuseum.ca/about-contact; "Museum and Discovery Center," Toronto Police Department, accessed September 21, 2020, http://www.torontopolice.on.ca/museum/; "Police Museum," Service de Police de la Ville de Mon-

treal (SPVM), accessed September 21, 2020, https://spvm.qc.ca/en/Pages/Discover
-SPVM/Police-museum; "Winnipeg Police Museum," City of Winnipeg, accessed
September 21, 2020, https://www.winnipeg.ca/police/museum/; Amy Chazkel,
"Police Museums in Latin America: Preface," *Radical History Review* 2012, no. 113
(May 1, 2012): 127–33.

4. Robert Buffington, "Institutional Memories: The Curious Genesis of the
Mexican Police Museum," *Radical History Review* 2012, no. 113: 155–69, 155.

5. "Museum," American Police Hall of Fame, accessed August 31, 2020, https://
www.aphf.org/museum

6. "Shooting Center," American Police Hall of Fame and Museum, accessed
September 5, 2020, https://www.aphf.org/shooting-center

7. The comparison of toy and real guns may be seen as making an implicit argument
that police shootings of those carrying toy guns are justified. On the police shooting of
Tamir Rice, a twelve-year-old boy carrying a toy gun, see Shaila Dewan and Richard Oppel
Jr., "In Tamir Rice Case, Many Errors by Cleveland Police, Then a Fatal One," *New York
Times*, January 22, 2015, https://www.nytimes.com/2015/01/23/us/in-tamir-rice-
shooting-in-cleveland-many-errors-by-police-then-a-fatal-one.html. Poet Reginald Betts
responds to the shooting in "When I Think of Tamir Rice While Driving," *Poetry Foundation*, https://www.poetryfoundation.org/poetrymagazine/poems/88739/when-i-think-
of-tamir-rice-while-driving. On the determination by another Ohio police department
that the officer who killed Rice could be hired with "no concerns," see Matthew Haag,
"Cleveland Officer Who Killed Tamir Rice Is Hired by an Ohio Police Department," *New
York Times*, October 8, 2018, https://www.nytimes.com/2018/10/08/us/timothy-
loehmann-tamir-rice-shooting.html

8. Jacqueline Rose, *States of Fantasy* (Oxford: Oxford University Press, 1996),
5.

9. Michael Rogin, "'Make My Day!': Spectacle as Amnesia in Imperial Politics,"
Representations 29 (Winter 1990): 99–123, 103.

10. Bianca Quilantan, "Trump Says U.S. 'Locked and Loaded' After Attack on
Saudi Oil," *Politico*, September 15, 2019, https://www.politico.com/story/2019/09
/15/trump-locked-loaded-iran-saudi-arabia-1497452; Colin Dwyer, "Donald
Trump: 'I Could . . . Shoot Somebody, And I Wouldn't Lose Any Voters,'" *National
Public Radio*, January 23, 2016, https://www.npr.org/sections/thetwo-way/2016/01
/23/464129029/donald-trump-i-could-shoot-somebody-and-i-wouldnt-lose-any
-voters

11. Rogin, "Make My Day!," 105.

12. Rogin, "Make My Day!," 104.

13. Barbara Kirshenblatt-Gimblett, "The Museum—A Refuge for Utopian
Thought," 2004, https://www.researchgate.net/profile/Barbara_Kirshenblatt-Gimbl
ett/publication/242493603_The_Museum--A_Refuge_for_Utopian_Thought/links
/5516d7ce0cf2d70ee276f574/The-Museum--A-Refuge-for-Utopian-Thought.pdf.
Appeared in German translation in *Die Unruhe der Kultur: Potentiale des Utopischen*, eds. Jörn Rüsen, Michael Fehr, and Annelie Ramsbrock (Velbrück Wissenschaft, 2004).

14. Marita Sturken, "Comfort, Irony, and Trivialization: The Mediation of Torture," *International Journal of Cultural Studies* 14, no. 4 (2011): 423–40.

15. "WATCH REPLAY: Brevard Sheriff's Office, American Police Hall of Fame to Honor Fallen Heroes During Memorial Service," *Space Coast Daily*, May 19, 2019, https://spacecoastdaily.com/2019/05/brevard-sheriffs-office-american-police-hall-of-fame-to-honor-fallen-heroes-during-memorial-service-2/,

16. "The Tomb of the Unknown Soldier," Arlington National Cemetery, http://www.arlingtoncemetery.mil/Explore/Tomb-of-the-Unknown-Soldier

17. Benedict Anderson, *Imagined Communities* (London: Verso, 1983), 9.

18. U.S. Bureau of Labor Statistics, "National Census of Fatal Occupational Injuries in 2018" (U.S. Department of Labor, USDL-19-2194), https://www.bls.gov/news.release/pdf/cfoi.pdf

19. Anderson, *Imagined Communities*, 9.

20. Jerome Skolnick, *Justice Without Trial: Law Enforcement in Democratic Society* (New York: MacMillan, 1994).

21. Skolnick, *Justice Without Trial*, 46.

22. For more on the division between citizens and "dirt-bags," see Lori Beth Way and Ryan Patten, *Hunting for "Dirt-Bags": Why Cops Over-police the Poor and Racial Minorities* (Boston: Northeastern University Press, 2013).

23. Michael Rogin, *Ronald Reagan*, 292.

24. "Causes of Law Enforcement Death," National Law Enforcement Officers' Memorial Fund, accessed June 21, 2019, https://nleomf.org/facts-figures/causes-of-law-enforcement-deaths

25. Gilbert Sandler, "A Neater Way to Kill," *Baltimore Sun*, November 2, 1993, https://www.baltimoresun.com/news/bs-xpm-1993-11-02-1993306212-story.html

26. "Capital Punishment History," Maryland Department of Public Safety and Correctional Services, accessed June 21, 2019, http://www.dpscs.state.md.us/public info/capitalpunishment/demographics_persons1923.shtml

27. "Hanging of Amy Spain," *Harper's Weekly* (September 30, 1865): 613.

28. Virginia Martinez, "Chicanas and the Law," *Latina Issues: Fragments of Historia (ella)(herstory)* 2 (1999): 205.

29. "Mapping Police Violence," Mapping Police Violence, accessed June 15, 2019, https://mappingpoliceviolence.org

30. Pat Reavy, "Man Announces Excessive Force Lawsuit then Gets Arrested," *DeseretNews*,December6,2017,https://www.deseret.com/2017/12/6/20637057/man-announces-excessive-force-lawsuit-against-police-then-gets-arrested#salt-lake-ci ty-police-officer-matt-roper-escorts-jackie-sanchez-out-of-attorney-robert-b-syk es-office-after-arresting-him-in-salt-lake-city-on-wednesday-dec-6-2017-sanchez -was-arrested-for-assault-against-a-police-officer-interference-with-arresting-offic er-and-disorderly-conduct-from-an-incident-in-july; Sanchez v. Hone et al., 2:17-cv-01257. Decided May 29, 2018.

31. "A Noise in the Night" IMDB, accessed June 15, 2019, https://www.imdb .com/title/tt7491984/?ref_=nm_flmg_act_2. Kayli Lasley, who was at home when her sister Bre was attacked, wrote critical Tweets about the reenactments, which

incorrectly cast the assailant as a black man and her best friend as a white man, https://twitter.com/kaylilasley/status/954167351657742336, accessed June 15, 2019.

32. Rogin, *Ronald Reagan, The Movie*, 292.

33. "Herstory," Black Lives Matter, accessed February 10, 2018, https://blacklive smatter.com/about/herstory/

34. Eliana Gil, "Understanding and Responding to Post-Trauma Play," *Association for Play Therapy Newsletter* 17, no. 1 (1998): 7–10.

35. Winnicott, *Playing and Reality*, 37, 43.

36. Donald Pease, *New American Exceptionalism* (Minneapolis: University of Minnesota Press, 2009), 4.

Chapter 6

1. "Brigadier General Albert Pike Statue," DC Historic Sites, accessed August 30, 2020, https://historicsites.dcpreservation.org/items/show/476

2. "Statue of Confederate General Albert Pike Toppled in Washington DC | George Floyd protests," *The Telegraph*, https://www.youtube.com/watch?v=NaBBm bKkQoc

3. Associated Press, "Protesters Topple Confederate General Statue in Washington DC and Set It on Fire," *The Guardian*, June 20, 2020, https://www.theguardi an.com/us-news/2020/jun/20/protesters-statue-washington-dc-albert-pike-junete enth-us

4. In Hawaii, a memorial has been approved by the state legislature but not yet constructed. For noncomprehensive lists of police memorials, see Amy Neuman, "List of Police Memorials," *lovetoknow*, undated, accessed September 7, 2020, https://dying.lovetoknow.com/Police_Memorials. In addition, see "Alabama Law Enforcement Memorial," Sweet Home Alabama, accessed September 7, 2020, https://alabama.travel/places-to-go/alabama-law-enforcement-memorial; "Arizona Peace Officers Memorial Board," Attorney General of the State of Arizona, accessed September 7, 2020, https://www.azag.gov/outreach/law-enforcement/pomb; "Law Enforcement Officers' Memorial," State of Arkansas, accessed September 7, 2020, https://portal.arkansas.gov/agency/law-enforcement-officers-memorial/; "Oregon Fallen Law Enforcement Officers' Memorial," State of Oregon, accessed September 7, 2020, https://www.oregon.gov/dpsst/Memorials/LawEnforcement/Pages/default .aspx; "Delaware State Police Memorial Vandalized—Dover," Delaware State Police, posted June 16, 2020, https://dsp.delaware.gov/2020/06/16/delaware-state-police -memorial-vandalized-dover/; "Fallen Heroes," Maine.gov, accessed September 7, 2020, https://www.maine.gov/dps/cim/crime_in_maine/dedication.html; "The Memorial," City of Missoula, accessed September 7, 2020, https://www.ci.missoula .mt.us/384/Law-Enforcement-Memorial; "Deaths in Line of Duty," North Carolina Department of Public Safety, accessed September 7, 2020, https://www.ncdps.gov/our-organization/law-enforcement/state-highway-patrol/history/deaths-in-line -of-duty; "Ohio Police & Fire Memorial Park: About the Park," Ohio Police & Fire

Pension Fund, accessed September 7, 2020, https://www.op-f.org/information/abo
utthepark; "Man Guards Police Memorial during Protests," WTVF, June 13, 2020,
https://www.newsbreak.com/tennessee/nashville/news/1583314432984/man-guar
ds-police-memorial-during-protest; "'He Deserves It:' Mom of Fallen Trooper
Wants Son Added to Vermont Memorial," NECN, May 17, 2019, https://www.necn
.com/news/local/vermont/mom-of-fallen-trooper-wants-son-added-to-vermont
-memorial/129777/; "New Mexico Fallen Police Officers Honored, Alamogordo
Police Department Officer's Name Added to Memorial Wall," Office of the Lt. Governor, State of New Mexico, press release dated May 22, 2019, https://www.ltgov.sta
te.nm.us/2019/05/22/new-mexico-fallen-police-officers-honored-alamogordo-pol
ice-department-officers-name-added-to-memorial-wall/; "The Memorial," Maryland Police & Correctional Fallen Officers Memorial, accessed September 7, 2020,
http://www.mdfallenofficers.org/the-memorial.html; "The Memorial . . . Vision
and Mission," The Hawaii Law Enforcement Memorial Foundation, accessed September 7, 2020, http://www.hlemf.org/the-memorial

5. "About the Memorial," National Law Enforcement Officer's Memorial Fund,
accessed June 10, 2017, www.nleomf.org

6. "About," National Law Enforcement Officers' Memorial Fund, accessed June
20, 2020, http://www.nleomf.org/about

7. Logan Strother, Spencer Piston, and Thomas Ogorzalek, "Pride or Prejudice? Racial Prejudice, Southern Heritage, and White Support for the Confederate
Battle Flag," *Du Bois Review: Social Science Research on Race* 14, no. 1 (2017):
295–323.

8. Judith Butler, *The Force of Nonviolence* (New York: Verso, 2020), 59.

9. Connie Clark, *The Making of a Memorial* (Columbia, MD, Potomac Publishing, 1992), 107–8.

10. Clark, *The Making of a Memorial*, 90.

11. Marita Sturken, "The Wall, the Screen, and the Image: The Vietnam Veterans Memorial," *Representations* 35 (1991): 118–42.

12. "National Memorial to Fallen Educators: About," National Teachers Hall of
Fame, accessed August 16, 2020, https://nthfmemorial.org/

13. "Memorial," National Law Enforcement Officers' Memorial Fund, accessed
June 20, 2020, https://nleomf.org/memorial

14. Lauren Berlant, *The Queen of America Goes to Washington City: Essays on
Sex and Citizenship* (Durham: Duke University Press, 1997), 27.

15. Marita Sturken, *Tourists of History: Memory, Kitsch, and Consumerism from
Oklahoma City to Ground Zero* (Durham: Duke University Press, 2007), 22.

16. "2019 Roll Call of Heroes," National Law Enforcement Officers Memorial,
searched July 20, 2019, https://nleomf.org/facts-figures/2019-roll-call-of-heroes

17. Russell G. Lande, *How to Build a Police Memorial*, PhD diss., Kutztown University of Pennsylvania (2006), ix.

18. Lande, *How to Build a Police Memorial*, ix–x.

19. Lande, *How to Build a Police Memorial*, x.

20. Travis Yates, "The Absence of a President," *LawOfficer.Com*, August 9, 2017,
https://lawofficer.com/leadership/absence-president/

21. Remarks by Attorney General Jeff Sessions at the National Law Enforcement Officers Memorial Fund 29th Annual Candlelight Vigil, May 13, 2017. Transcript: https://www.justice.gov/opa/speech/remarks-attorney-general-jeff-sessions-national-law-enforcement-officers-memorial-fund

22. Barack Obama, "Open Letter to America's Law Enforcement Community," posted July 19, 2016, https://obamawhitehouse.archives.gov/blog/2016/07/19/read-president-obamas-open-letter-americas-law-enforcement-community

23. Twitter post by @NLEOMF, posted May 14, 2019, https://twitter.com/NLEOMF/status/1128381079365222401

24. The context of the revolt and the imprisoned people who died at Attica are not mentioned. For more on the Attica revolt see Heather Ann Thompson, *Blood in the Water: The Attica Prison Uprising of 1971 and Its Legacy* (New York: Pantheon Books, 2016).

25. Marita Sturken discusses the teddy bear in the 9/11 gift shop in *Tourists of History*.

26. Linda Mobolio-Keeling, *Feeling Safe with Officer Frank* (Herndon, VA: Mascot Books, 2011).

27. Ellen Kirschman, *I Love a Cop: What Police Families Need to Know* (New York: Guilford Publications, 2018); Allen R. Kates, *CopShock: Surviving Posttraumatic Stress Disorder (PTSD)*. (Cortaro, AZ: Holbrook Street Press, 1999).

28. "Criteria for Inclusion," National Law Enforcement Officers' Memorial, accessed April 2, 2016, http://www.nleomf.org/assets/pdfs/officer-data/formatted_criteria_for_inclusion_received_12_10_15.pdf

29. "Criteria for Inclusion," National Law Enforcement Officers' Memorial.

30. Hope Tiesman, "Workplace Suicide," *NIOSH Science Blog*, posted on April 13, 2015, https://blogs-origin.cdc.gov/niosh-science-blog/2015/04/13/workplace-suicide/

31. Annelise M. Mennicke and Katie Ropes, "Estimating the Rate of Domestic Violence Perpetrated by Law Enforcement Officers: A Review of Methods and Estimates," *Aggression and Violent Behavior* 31 (2016): 157–64.

32. See Conor Friedersdorf, "Police Have a Much Bigger Domestic Violence Problem than the NFL Does," *The Atlantic*, September 19, 2014, https://www.theatlantic.com/national/archive/2014/09/police-officers-who-hit-their-wives-or-girlfriends/380329/

33. "Outrage Grows After Wis. Officer Left Off Wall," *Officer.com*, March 22, 2013, https://www.officer.com/home/news/10898459/outrage-grows-after-wauwatosa-wis-police-officer-jennifer-sebena-left-off-memorial; Associated Press and Jeff Karoub, "National Police Memorial Wall Comes with Some Tough Calls," *Mercury News*, May 12, 2013, www.mercurynews.com/2013/05/12/national-police-memorial-wall-comes-with-some-tough-calls/; Dinesh Ramde, "Wisconsin Police Officer to Be Honored in Memorial," *Pioneer Press*, April 3, 2013, https://www.twincities.com/2013/04/03/wisconsin-police-officer-to-be-honored-in-memorial/

34. Bruce Vielmetti, "Husband Pleads Guilty to Killing Wauwatosa Police Officer Jennifer Sebena," *Milwaukee Journal-Sentinel*, June 26, 2013, archive.jsonline.com/news/crime/plea-expected-in-killing-of-wauwatosa-police-officer-jennifer-sebena-b9942397z1-213112411.html

35. Pauline Kael, "Dirty Harry: Saint Cop," *New Yorker*, January 15, 1972.

36. "Clint Eastwood Accepts Honorary Role with NLEOMF," *Police: The Law Enforcement Magazine* July 11, 2011, https://www.policemag.com/348577/clint-eas twood-accepts-honorary-role-with-nleomf?page=77, searched June 16, 2019.

37. "Craig Floyd, Founding CEO of the National Law Enforcement Officers' Memorial Fund, to Retire at End of 2018," news release, undated, National Law Enforcement Officers' Memorial Fund, accessed September 13, 2020, https://nleo mf.org/newsroom/news-releases/craig-w-floyd-founding-ceo-of-the-national-law -enforcement-officers-memorial-fund-to-retire-at-end-of-2018

38. "Former U.S. Attorney General John Ashcroft Appointed Chairman of National Law Enforcement Officers Memorial Fund," National Law Enforcement Officers' Memorial Fund, press release, September 19, 2016, http://www.nleomf.org /newsroom/news-releases/ashcroft-appointed-chairman.html

39. "Officer Deaths by Year," National Law Enforcement Officers Memorial, accessed September 23, 2020, https://nleomf.org/facts-figures/officer-deaths-by -year

40. "National Law Enforcement Memorial and Museum Unveils Virtual Bulle-tin Board for Law Enforcement and Community Relations," National Law Enforce-ment Memorial and Museum, accessed September 7, 2020, https://nleomf.org/new sroom/news-releases/national-law-enforcement-memorial-and-museum-unveils -virtual-bulletin-board-for-law-enforcement-and-community-relations

41. Pease, *New American Exceptionalism*, 4.

Conclusion

1. The majority had experienced poverty, both physical and sexual violence, and had run away from home. The majority had attempted suicide at some point in their young lives. Bernadine Dohrn, "All Ellas: Girls Locked Up," *Feminist Studies* 30, no 2. (Summer 2004): 302–24.

2. INCITE! Women of Color Against Violence, ed., *The Revolution Will Not be Funded: Beyond the Non-profit Industrial Complex* (Cambridge, MA: South End Press, 2007).

3. Sarah Barr, "National Campaign Calls for Schools to Remove All Law Enforcement Officers," *Youth Today*, September 21, 2016, https://youthtoday.org/20 16/09/national-campaign-calls-for-schools-to-remove-all-law-enforcement-offic ers/

4. "Mission," Dignity in Schools, accessed September 26, 2020, https://dignityi nschools.org/about-us/mission/

5. Amir Whitaker, Sylvia Torres-Guillén, Michelle Morton, Harold Jordan, Stefanie Coyle, Angela Mann, and Wei-Ling Sun, "Cops and No Counselors: How the Lack of School Mental Health Staff Is Harming Students," American Civil Liber-ties Union, March 4, 2019, https://www.aclu.org/report/cops-and-no-counselors

6. Whitaker et al., "Cops and No Counselors," 4.

7. Michael Rembis, "The New Asylums: Madness and Mass Incarceration in

the Neoliberal Era," in *Disability Incarcerated: Imprisonment and Disability in the United States and Canada*, eds. Liat Ben-Moshe, Chris Chapman, and Allison C. Carey (New York: Palgrave MacMillan, 2014).

8. For a discussion of the overlap between deinstitutionalization struggles and abolitionist struggles, and what abolitionists can learn from disability/madness studies, see Liat Ben Moshe, *Decarcerating Disability: Deinstitutionalization and Prison Abolition* (Minneapolis: University of Minnesota Press, 2020).

9. Angela Davis, *Are Prisons Obsolete?* (New York: Seven Stories Press. 2003), 107.

10. "Help & Guidance," Stop It Now!, accessed September 27, 2020, https://www.stopitnow.org/help-guidance

11. "Toolkit," Creative Interventions, accessed September 27, 2020, https://www.creative-interventions.org/tools/toolkit/; "Stories," Creative Interventions, accessed September 27, 2020, https://www.creative-interventions.org/stories/

12. "Our Work," FreeFrom, https://www.freefrom.org/about, accessed November 22, 2020.

13. Meenakshi Mannoe, Dylan Lambi-Raine, and Donna Baines, "Defund the Police and Social Work's Relationship to State Coercion and Control," *The Social Lens: A Social Work Action Blog*, April 8, 2021, https://socialwork.ubc.ca/news/defund-the-police-and-social-works-relationship-to-state-coercion-and-control/; Leah A. Jacobs, Mimi E. Kim, Darren L. Whitfield, Rachel E. Gartner, Meg Panichelli, Shanna K. Kattari, Margaret Mary Downey, Shanté Stuart McQueen, and Sarah E. Mountz, "Defund the Police: Moving towards an Anti-Carceral Social Work," *Journal of Progressive Human Services* 32, no. 1 (2021): 37–62; Mimi E. Kim, "Anti-Carceral Feminism: The Contradictions of Progress and the Possibilities of Counter-Hegemonic Struggle," *Affilia* 35, no. 3 (2020): 309–26.

14. Andrew Ivsins, Jade Boyd, Leo Beletsky, and Ryan McNeil, "Tackling the Overdose Crisis: The Role of Safe Supply," *International Journal of Drug Policy* 80 (2020): 102769; Mohammad Karamouzian, Carolyn Dohoo, Sara Forsting, Ryan McNeil, Thomas Kerr, and Mark Lysyshyn, "Evaluation of a Fentanyl Drug Checking Service for Clients of a Supervised Injection Facility, Vancouver, Canada," *Harm Reduction Journal* 15, no. 1 (2018): 1–8; Bruce Wallace, Flora Pagan, and Bernadette Bernie Pauly, "The Implementation of Overdose Prevention Sites as a Novel and Nimble Response during an Illegal Drug Overdose Public Health Emergency," *International Journal of Drug Policy* 66 (2019): 64–72.

15. Tracey Wade, Anna Frayne, Sally-Anne Edwards, Therese Robertson, and Peter Gilchrist, "Motivational Change in an Inpatient Anorexia Nervosa Population and Implications for Treatment," *Australian & New Zealand Journal of Psychiatry* 43, no. 3 (2009): 235–43. With regard to suicide and self-harm, I am referring to Marsha Linehan's dialectical behavior therapy. Marsha Linehan, *Cognitive Behavioral Treatment for Borderline Personality Disorder* (New York: Guilford, 1993).

16. Rojas, "Are the Cops in Our Heads and Hearts?"

17. For more on clinical work to address problematic and harmful sexual behaviors with children, see William Friedrich, *Children with Sexual Behavior Problems:*

Family-Based Attachment-Focused Therapy (New York: W. W. Norton, 2007); Eliana Gil and Jennifer Shaw, *Working with Children with Sexual Behavior Problems* (New York: Guilford, 2013); for work with adolescents see National Center on the Sexual Behavior of Youth, "Professionals," http://www.ncsby.org/content/professionals; Adolescent Practice Guidelines, available at Association for the Treatment of Sexual Abusers, "Effective Practice," https://www.atsa.com/practice; Scott Henggeler, Sonja K. Schoenwald, Charles M. Borduin, Melisa D. Rowland, and Phillippe B. Cunningham, *Multisystemic Therapy for Antisocial Behavior in Children and Adolescents* (New York: Guilford Press, 2009.)

18. Audre Lorde, *The Black Unicorn: Poems* (New York: Norton, 1978).

BIBLIOGRAPHY

Adorno, Theodor, Else Frenkel-Brenswik, Daniel J. Levinson, and R. Nevitt Sanford. *The Authoritarian Personality*. New York: Verso Books, 2019.

Ahmed, Sara. "The Nonperformativity of Antiracism." *Meridians: Feminism, Race, Transnationalism* 7, no. 1 (2006): 104–26.

Ahmed, Sara. *On Being Included: Racism and Diversity in Institutional Life*. Durham: Duke University Press, 2012.

Altman, Neil. *White Privilege: Psychoanalytic Perspectives*. London: Routledge, 2021.

Amidon, Kevin, and Dan Krier. "On Rereading Klaus Theweleit's Male Fantasies." *Men and Masculinities* 11, no. 4 (2009): 488–96.

Andersen, Benedict. *Imagined Communities: Reflections on the Origin and Spread of Nationalism*. New York: Verso, 1983.

Anderson, Jessica. "County Police Move to Keep Their Old Guns Off the Street—But at a Cost." *Baltimore Sun*. September 25, 2013.

Anzaldua, Gloria. *Borderlands La Frontera*. San Francisco: Aunt Lute, 1987.

Arias, Elizabeth, Betzaida Tejada-Vera, and Farida Ahmad. "Provisional Life Expectancy Estimates for January through June, 2020." *Vital Statistics Rapid Release*, February 2021. https://www.cdc.gov/nchs/data/vsrr/VSRR10-508.pdf

Artwohl, Alexis, and Loren W. Christensen. *Deadly Force Encounters: What Cops Need to Know to Mentally and Physically Prepare for and Survive a Gunfight*. Boulder, CO: Paladin Press, 1997.

Associated Press. "DOJ: No Civil Rights Charge in Police Shooting." *AP News*, March 1, 2019, https://apnews.com/article/e8b98d48130a4426b193a514280320d5

Associated Press. "Protesters Topple Confederate General Statue in Washington DC and Set It on Fire." *The Guardian*. June 20, 2020. https://www.theguardian.com/us-news/2020/jun/20/protesters-statue-washington-dc-albert-pike-juneenth-us

Associated Press and Jeff Karoub. "National Police Memorial Wall Comes with Some Tough Calls," *Mercury News*. May 12, 2013. www.mercurynews.com/2013/05/12/national-police-memorial-wall-comes-with-some-tough-calls/, accessed November 10, 2016.

Austin, J. L. *How to Do Things with Words*. 2nd ed. Cambridge: Harvard University Press, 1975.

Baker, Al. "Confronting Implicit Bias in the New York Police Department." *New York Times*. July 15, 2018.

Banks, Duren, Joshua Hendrix, Matthew Hickman, and Tracey Kyckelhahn. "National Sources of Law Enforcement Employment Data." Bureau of Justice Statistics, US Department of Justice. April 2016, Revised October 4, 2016. www.bjs.gov/content/pub/pdf/nsleed.pdf, accessed October 3, 2016.

Barr, Sarah. "National Campaign Calls for Schools to Remove All Law Enforcement Officers." *Youth Today*. September 21, 2016. https://youthtoday.org/2016/09/national-campaign-calls-for-schools-to-remove-all-law-enforcement-officers/

Bartol, Curt R., and Anne M. Bartol. "History of Forensic Psychology." In *The Handbook Of Forensic Psychology*, edited by A. K Heiss and I. B. Weiner, 3–23. Hoboken: John Wiley and Sons, 1999.

Bateson, Gregory. *Steps to an Ecology of the Mind: A Revolutionary Approach to Man's Understanding of Himself*. Chicago: University of Chicago Press, 1972.

Beckett, Katherine, and Naomi Murakawa. "Mapping the Shadow Carceral State: Toward an Institutionally Capacious Approach to Punishment." *Theoretical Criminology* 16, no. 2 (2012): 221–44.

Benforado, Adam. *Unfair: The New Science of Criminal Injustice*. New York: Crown Publishers, 2015.

Benjamin, Walter. *Reflections: Essays, Aphorisms, Autobiographical Writings*. New York: Schocken, 1986.

Ben Moshe, Liat. *Decarcerating Disability: Deinstitutionalization and Prison Abolition*. Minneapolis: University of Minnesota Press, 2020.

Berlant, Lauren Gail. *Cruel Optimism*. Durham: Duke University Press, 2011.

Berlant, Lauren. "The Epistemology of State Emotion." In *Dissent in Dangerous Times*, edited by Austin Sarat. Ann Arbor: University of Michigan Press, 2005.

Berlant, Lauren. *The Queen of America Goes to Washington City: Essays on Sex and Citizenship*. Durham: Duke University Press, 1997.

Berman, Jay Stuart, *Police Administration and Progressive Reform: Theodore Roosevelt as Police Commissioner of New York*. Westport, CT: Greenwood Press, 1987.

Bernstein, Elizabeth. "Carceral Politics as Gender Justice? The 'Traffic in Women' and Neoliberal Circuits of Crime, Sex, and Rights." *Theory and Society* 41, no. 3 (2012): 233–59.

Bernstein, Elizabeth. "Militarized Humanitarianism Meets Carceral Feminism: The Politics of Sex, Rights, and Freedom in Contemporary Antitrafficking Campaigns." *Signs: Journal of Women in Culture and Society* 36, no. 1 (2010): 45–71.

Bernstein, Robin. *Racial Innocence: Performing American Childhood and Race from Slavery to Civil Rights*. New York: NYU Press, 2011.

Betts, Reginald. "When I Think of Tamir Rice While Driving." *Poetry Foundation*. https://www.poetryfoundation.org/poetrymagazine/poems/88739/when-i-think-of-tamir-rice-while-driving

Biden, Joseph. "Executive Order on Advancing Racial Equity and Support for Underserved Communities Through the Federal Government," January 20, 2021. https://www.whitehouse.gov/briefing-room/presidential-actions/2021/01/20/executive-order-advancing-racial-equity-and-support-for-underserved-communities-through-the-sfederal-government/

Bittner, Egon. "Capacity to Use Force as the Core of the Police Role." In *Moral Issues in Police Work*, edited by Fredrick A Elliston and Michael Feldberg. Lanham, MD: Rowman & Littlefield, 1985, 15–25.

Black Lives Matter. "Herstory." BlackLivesMatter.com.

Bland, Nick, Gary Mundy, Jacqueline Russell, and Rachel Tuffin. *Career Progression of Ethnic Minority Police Officers*. Great Britain Home Office, Policing and Reducing Crime Unit, 1999.

Bonifacio, Philip. *The Psychological Effects of Police Work: A Psychodynamic Approach*. New York: Springer, 1991.

Bonilla-Silva, Eduardo. *Racism without Racists: Color-blind Racism and the Persistence of Racial Inequality in the United States*. Lanham, MD: Rowman & Littlefield Publishers, 2006.

Bosman, Julie, and John Goldstein. "Timeline for a Body: 4 hours in the Middle of a Ferguson Street." *New York Times*. August 23, 2014.

Brickman, Celia. *Aboriginal Populations of the Mind: Race and Primitivity in Psychoanalysis*. New York: Columbia University Press, 2003.

Brodeur, Jean Paul, and Benoit Dupont. "Knowledge Workers or 'Knowledge' Workers?" *Policing & Society* 16, no. 1.

Brown, Bill. "Thing Theory." *Critical Inquiry* 28, no 1 (Autumn 2001): 1–22.

Buffington, Robert. "Institutional Memories: The Curious Genesis of the Mexican Police Museum." *Radical History Review* 113 (2012): 155–69.

Bureau of Justice Statistics. *Correctional Populations in the United States, 2014*. Department of Justice, 2016. www.bjs.gov/content/pub/pdf/cpus14.pdf

Bureau of Justice Statistics. "One in 34 Adults under Correctional Supervision in 2011, Lowest Rate Since 2000." Press release. November 29, 2012. www.bjs.gov/content/pub/press/cpus11ppus11pr.cfm

Bureau of Labor Statistics. "Illnesses, Injuries, and Fatalities: Fact Sheet, Police Officers." August 2016. https://www.bls.gov/iif/oshwc/cfoi/police-officers-2014.htm

Bureau of Labor Statistics. *Occupational Employment Statistics*. U.S. Department of Labor, 2015.

Bureau of Labor Statistics, U.S. Department of Labor. *Occupational Outlook Handbook*. https://www.bls.gov/ooh

Burns, Mason D., Margo J. Monteith, and Laura R. Parker. "Training Away Bias: The Differential Effects of Counterstereotype Training and Self-Regulation on Stereotype Activation and Application." *Journal of Experimental Social Psychology* 73 (2017): 97–110.

Butler, Judith, *The Force of Non-Violence*. New York: Verso, 2020.

Butler, Judith. *Gender Trouble: Feminism and the Subversion of Identity*. New York: Routledge, 1990.

Butler, Judith. *Notes Toward a Performative Theory of Assembly*. Cambridge, MA: Harvard University Press, 2015.

Caimari, Lila. "Vestiges of a Hidden Life: A Visit to the Buenos Aires Police Museum." *Radical History Review* 113 (2012): 143–54.

California Public Employees Retirement Fund Actuarial Office. *CalPERS Experience Study*, April 2010. https://www.calpers.ca.gov/docs/forms-publications/calpers-experience-study-2010.pdf

Case, Ann, and Angus Deaton. *Deaths of Despair and the Future of Capitalism*. Princeton: Princeton University Press, 2020.

Charles, Sam. "Days After Acquittal, Robert Rialmo Involved in Another Bar Scuffle." *Chicago Sun-Times*, July 13, 2018. https://chicago.suntimes.com/2018/7/13/18327514/days-after-acquittal-chicago-cop-robert-rialmo-involved-in-another-bar-scuffle

Chawkins, Steve. "Martin Reiser Dies at 87; LAPD's First Staff Psychologist." *LA Times*. April 16, 2015. https://www.latimes.com/local/obituaries/la-me-martin-reiser-20150417-story.html

Chazkel, Amy. "Police Museums in Latin America: Preface." *Radical History Review* 113, no. 1 (May 2012): 127–33.

Clark, Connie. *The Making of a Memorial*. Potomac Publishing. 1992.

Cochrane, Robert E., Robert P. Tett, and Leon Vandecreek. "Psychological Testing and the Selection of Police Officers: A National Survey." *Criminal Justice and Behavior* 30, no. 5, 2003: 511–37.

Cole, Alyson. *The Cult of True Victimhood: From the War on Welfare to the War on Terror*. Palo Alto: Stanford University Press, 2007.

Cooper, Frank Rudy. "Who's the Man—Masculinities Studies, Terry Stops, and Police Training." *Columbia Journal of Gender and Law* 18 (2008): 671–742.

Correll, Joshua, Bernadette Park, Charles M. Judd, Bernd Wittenbrink, Melody S. Sadler, and Tracie Keesee. "Across the Thin Blue Line: Police Officers and Racial Bias in the Decision to Shoot." *Journal of Personality and Social Psychology* 92, no. 6 (2007): 1006–23.

Crenshaw, Kimberlé Williams, and Andrea J. Ritchie. *Say Her Name: Resisting Police Brutality Against Black Women*. New York: African American Policy Forum, Center for Intersectionality and Social Policy Studies. 2015.

Crouch, Stanley. "Some Lessons about Why Cops Have the Blues." *NY Daily News*. September 8, 1996.

Cunningham, Timothy J., Janet Croft, Yong Liu, Hua Lu, Paul Eke, and Wayne Gils. "Vital Signs: Racial Disparities in Age-Specific Mortality among Blacks or African Americans—United States, 1999–2015." *MMWR. Morbidity and Mortality Weekly Report* 66(17) (2017).

Das, Veena. *Life and Words: Violence and the Descent into the Ordinary*. Berkeley: University of California Press, 2007.

Davie, Monica, and Julie Bosman, "Protests Flare After Ferguson Police Officer Is Not Indicted." *New York Times*. November 25, 2014. https://www.nytimes.com/2014/11/25/us/ferguson-darren-wilson-shooting-michael-brown-grand-jury.html

Davis, Angela. *Are Prisons Obsolete?* New York: Seven Stories, 2003.

DeLord, Ron, and Ron York. *Law Enforcement, Police Unions, and the Future.* Springfield, IL: Charles C. Thomas, Publisher, 2017.

Devine, Patricia, Patrick S. Forscher, Anthony J. Austin, and William TL Cox. "Long-Term Reduction in Implicit Race Bias: A Prejudice Habit-Breaking Intervention." *Journal of Experimental Social Psychology* 48, no. 6 (2012): 1267–78.

Dewan, Shaila, and Richard Oppel Jr. "In Tamir Rice Case, Many Errors by Cleveland Police, Then a Fatal One." *New York Times.* January 22, 2015. https://www.nytimes.com/2015/01/23/us/in-tamir-rice-shooting-in-cleveland-many-errors-by-police-then-a-fatal-one.html

Dimen, Muriel. "*Lapsus Linguae* or a Slip of the Tongue? A Sexual Violation in an Analytic Treatment and Its Personal and Theoretical Aftermath." *Contemporary Psychoanalysis* 47, no. 1 (2011): 35–79.

Dimen, Muriel. "Rotten Apples and Ambivalence: Sexual Boundary Violations Through a Psychocultural Lens." *Journal of the American Psychoanalytic Association* 64, no. 2 (2016): 361–73.

Dimon, Laura, and Rocco Parascandola. "NYPD to Start 'Implicit Bias Training.'" *PoliceOne.* February 18, 2018. https://www.policeone.com/patrol-issues/articles/470642006-NYPD-to-start-implicit-bias-training/

Doerner, William G. "Officer Retention Patterns: An Affirmative Action Concern for Police Agencies?" *American Journal of Police* 14, nos. 3/4 (1995): 197–210.

Dohrn, Bernadine. "All Ellas: Girls Locked Up." *Feminist Studies* 30, no 2 (Summer 2004): 302–24.

Douglas, Tanisha "Wakumi." Comments at "Abolitionist Social Work: Possibilities, Paradox, and Praxis." Online panel hosted by Haymarket Books, February 25, 2021. https://www.haymarketbooks.org/blogs/284-abolitionist-social-work-possibilities-paradox-and-praxis

Dowling, F. G., G. Moynihan, B. Genet, and J. Lewis. "A Peer-Based Assistance Program for Officers with the New York City Police Department: Report of the Effects of Sept. 11, 2001." *American Journal of Psychiatry* 163 (2006): 151–53.

Drowosa, Joanna, Charles H. Hennekens, Robert S. Levine. "Variations in Mortality from Legal Intervention in the United States—1999 to 2013." *Preventive Medicine* 81 (December 2015): 290–93.

Dwyer, Colin. "Donald Trump: 'I Could . . . Shoot Somebody, And I Wouldn't Lose Any Voters.'" *National Public Radio.* January 23, 2016. https://www.npr.org/sections/thetwo-way/2016/01/23/464129029/donald-trump-i-could-shoot-somebody-and-i-wouldnt-lose-any-voters

Edwards, Frank, Michael H. Esposito, and Hedwig Lee. "Risk of Police-Involved Death by Race/Ethnicity and Place, United States, 2012–2018." *American Journal of Public Health* 108, no. 9 (2018): 1241–48.

8 to Abolition, "Why." https://www.8toabolition.com/why, accessed September 19, 2020.

Epp, Charles, Steven Maynard-Moody, and Donald Haider-Markel. *Pulled Over: How Police Stops Define Race and Citizenship.* Chicago: University of Chicago Press, 2014.

Ericson, Richard, and Kevin Haggerty. *Policing the Risk Society*. Oxford: Oxford University Press, 1997.

Estepa, Jessica. "President Trump Thanks 'Deplorables' for Helping Him Win the 2016 Election." *USA Today*, November 8, 2017. https://www.usatoday.com/story/news/politics/onpolitics/2017/11/08/president-trump-thanks-deplorables-helping-him-win-2016-election/844744001/

Fanon, Frantz. *Black Skin, White Masks*. Translated by Richard Philcox. New York: Grove Press, 2008.

Fanon, Frantz. *The Wretched of the Earth*. Translated by Richard Philcox. New York: Grove Press, 2004.

Fassin, Didier. *Enforcing Order: An Ethnography of Urban Policing*. Cambridge, UK: Polity, 2013.

Federal Bureau of Investigation. 2013. "Uniform Crime Statistics, 2013." https://ucr.fbi.gov/crime-in-the-u.s/2013/crime-in-the-u.s.-2013

"Forums." *NJ Lawman: Law Enforcement Magazine*. forums.njlawman.com/post/fitness-for-duty-examination-by-a-psychologist-on-a-policeman-386164?&trail=30

Foucault, Michel. *The History of Sexuality: Volume 1*. Translated by Robert Hurley. New York: Vintage, 1990.

Fournier, Lauren. *Autotheory as Feminist Practice in Art, Writing, and Criticism*. Cambridge: MIT Press, 2021.

Fox, Dennis, Isaac Prilleltensky, and Stephanie Austin. "Critical Psychology for Social Justice: Concerns and Dilemmas." In *Critical Psychology: An Introduction*, edited by D. Fox, I. Prilleltensky, and S. Austin, 3–19. Thousand Oaks, CA: Sage, 2009.

Freedman, Estelle. *Their Sister's Keepers*. Ann Arbor: University of Michigan Press, 1981.

Freud, Sigmund, *Dora: An Analysis of a Case of Hysteria*. New York: Touchstone, 1967.

Freud, Sigmund. *The Interpretation of Dreams*. Translated by James Strachey. New York: Basic Books, 2010.

Freud, Sigmund. "Mourning and Melancholia." In *The Standard Edition of the Complete Psychological Works of Sigmund Freud, Volume XIV (1914–1916): On the History of the Psycho-Analytic Movement, Papers on Metapsychology and Other Works*. 1957. 237–58.

Freud, Sigmund. "An Outline of Psychoanalysis." *International Journal of Psychoanalysis XXI*, 1940.

Friedersdorf, Conor. "Police Have a Much Bigger Domestic Violence Problem than the NFL Does." *The Atlantic*, September 19, 2014, https://www.theatlantic.com/national/archive/2014/09/police-officers-who-hit-their-wives-or-girlfriends/380329/

Friedrich, William. *Children with Sexual Behavior Problems: Family-Based Attachment-Focused Therapy*. New York: W. W. Norton, 2007.

Frizell, Sam. "Ferguson Police Are Testing 'Less-Lethal' Attachments For Guns."

Time Magazine. February 4, 2015. http://time.com/3695435/ferguson-police -michael-brown-guns/

Fuss, Diana. "Interior Colonies: Frantz Fanon and the Politics of Identification." *Diacritics* 24 (1994): 19–42.

Gamble, Oscar. "Montgomery County Police, Community, and NAACP Attend Training on Fair, Unbiased Policing." *The Times-Herald*. April 11, 2017. https:// www.timesherald.com/news/montgomery-county-police-community-and-na acp-attend-training-on-fair/article_d49eb05a-d482-594f-8161-b12eba5ed4f5 .html

Gandbhir, Geeta, and Blair Foster. "A Conversation with My Black Son." *New York Times*. March 17, 2015. https://www.nytimes.com/video/opinion/10000000357 5589/a-conversation-with-my-black-son.html

Garot, Robert. "'You're Not a Stone': Emotional Sensitivity in a Bureaucratic Setting." *Journal of Contemporary Ethnography* 33, no. 6 (2004): 735–66.

Gates, Daryl. *Chief: My Life in the LAPD*. New York: Bantam, 1992.

Gherovici, Patricia. *Transgender Psychoanalysis: A Lacanian Perspective on Sexual Difference*. New York: Routledge, 2017.

Gil, Eliana. "Understanding and Responding to Post-Trauma Play." *Association for Play Therapy Newsletter* 17, no. 1 (1998).

Gil, Eliana, and Jennifer Shaw. *Working with Children with Sexual Behavior Problems*. New York: Guilford, 2013.

Gilmartin, Kevin. *Emotional Survival for Law Enforcement*. Boulder, CO: Paladin Press, 2002.

Gilmore, Ruth Wilson. "Globalisation and US Prison Growth: From Military Keynesianism to Post-Keynesian Militarism." *Race & Class* 40, nos. 2–3 (1999): 171–88.

Gilmore, Ruth Wilson. *Golden Gulag*. Berkeley: University of California Press, 2006.

Gilmore, Ruth Wilson, and Craig Gilmore. "Restating the Obvious." In *Indefensible Sspace: The Architecture of the National Insecurity State*, edited by Michael Sorkin. New York: Routledge, 2008, 141–62.

Gladwell, Malcolm. *Blink: The Power of Thinking without Thinking*. New York: Little, Brown, and Company. 2005.

Gorner, Jeremy, and Gregory Pratt. "Cop Who Shot Quintonio LeGrier and Neighbor Sues Teen's Estate, Claiming Trauma." *Chicago Tribune*. February 6, 2016. http://www.chicagotribune.com/news/local/breaking/ct-robert-rialmo-quinto nio-legrier-20160206-story.html

Gorz, Andre. *Strategy for Labor*. Boston: Beacon Press, 1967.

Graeber, David. *The Utopia of Rules: On Technology, Stupidity, and the Secret Joys of Bureaucracy*. Brooklyn: Melville House Press, 2015.

Green, Emily. "Melanie Klein and the Black Mammy: An Exploration of the Influence of the Mammy Stereotype on Klein's Maternal and Its Contribution to the 'Whiteness' of Psychoanalysis." *Studies in Gender and Sexuality* 19, no. 3 (2018): 164–82.

Grim, Ryan, and Aida Chávez. "Minneapolis Police Union President: 'I've Been Involved in Three Shootings Myself, and Not One of Them Has Bothered Me.'" *The Intercept*. June 2, 2020. https://theintercept.com/2020/06/02/minneapolis-police-union-bob-kroll-shootings/

Haag, Matthew. "Cleveland Officer Who Killed Tamir Rice Is Hired by an Ohio Police Department." *New York Times*. October 8, 2018. https://www.nytimes.com/2018/10/08/us/timothy-loehmann-tamir-rice-shooting.html

Haarr, Robin. "Factors Affecting the Decision of Police Recruits to 'Drop Out' of Police Work." *Police Quarterly* 8, no. 4 (2005): 431–53.

Haney, Lynne. "Motherhood as Punishment: The Case of Parenting in Prison." *Signs* 39, no. 1 (Autumn 2013).

Haney, Lynne. *Offending Women: Power, Punishment, and the Regulation of Desire.* Berkeley: University of California Press, 2010.

"Hanging of Amy Spain." *Harper's Weekly* (September 30, 1865), 613.

Harris, Adrienne, and Steven Boticelli, eds. *First Do No Harm: The Paradoxical Encounters of Psychoanalysis, Warmaking, and Resistance.* London: Taylor and Francis Group, 2010.

Harris, Angela P., "Gender, Violence, Race, and Criminal Justice." *Stanford Law Review* 52, no. 4 (1999): 777–807.

Hartman, Saidiya V. *Lose Your Mother: A Journey along the Atlantic Slave Route.* New York: Macmillan, 2008.

Hartman, Saidiya V. *Scenes of Subjection: Terror, Slavery, and Self-making in Nineteenth-Century America.* New York: Oxford University Press, 1997.

Hegeman, Elizabeth. "Institutional Betrayal and the Case of the American Psychological Association." In *Psychoanalysis, Trauma, and Community: History and Contemporary Reappraisals*, edited by Judith Alpert and Elizabeth Goren, 214–30. London: Taylor and Francis Group, 2016.

Henggeler, Scott, Sonja K. Schoenwald, Charles M. Borduin, Melisa D. Rowland, and Phillippe B. Cunningham. *Multisystemic Therapy for Antisocial Behavior in Children and Adolescents.* New York: Guilford Press, 2009.

Henry, Vincent. *Death Work: Police, Trauma, and the Psychology of Survival.* New York: Oxford University Press, 2004.

Herman, Judith. *Trauma and Recovery: The Aftermath of Violence—From Domestic Abuse to Political Terror.* New York: Basic Books, 2015.

Hinkel, Dan. "Benefit for Robert Rialmo, Cop Who Fatally Shot Teenager and Bystander, Will Raffle Gift Certificates for Guns." *Chicago Tribune*, May 2, 2019. https://www.chicagotribune.com/news/ct-met-chicago-police-union-shooting-robert-rialmo-raffle-guns-20190502-story.html

Hoffman, K. M., S. Trawalter, J. Axt, and M. N. Oliver. "Racial Bias in Pain Assessment and Treatment Recommendations, and False Beliefs about Biological Differences between Blacks and Whites." *Proceedings of the National Academy of Sciences of the United States of America* 113, no. 16 (2016): 4296–301. https://doi.org/10.1073/pnas.1516047113

Holmes, Dorothy Evans. "Culturally Imposed Trauma: The Sleeping Dog Has

Awakened. Will Psychoanalysis Take Heed?" *Psychoanalytic Dialogues* 26, no. 6 (2016): 641–54. DOI:10.1080/10481885.2016.1235454

Hook, Derek. *Foucault, Psychology, and the Analytics of Power*. New York: Palgrave MacMillan, 2007.

Hook, Derek, and Ross Truscott. "Fanonian Ambivalence: On Psychoanalysis and Postcolonial Critique." *Journal of Theoretical and Philosophical Psychology* 13, no. 3 (2013):155–69.

hooks, bell. *Feminist Theory: From Margin to Center*. London: Pluto Press, 2000.

Huey, Laura, and Rose Riciardelli. "'This Isn't What I Signed Up For': When Police Officer Role Expectations Conflict with the Realities of General Duty Police Work in Remote Communities." *International Journal of Police Science & Management* 17 no. 3 (2015): 194–203.

Hughes, David. "I'm a Black Police Officer. Here's How to Change the System." *New York Times*. July 16, 2020. https://www.nytimes.com/2020/07/16/opinion/poli ce-funding-defund.html

Hunn, David, and Kim Bell. "Why Was Michael Brown's Body Left There for Hours?" *St. Louis Post-Dispatch*. September 14, 2014.

Imarisha, Walidah, Alexis Pauline Gumbs, Leah Lakshmi Piepzna-Samarasinha, Adrienne Maree Brown, and Mia Mingus. "The Fictions and Futures of Transformative Justice." *The New Inquiry* (April 20, 2017). https://thenewinquiry.com /the-fictions-and-futures-of-transformative-justice/

INCITE! Women of Color Against Violence, ed. *The Revolution Will Not be Funded: Beyond the Non-profit Industrial Complex*. Cambridge, MA: South End Press, 2007.

International Association of Chiefs of Police. *Officer-Involved Shootings: A Guide for Law Enforcement Leaders*. Washington, DC: Office of Community Oriented Policing Services, 2016.

International Police Association. "Police Museums USA, Updated July 2015." www .ipa-usa.org/?page=Museums

Ioanide, Paula. "Defensive Appropriations." In *Antiracism Inc.: Why the Way We Talk about Racial Justice Matters*, edited by Felicia Blake, Paula Ioanide, and Alison Reed. Santa Barbara: Punctum, 2019.

Ioanide, Paula. *The Emotional Politics of Racism: How Feelings Trump Facts in an Era of Colorblindness*. Palo Alto, CA: Stanford University Press, 2015.

Ivsins, Andrew, Jade Boyd, Leo Beletsky, and Ryan McNeil. "Tackling the Overdose Crisis: The Role of Safe Supply." *International Journal of Drug Policy* 80 (2020).

Jackson, Jessi Lee. "The Necropolitics of Prison Rape Elimination." *Signs* 39, no. 1 (Autumn 2013).

Jacobs, Leah A., Mimi E. Kim, Darren L. Whitfield, Rachel E. Gartner, Meg Panichelli, Shanna K. Kattari, Margaret Mary Downey, Shanté Stuart McQueen, and Sarah E. Mountz. "Defund the Police: Moving Towards an Anti-Carceral Social Work." *Journal of Progressive Human Services* 32, no. 1 (2021).

Jacobs, Lynne M. "Learning to Love White Shame and Guilt: Skills for Working as a White Therapist in a Racially Divided Country." *International Journal of Psychoanalytic Self Psychology* 9, no. 4 (2014): 297–312.

James, Lois, Stephen James, and Bryan Vila. "The Reverse Racism Effect: Are Cops More Hesitant to Shoot Black than White Suspects?" *Criminology & Public Policy* 15, no. 2 (2016).

Janofsky, Jeffrey. "Lies and Coercion: Why Psychiatrists Should Not Participate in Police and Intelligence Interrogations." *Journal of the American Academy of Psychiatry and Law* 34 (2006): 472–78.

Jeffrey Janofsky. "Reply to Schafer: Exploitation of Criminal Suspects by Mental Health Professionals Is Unethical." Journal of the American Academy of Psychiatry and the Law 29, no. 4 (2001): 449–51. PMID: 11785618.

Johnson, Kevin. "Women Move into Law Enforcement's Highest Ranks." *USA Today*, December 2, 2015.

Jones, Daniel J. "The Potential Impacts of Pandemic Policing on Police Legitimacy: Planning Past the Covid-19 Crisis." *Policing: A Journal of Policy and Practice* (June 2020). doi: 10.1093/police/paaa026

Kaba, Mariame. "Yes, We Mean Literally Abolish the Police." *New York Times.* June 12, 2020. https://www.nytimes.com/2020/06/12/opinion/sunday/floyd-abolish-defund-police.html

Kael, Pauline. "Dirty Harry: Saint Cop." *New Yorker* (January 15, 1972).

Karamouzian, Mohammad, Carolyn Dohoo, Sara Forsting, Ryan McNeil, Thomas Kerr, and Mark Lysyshyn. "Evaluation of a Fentanyl Drug Checking Service for Clients of a Supervised Injection Facility, Vancouver, Canada." *Harm Reduction Journal* 15, no. 1 (2018).

Karimi, Faith, Eric Levenson, and Justin Gamble. "Tulsa Cop Not Guilty in Fatal Shooting of Unarmed Black Man." *CNN*, May 17, 2017. https://www.cnn.com/2017/05/17/us/tulsa-police-shooting-trial/index.html

Kates, Allen R. *CopShock: Surviving Posttraumatic Stress Disorder (PTSD)*. Cortaro, AZ: Holbrook Street Press, 1999.

Kennedy, Angie. "Eugenics, 'Degenerate Girls,' and Social Workers During the Progressive Era." *Affilia: Journal of Women and Social Work* 23, no. 1 (February 2008): 22–37.

Kerner Commission. *National Advisory Commission on Civil Disorder*. Washington, DC: US Government Printing Office, 1968.

Khanna, Ranjana. *Dark Continents: Psychoanalysis and Colonialism*. Durham, NC: Duke University Press, 2003.

Kim, Mimi E. "Anti-carceral Feminism: The Contradictions of Progress and the Possibilities of Counter-hegemonic Struggle." *Affilia* 35, no. 3 (2020): 309–26.

Kim, Mimi. "From Carceral Feminism to Transformative Justice: Women-of-color Feminism and Alternatives to Incarceration." *Journal of Ethnic & Cultural Diversity in Social Work* 27, no. 3 (2018): 219–33.

Kirschman, Ellen. *I Love a Cop, Revised Edition: What Police Families Need to Know*. New York: Guilford Press, 2006.

Kirschman, Ellen, Mark Kamena, and Joel Fay. *Counseling Cops: What Clinicians Need to Know*. New York: Guilford Press, 2014.

Kirshenblatt-Gimblett, Barbara. "The Museum—A Refuge for Utopian Thought."

in Jörn Rüsen, Michael Fehr, and Annelie Ramsbrock, *Die Unruhe de Kulture: Potentiales des Utopischen*. Weilerswist, Germany: Velbrück Wissenschaft, 2004.

Kivland, Chelsey L. "The Magic of Guns: Scriptive Technology and Violence in Haiti." *American Ethnologist* 45, no. 3 (2018): 354–66.

Klein, Melanie. *Envy and Gratitude and Other Works 1946–1963*. New York: The Free Press, 1975.

Klein, Melanie. *Love, Guilt, and Reparation and Other Works 1921–1945*. New York: The Free Press, 1975.

Kochanek, Kenneth D., Jiaquan Xu, and Elizabeth Arias, *Mortality in the United States, 2019*. NCHS Data Brief No. 395, December 2020. Hyattsville, MD: National Center for Health Statistics, 2020.

Kolata, Gina. "The Price for 'Predatory' Publishing? $50 Million." *New York Times*, April 3, 2019.

Kuchuk, Steven, Dan Friedlander, and Tami Dror-Schieber. "Eyes Wide Open: Report from the 2019 Tel Aviv Conference Committee." International Association for Relational Psychoanalysis and Psychotherapy. http://iarpp.net/article/imagining-with-eyes-wide-open-report-from-the-2019-tel-aviv-conference-committee/, accessed September 15, 2020.

Kurke, Martin I., and Ellen M. Scrivner, eds. *Police Psychology into the 21st Century*. Hillsdale, NJ: Lawrence Erlbaum Associates, 1995.

Lacan, Jacques. *Ecrits*. Translated by Bruce Fink. New York: W. W. Norton, 2002.

Lande, Russell G. *How to Build A Police Memorial*. PhD diss. Kutztown University of Pennsylvania, 2006.

Laubender, Carolyn. "Speak for Your Self: Psychoanalysis, Autotheory, and The Plural Self," *Arizona Quarterly: A Journal of American Literature, Culture, and Theory* 76, no. 1 (2020): 39–64.

"Lauren Berlant on Her Book *Cruel Optimism*." *ROROTOKO*, June 4, 20102, http://rorotoko.com/interview/20120605_berlant_lauren_on_cruel_optimism

Lauzon, Claudette. "Drones Gone Wild, and Other Unruly Bodies of War: A Contemporary Art History." Lecture at the Vancouver Institute for Social Research, November 14, 2016.

Lepecki, Andre. "Choreopolicing and Choreopolitics; or, the Task of the Dancer." *TDR* 57, no. 4 (Winter 2013).

Linehan, Marsha. *Cognitive Behavioral Treatment for Borderline Personality Disorder*. New York: Guilford, 1993.

Linville, Kelli, and Cliff Cook. "Here's What Makes a Successful Partnership between a Police Department and a Community." *Bellingham Herald*. January 4, 2017. https://www.bellinghamherald.com/opinion/op-ed/article124398014.html

Lorde, Audre. *Zami: A New Spelling of My Name*. Watertown, MA: Persephone, 1982.

Lorde, Audre. *The Black Unicorn: Poems*. New York: Norton, 1978.

Lugones, María, *Pilgrimages/Peregrinajes: Theorizing Coalitions Against Multiple Oppressions*. Lanham, MD: Rowman & Littlefield, 2003.

Mannoe, Meenakshi, Dylan Lambi-Raine, and Donna Baines. "Defund the Police and Social Work's Relationship to State Coercion and Control." *The Social Lens: A Social Work Action Blog.* April 8, 2021. https://socialwork.ubc.ca/news/defu nd-the-police-and-social-works-relationship-to-state-coercion-and-control/

Martinez, Virginia. "Chicanas and the Law." *Latina Issues: Fragments of Historia (ella)(herstory)* 2 (1999): 205.

Maruschak, Laura, and Todd D. Hinton. "Correctional Populations in the United States, 2017–2018," *BJS Bulletin.* Washington DC: Bureau of Justice Statistics, Department of Justice, 2016. https://www.bjs.gov/content/pub/pdf/cpus1718 .pdf

Mathiesen, Thomas. *The Politics of Abolition.* New York: John Wiley & Sons, 1974.

McCoy, Terrence. "Darren Wilson Explains Why He Killed Michael Brown." *Washington Post.* November 25, 2014.

Meiners, Erica. *Right to Be Hostile: Schools, Prisons, and the Making of Public Enemies.* New York: Routledge, 2010.

Meiners, Erica, and Charity Tolliver. "Refusing to be Complicit in Our Prison Nation: Teachers Rethinking Mandated Reporting." *Radical Teacher* 106 (Fall 2016): 106–14, 107.

Meiners, Erica, and Maisha T. Winn. "Resisting the School to Prison Pipeline: The Practice to Build Abolition Democracies." *Race Ethnicity and Education* 13, no. 3 (2010): 271–76.

Menjoge, Sujata S. "Testing the Limits of Anti-Discrimination Law: How Employers' Use of Pre-Employment Psychological and Personality Test Can Circumvent Title VII and the ADA." *North Carolina Law Review.* 82 (2003): 326–65.

Mennicke, Annelise M., and Katie Ropes. "Estimating the Rate of Domestic Violence Perpetrated by Law Enforcement Officers: A Review of Methods and Estimates." *Aggression and Violent Behavior* 31 (2016): 157–64.

Metzl, Jonathan. *Dying of Whiteness: How the Politics of Racial Resentment Is Killing America's Heartland.* New York: Basic Books, 2019.

Mitchell, Juliet. *Feminism and Psychoanalysis: A Radical Reassessment of Freudian Psychoanalysis.* New York: Basic Books, 2000.

Mobolio-Keeling, Linda. *Feeling Safe with Officer Frank.* Herndon, VA: Mascot Books, 2011.

Mogul, Joey L., Andrea J. Ritchie, and Kay Whitlock. *Queer (In)Justice: The Criminalization of LGBT People in the United States.* Boston: Beacon, 2011.

Monkkonen, Eric. "History of Urban Police." *Crime and Justice* 15 (1992): 547–80.

Moskos, Peter. *Cop in the Hood: My Year Policing in Baltimore's Eastern District.* Princeton: Princeton University Press, 2008.

Murakawa, Naomi. *The First Civil Right: How Liberals Built Prison America.* New York: Oxford University Press, 2014.

Murakawa, Naomi, and Katherine Beckett. "The Penology of Racial Innocence: The Erasure of Racism in the Study and Practice of Punishment." *Law & Society Review* 44, nos. 3–4 (2010): 695–730.

Nast, Heidi. "The Machine-Phallus: Psychoanalyzing the Geopolitical Economy of Masculinity and Race." *Psychoanalytic Inquiry* 35 (2015): 766–85.

National Center for Health Statistics. "Health, United States, 2017: With Special Features on Mortality." Hyattsville, MD: US Department of Health and Human Services, 2018.

National Law Enforcement Officers' Memorial Fund, www.nleomf.org

Navarro, Chantelle. "UI Police Invites Public to Attend Implicit-bias Training Next Week." Friday, July 6, 2018. *KCRG-TV*, http://www.kcrg.com/content/news/UI -Police--487548671.html

Nelson, Maggie. *The Argonauts*. Minneapolis: Graywolf, 2015.

Neocleous, Mark. *The Fabrication of Social Order: A Critical Theory of Police Power*. London: Pluto, 2000.

Noack, Rick. "Five Countries Where Most Police Officers Do Not Carry Guns—and It Works Well." *Washington Post*. July 8, 2016. www.washingtonpost.com/news /worldviews/wp/2015/02/18/5-countries-where-police-officers-do-not-carry -firearms-and-it-works-well/?utm_term=.e48d2981a7cf

Obama, Barack. "Open Letter to America's Law Enforcement Community," posted July 19, 2016. https://obamawhitehouse.archives.gov/blog/2016/07/19/read-pr esident-obamas-open-letter-americas-law-enforcement-community

Office of Community Oriented Policing Services. *The President's Task Force on 21st Century Policing Implementation Guide: Moving from Recommendations to Action*. Washington, DC: Office of Community Oriented Policing Services, 2015. https://cops.usdoj.gov/RIC/Publications/cops-p341-pub.pdf

Payne, Stetson. "Former Tulsa Police Officer Betty Shelby to Teach Basic NRA Pistol Course with Husband." *Tulsa World*, April 24, 2019. https://tulsaworld.com /news/local/former-tulsa-police-officer-betty-shelby-to-teach-basic-nra-pistol -course-with-husband/article_0380c8b4-fdd3-5a59-80f9-b4bd2ec9ce40.html

Pease, Donald. *New American Exceptionalism*. Minneapolis: University of Minnesota Press, 2009.

Peery, Destiny. "Implicit Bias Training for Police May Help, But It's Not Enough." *Huffington Post*. March 14, 2016. www.huffingtonpost.com/destiny-peery/impl icit-bias-training-fo_b_9464564.html

Pérez-Peña, Richard, "Why First Aid Is Often Lacking in the Moments After a Police Shooting." *New York Times*. September 21, 2016. https:// www.nytimes.com/2016/09/22/us/why-first-aid-is-often-lacking-in-the- moments-after-a-police-shooting.html

Perry, Steven W., and Duren Banks. "Prosecutors in State Courts, 2007." *Bureau of Justice Statistics—Statistical Tables*. US Department of Justice: December 2011. https://www.bjs.gov/index.cfm?ty=pbdetail&iid=1749

"Police and Detectives." Bureau of Labor Statistics, U.S. Department of Labor, *Occupational Outlook Handbook*. https://www.bls.gov/ooh/protective-service/police -and-detectives.htm, accessed February 22, 2019.

Preciado, Paul. *Testo Junkie: Sex, Drugs, and Biopolitics in the Pharmacopornographic Era*. New York: Feminist Press, 2013.

President's Commission on Law Enforcement and Administration of Justice. *The Challenge of Crime in a Free Society*. Washington DC: US Government Printing Office, 1967. https://www.ncjrs.gov/pdffiles1/nij/42.pdf

President's Task Force on 21st Century Policing. *Final Report of the President's Task Force on 21st Century Policing*. Washington, DC: Office of Community Oriented Policing Services, 2015.

Probyn Ramsey, Fiona. "Complicity, Critique And Methodology." *ARIEL* 38, no. 2–3 (2007).

Quilantan, Bianca. "Trump Says U.S. 'Locked and Loaded' After Attack on Saudi Oil." Politico. September 15, 2019. https://www.politico.com/story/2019/09/15/trump-locked-loaded-iran-saudi-arabia-1497452

Ramde, Dinesh. "Wisconsin Police Officer to Be Honored in Memorial." *CNSNews.com* April 3, 2013. www.cnsnews.com/news/article/wisconsin-police-officer-be-honored-memorial

Rankine, Claudia. *Citizen: An American Lyric*. Minneapolis: Graywolf Press, 2015.

Rankine, Claudia. "The Condition of Black Life Is One of Mourning," *New York Times Magazine*. June 22, 2015. https://www.nytimes.com/2015/06/22/magazine/the-condition-of-black-life-is-one-of-mourning.html

Raub, R. A. *Police Officer Retirement: The Beginning of a Long Life*. Illinois State Police, Division of Administration, 1987.

Reavy, Pat. "Man Announces Excessive Force Lawsuit then Gets Arrested." *Deseret News*. December 6, 2017. https://www.deseret.com/2017/12/6/20637057/man-announces-excessive-force-lawsuit-against-police-then-gets-arrested#salt-lake-city-police-officer-matt-roper-escorts-jackie-sanchez-out-of-attorney-robert-b-sykes-office-after-arresting-him-in-salt-lake-city-on-wednesday-dec-6-2017-sanchez-was-arrested-for-assault-against-a-police-officer-interference-with-arresting-officer-and-disorderly-conduct-from-an-incident-in-july

Reed, Alison. "Caption This: Police in Pussyhats, White Ladies, and Carceral Psychology Under Trump." *Abolition Journal* (September 24, 2017). https://abolitionjournal.org/caption-this/

Reiner, Robert. *The Politics of the Police*, 2nd ed. London: Harvester Wheatsheaf, 1992.

Reiser, Martin. *The Police Department Psychologist*. Springfield, IL: Thomas, 1972.

Rembis, Michael. "The New Asylums: Madness and Mass Incarceration in the Neoliberal Era." In *Disability Incarcerated*, eds. Liat Ben-Moshe, Chris Chapman, and Allison Carey, 139–59. New York: Palgrave Macmillan US, 2014.

Risen, James. "American Psychological Association Bolstered C.I.A. Torture Program, Report Says." *New York Times*. April 30, 2015. https://www.nytimes.com/2015/05/01/us/report-says-american-psychological-association-collaborated-on-torture-justification.html

Risen, James. "Three Leave Jobs over Psychologists' Involvement in Torture." *New York Times*. July 15, 2015. https://www.nytimes.com/2015/07/15/us/politics/3-leave-jobs-over-psychologists-involvement-in-bush-era-interrogations.html

Ritchie, Andrea. *Invisible No More: Police Violence Against Black Women and Women of Color*. Boston: Beacon, 2017.

Roberts, Dorothy E. "Prison, Foster Care, and the Systemic Punishment of Black Mothers." *UCLA Law Review* 59 (2011): 1474–500.

Roberts, Dorothy. *Shattered Bonds: The Color of Child Welfare*. New York: Basic Civitas Books, 2003.

Robinson, Cedric. *Black Marxism: The Making of the Black Radical Tradition*. Chapel Hill: University of North Carolina Press, 2000.

Rogin, Michael. *"Ronald Reagan," the Movie: And Other Episodes in Political Demonology*. Berkeley: University of California Press, 1987.

Rogin, Michael. "'Make My Day!' Spectacle as Amnesia in Imperial Politics." *Representations* 29 (Winter 1990): 99–123.

Rojas, Paula. "Are the Cops in Our Heads and Hearts?" In *The Revolution Will Not Be Funded*, edited by INCITE! Women of Color Against Violence, 197–214. Boston: South End Press, 2009.

Rose, Jacqueline. *States of Fantasy*. Oxford: Oxford University Press, 1996.

Sandler, Gilbert. "A Neater Way to Kill." *Baltimore Sun*. November 2, 1993. https://www.baltimoresun.com/news/bs-xpm-1993-11-02-1993306212-story.html

Scannell, Joshua. "Broken Windows, Broken Code." *Real Life*. August 29, 2016. http://reallifemag.com/broken-windows-broken-code/

Schaper, David. "Claiming Emotional Trauma, Chicago Officer Countersues Victim's Estate." *NPR Morning Edition*. February 10, 2016. http://www.npr.org/2016/02/10/466250515/claiming-emotional-trauma-chicago-officer-countersues-estate-of-victim-he-shot

Schept, Judah, Tyler Wall, and Avi Brisman. "Building, Staffing, and Insulating: An Architecture of Criminological Complicity in the School-to-Prison Pipeline." *Social Justice* 41, no. 4 (2014): 96–115.

"Security Guards and Gaming Surveillance Officers." Bureau of Labor Statistics, U.S. Department of Labor, *Occupational Outlook Handbook*. https://www.bls.gov/ooh/protective-service/security-guards.htm, accessed March 12, 2019.

Sedgwick, Eve Kosofsky. *Touching Feeling: Affect, Pedagogy, Performativity*. Durham: Duke University Press, 2003.

Seigal, Micol. *Violence Work: Policing and Power*. Durham: Duke University Press, 2018.

Sharpe, Christina. *In the Wake: On Blackness and Being*. Durham: Duke University Press, 2016.

Silliman, Jael, Anannya Bhattacharjee, and Angela Yvonne Davis, eds. *Policing the National Body: Sex, Race, and Criminalization*. Boston: South End Press, 2002.

Skolnick, Jerome. *Justice Without Trial: Law Enforcement in Democratic Society*. New York: MacMillan, 1994.

Sontag, Susan. *On Photography*. New York: Farrar, Strauss, and Giroux, 1977.

Southall, Ashley. "New York Police Department Is Retiring the Revolver." *New York Times*. May 31, 2018. https://www.nytimes.com/2018/05/31/nyregion/new-york-police-revolver.html

Spade, Dean. *Normal Life: Administrative Violence, Critical Trans Politics, and the Limits of Law*. Boston: South End Press, 2011.

Spillers, Hortense. "Mama's Baby, Papa's Maybe: An American Grammar Book." *diacritics* 17, no. 2 (1987): 65–81.

Stamper, Norm. *Breaking Rank: A Top Cop's Exposé of the Dark Side of American Policing*. New York: Nation Books, 2005.

Stamper, Norm. *To Protect and Serve: How to Fix America's Police*. New York: Nation Books, 2016.

Stanley, Eric A., Dean Spade, and Queer (In)Justice. "Queering Prison Abolition, Now?" *American Quarterly* 64, no. 1 (2012): 115–27.

Stanley-Becker, Isaac. "She Fatally Shot an Unarmed Black Man. Now She's Teaching Other Police Officers How to 'Survive' Such Incidents." *Washington Post*, August 28, 2018, https://www.washingtonpost.com/news/morning-mix/wp/20 18/08/28/she-fatally-shot-an-unarmed-black-man-now-shes-teaching-other -cops-how-to-survive-such-incidents/

Stern, Alexandra Minna. *Eugenic Nation: Faults and Frontiers of Better Breeding in Modern America*. Berkeley: University of California Press, 2015.

Strother, Logan, Spencer Piston, and Thomas Ogorzalek. "Pride or Prejudice? Racial Prejudice, Southern Heritage, and White Support for the Confederate Battle Flag." *Du Bois Review: Social Science Research on Race* 14, no. 1 (2017): 295–323.

Sturken, Marita. "Comfort, Irony, and Trivialization: The Mediation of Torture." *International Journal of Cultural Studies* 14, no. 4 (2011): 423–40.

Sturken, Marita. *Tourists of History: Memory, Kitsch, and Consumerism from Oklahoma City to Ground Zero*. Durham: Duke University Press, 2007.

Sturken, Marita. "The Wall, the Screen, and the Image: The Vietnam Veterans Memorial." *Representations* 35: 1991, 118–42.

Sue, Derald Wing. *Microaggressions in Everyday Life: Race, Gender, and Sexual Orientation*. New York: John Wiley and Sons, 2010.

Sue, Derald Wing, Patricia Arredondo, and Roderick J. McDavis. "Multicultural Counseling Competencies and Standards: A Call to the Profession." *Journal of Counseling & Development* 70, no. 4 (1992): 477–86.

Sullivan, Shannon. *Good White People: The Problem with Middle-Class White Anti-Racism*. Albany: SUNY Press, 2014.

Swartz, Sally. *Ruthless Winnicott: The Role of Ruthlessness in Psychoanalysis and Political Protest*. London: Routledge, 2019.

Tavernise, Sabrina, and Abby Goodnough. "American Life Expectancy Rises for First Time in Three Years." *New York Times*. January 30, 2020. https://www.nyti mes.com/2020/01/30/us/us-life-expectancy.html

Taylor, Diana. *The Archive and the Repertoire: Performing Cultural Memory in the Americas*. Durham, NC: Duke University Press, 2003.

Terman, Lewis. *The Measurement of Intelligence*. Boston: Houghton, Mifflin and Company, 1916. https://doi.org/10.1037/10014-000

Terman, Lewis, Arthur Otis, Virgil Dickson, O. Hubbard, J. Norton, Lowry Howard, J. Flanders, and C. Cassingham. "A Trial of Mental and Pedagogical Tests in a Civil Service Examination for Policemen and Firemen." *Journal of Applied Psychology* 1 (no. 1: 1917).

Theweleit, Klaus. *Male Fantasies, Volume 1: Women Floods Bodies History*. Minneapolis: University of Minnesota Press, 1987.

Theweleit, Klaus. *Male Fantasies, Volume 2: Psychoanalyzing the White Terror*. Minneapolis: University of Minnesota Press, 1989.

Thompson, Heather Ann. *Blood in the Water: The Attica Prison Uprising of 1971 and Its Legacy*. New York: Pantheon Books, 2016.

Tiesman, Hope M. "Workplace Suicide" NIOSH Science Blog, April 13, 2015. https://blogs-origin.cdc.gov/niosh-science-blog/2015/04/13/workplace-suicide

Tuck, Eve, and K. Wayne Yang, "Decolonization Is Not a Metaphor." *Decolonization: Indigeneity, Education & Society* 1, no. 1 (2012).

U.S. Bureau of Labor Statistics. "Union Members Summary." *Economic New Release*, January, 1, 2020. https://www.bls.gov/news.release/union2.nr0.htm

United States Department of Justice, Federal Bureau of Investigation. (September 2011). *Crime in the United States, 2010*. Retrieved Dec. 20, 2016, from https://ucr.fbi.gov/crime-in-the-u.s/2010/crime-in-the-u.s.-2010/tables/10tbl74.xls

Vielmetti, Bruce. "Husband Pleads Guilty to Killing Wauwatosa Police Officer Jennifer Sebena." *Milwaukee Journal Sentinel*, June 26, 2013. archive.jsonline.com /news/crime/plea-expected-in-killing-of-wauwatosa-police-officer-jennifer-se bena-b9942397z1-213112411.html

Violanti, John M. "Suicide and the Police Role: A Psychosocial Model." *An International Journal of Police Strategies and Management* 20 (1997): 698–715.

Violanti, John M., Tara Hartley, Desta Fekedulegn, Michael Andrew, and Cecil Burchiel. "Life Expectancy in Police Officers: A Comparison with the US General Population." *International Journal of Emergency Mental Health* 15, no. 4 (2013): 217–28.

Violanti, John M., John E. Vena, and Sandra Petralia. "Mortality of a Police Cohort: 1950–1990." *American Journal of Industrial Medicine* 33, no. 4 (1998): 366–73.

Wade, Tracey, Anna Frayne, Sally-Anne Edwards, Therese Robertson, and Peter Gilchrist. "Motivational Change in an Inpatient Anorexia Nervosa Population and Implications for Treatment." *Australian & New Zealand Journal of Psychiatry* 43, no. 3 (2009): 235–43.

Wagner, Bryan. *Disturbing the Peace: Black Culture and the Police Power after Slavery*. Cambridge: Harvard University Press, 2009.

Wall, Tyler. "The Police Invention of Humanity: Notes on the 'Thin Blue Line.'" *Crime, Media, Culture: An International Journal* (September 17, 2019). https://doi.org/10.1177/1741659019873757

Wallace, Bruce, Flora Pagan, and Bernadette Bernie Pauly. "The Implementation of Overdose Prevention Sites as a Novel and Nimble Response During an illegal Drug Overdose Public Health Emergency." *International Journal of Drug Policy* 66 (2019): 64–72.

Wang, Jackie. *Carceral Capitalism*. Los Angeles: semiotext(e), 2018.

Ware, Vron. *Beyond the Pale: White Women, Racism, and History*. New York: Verso Books, 2015.

Way, Lori Beth, and Ryan Patten. *Hunting for "Dirt-Bags": Why Cops Over-police the Poor and Racial Minorities*. Boston: Northeastern University Press, 2013.

Weber, Max. *From Max Weber: Essays in Sociology*. New York: Oxford University Press, 1946.

Weiss, Peter, and Robin Inwald. "A Brief History of Personality Assessment in Police Psychology." In *Personality Assessment in Police Psychology: A 21st Century Perspective*, edited by Peter Weiss, 5–28. Springfield, IL: Charles C. Thomas, 2010.

Weiss, William U., Kevin Buehler, and David Yates. "The Psychopathic Deviate Scale of the MMPI in Police Selection." *Journal of Police and Criminal Psychology* 10, no. 4 (1995): 57–60.

Wender, Jonathan M. *Policing and the Poetics of Everyday Life*. Urbana: University of Illinois Press, 2008.

Whitaker, Amir, Sylvia Torres-Guillén, Michelle Morton, Harold Jordan, Stefanie Coyle, Angela Mann, and Wei-Ling Sun. "Cops and No Counselors: How the Lack of School Mental Health Staff Is Harming Students." American Civil Liberties Union, March 4, 2019, https://www.aclu.org/report/cops-and-no-counselors

"Who We Are." Immigration and Customs Enforcement. https://www.ice.gov /about, accessed March 12, 2019.

Wiegman, Robyn. "Introduction: Autotheory Theory." *Arizona Quarterly: A Journal of American Literature, Culture, and Theory* 76, no. 1 (2020): 1–14.

Wilkins, Vicky, and Brian N. Williams. "Black or Blue: Racial Profiling and Representative Bureaucracy." *Public Administration Review* 68, no. 4 (2008): 654–64.

Wilkins, Vicky, and Brian N. Williams. "Representing Blue: Representative Bureaucracy and Racial Profiling in the Latino Community." *Administration & Society* 40, no. 8 (2009): 775–98.

Wilkinson, Alec. "The Dark Presence of Guns." *The New Yorker*. December 22, 2012.

Winnicott, D. W. "Hate in the Counter-transference." *International Journal of Psychoanalysis* 30 (1949): 69–74.

Winnicott, D. W. *Playing and Reality*. London: Routledge Classics, 2005.

Woods, Alexandra. "The Work Before Us: Whiteness and the Psychoanalytic Institute." *Psychoanalysis, Culture & Society* 25 (2020): 230–49.

Wynter, Sylvia. "Unsettling the Coloniality of Being/Power/Truth/Freedom: Towards the Human, after Man, Its Overrepresentation—An Argument." *CR: The New Centennial Review* 3, no. 3 (2003).

Xu, J .Q., S. L. Murphy, K. D. Kochanek, and E. Arias. "Mortality in the United States, 2018," *NCHS Data Brief*, no 355. Hyattsville, MD: National Center for Health Statistics, 2020.

Yancy, George. *Look, a White! Philosophical Essays on Whiteness*. Philadelphia: Temple University Press, 2012.

Young, Hershini Bhana. "Inheriting the Criminalized Black Body: Race, Gender, and Slavery in 'Eva's Man.'" *African American Review* 39, no. 3 (2005): 377–94.

INDEX

abolition, 15, 147–52
abolitionist psychology, 151–52
Ahmed, Sara, 25, 91
Altman, Neil, 21
American Psychological Association, 16–17, 71, 75–77
Austin, J.L., 91
autotheory, 4, 5–6

Berlant, Lauren, 55, 61, 63, 131–32
Black Lives Matter, 3, 122–23, 124, 126–27, 141–43, 148
blue mourning, 25, 128, 140–41
Bonilla-Silva, Eduardo, 74, 92
Brown, Michael, 3, 45–46, 76, 83
bureaucratic emotional labor, 9, 10, 24, 60–62, 64, 151
Butler, Judith, 41, 56–57, 128
Buffington, Robert, 105–6

carceral fantasy, 107, 113, 124
carceral feminism, 14, 39
carceral psychology, 13, 14, 47, 60, 146
Case, Anne and Angus Deaton, 53
Cole, Alyson, 11, 56
complicity, 4, 5, 14–15, 20, 26, 32, 37–38, 40, 146, 147, 149
Confederate monuments, 126, 128
Correll, Joshua, 99
cops in our heads and hearts, 13, 150
Counseling Cops, 33–36
Crash (film), 93–94
critical psychology, 16, 70, 77, 88
Crutcher, Terence, 3, 69

Das, Veena, 61–62
Davis, Angela, 15, 147

Diallo, Amadou, 91
Dimen, Muriel, 5
Dirty Harry, 108–9, 139–40
Douglas, Tanisha Wakumi, 23

Fanon, Frantz, 19–20, 42, 86–88
fantasying, 109–10, 124
Floyd, George, 3, 76–77
Foucault, Michel, 70
Fox, Dennis with Isaac Prilleltensky and Stephanie Austin, 70
Frazier, Darnella, 3
Freud, Sigmund, 5–6, 35, 50

gas chamber, 114–15
gift shop, 107, 136
Gilmore, Ruth Wilson, 53, 101
Graeber, David, 61
grievability, 128–29, 136–37, 141, 147
guilt, 2, 20–21, 23, 66, 91, 98
Gumbs, Alexis Pauline, 23

Harris, Angela, 42
Hartman, Saidiya, 10
Hook, Derek, 70; with Ross Truscott, 16
Holmes, Dorothy Evans, 18

innocence, 11, 19, 22, 24, 42, 46, 78, 88, 90, 110, 125, 148
International Association for Relational Psychoanalysis and Psychotherapy, 27
intersectionality, 14, 92, 100–101, 148
intimate partner violence, 78, 138–39, 148–49

Jacobs, Lynne, 20
Jonie, Bettie, 3, 85

Kaba, Mariame, 8
Kerner commission, 73, 76
Kim, Mimi, 14, 149
Kirshenblatt-Gimblett, Barbara, 109
Kivland, Chelsey, 29
Klein, Melanie, 21–23, 66, 98

Lacan, Jacques, 18–19, 41–42
Lande, Russell, 133–134
Legrier, Quintonio, 3, 85
"line of duty" death, 49–52, 58, 104, 110–111,
    113, 127, 130, 131, 133, 136, 141
lion statues, 131–33
Lorde, Audre, 6, 152
lynching, 117

mandated reporting, 2, 14, 147
Meiners, Erica and Charity Tolliver, 14
Menjoge, Sujata, 74
Metzl, Jonathan, 34–35, 40–41
Mitchell, Stephen, 2
mourning, 25–26, 125, 127–28, 140, 148
Murakawa, Naomi and Katherine Beckett, 11,
    24, 78, 90

nonperformative speech acts, 25, 91

Pease, Donald, 125
penology of racial innocence, 11, 24, 78, 90
personality testing, 72–73, 74
phallus, 41–43
police culture; challenges to, 26, 151–52; defi-
    nition 12–16; in psychology and psycho-
    analysis, 16, 34, 36, 146, 150; and Melanie
    Klein, 22–23; and museums, 105, 107, 113;
    and grief, 128; and memorials, 139
police power, 6–10, 19–20, 21, 140, 143–44;
    complicity with, 146–47, 152; guns and 47–
    48; psychology and, 70–71, 88, 91, 99; fan-
    tasy and, 108, 124–25, 139, 142
President's Task Force on 21st Century Policing, 76
psychology of racial innocence, 24, 78, 88, 90
psychoanalysis, 16–23, 150, 151

Rankine, Claudia, 31–32, 84
Rapsey, Fiona Probyn, 4
Reed, Alison, 13
Ritchie, Andrea, 42
Roberts, Dorothy, 14
Rogin, Michael, 21, 109, 113, 122
Rojas, Paula X., 13, 150
Rose, Jacqueline, 108
rubber ducky, 107

Sebena, Jennifer, 138–39
Sedgwick, Eve Kosofsky, 21, 23, 66
Seigal, Micol, 8, 13, 60
Skolnick, Jerome, 113
shame, 11, 20–21, 41
Spillers, Hortense, 42
splitting, 22, 113, 122, 151
Stamper, Norm, 9, 40, 61
Sturken, Marita, 110, 132–33
suicide, 64, 137, 148
Sullivan, Shannon, 32–33

Taylor, Diana, 6, 12
Terman, Lewis, 72
Theweleit, Klaus, 21
Thompson, Wenona, 145
Tomb of the Unknown Peace Officer,
    111–12
trauma, 57–60, 64, 69–70, 79, 80, 81, 83–84,
    85, 124

Vietnam Veteran's Memorial, 129
vulnerable protectors, 11–12, 25, 84, 114, 120,
    124–125, 128, 134, 147, 150, 152

Wang, Jackie, 9, 11
Wender, Jonathon, 9
Winnicott, DW, 23, 28–31, 48, 109–10,
    124

Yancy, George, 19
Young, Hershini, 94